"*Is This Autism?* is a towering acco⌐ [the state] of the art of scientific and cl⌐ the lived experience and perspectives ⌐. ⌐ written, meticulously observed, and profoundly compassionate, this book will transform your understanding of autism, whether you're a clinician, a family member, or an autistic person yourself."

– **Steve Silberman,** *author of* NeuroTribes: The Legacy of Autism and the Future of Neurodiversity

"*Is This Autism?* is just brilliant – genuinely one of the best books I have ever read! Drs. Henderson and Wayland embrace neuro-affirming practice, bringing together their clinical and life experience to give a richness that is much needed within the medical and therapeutic field of autism."

– **Barb Cook, MAut, DipHSc,** *developmental educator, Director NeuroEmploy Pty Ltd & NeuroDiversity Hub, founder Spectrum Women*

"*Is This Autism?* integrates the voices of autistic people and the latest research to provide a readable, empowering, and comprehensive resource for clinicians of all kinds. Its emphasis on autistic strengths and the value of neurodiversity is especially welcome."

– **Lauren Kenworthy, PhD,** *pediatric neuropsychologist, Director, Center for Autism Spectrum Disorders, Children's National Hospital*

"You could spend years finding the patterns in first-person accounts of how autism manifests in various individuals – or you could read this book. As a late-diagnosed autistic woman, I wish it existed earlier. For other adult women seeking an autism evaluation, I would confidently recommend any clinician who reads this book. (That's a big leap from my previous recommendation, which was to only see a clinician who has previously diagnosed another autistic woman!)"

– **Annie Kotowicz,** *author of* What I Mean When I Say I'm Autistic: Unpuzzling a Life on the Autism Spectrum

"This book presents a respectful, rich, and expansive description of what autism really looks like across individuals. It provides an invaluable resource to help clinicians move past the often inaccurate, restricted, and stereotypical expectations that have historically limited an appreciation for the full 'spectrum' of this diagnosis. It is a must-read for all neuropsychologists as well as all who work with this population, whether they know it or not."

– **Kira Armstrong,** *pediatric neuropsychologist, co-editor of* The Clinical Neuropsychologist's Special Issue: Assessment and Diagnosis of Autism Spectrum Disorders

"Is This Autism? is a wonderful contribution to the field, guiding clinicians to better understand, appreciate, and describe autistic individuals as they support each unique individual's journey of self-discovery through the assessment process."

– **Marilyn J. Monteiro, PhD,** *author of* Monteiro Interview Guidelines for Diagnosing the Autism Spectrum, second edition (MIGDAS-2)

"This book is a MASTERPIECE. The information is new, beautifully stated, organized, important, helpful. Just gorgeous. I love it very much."

– **Carol Stock Kranowitz,** *author of* The Out-of-Sync Child

"I found the expertise in this book crucial for anyone interested in autism, a necessary resource for clinicians, researchers, and diagnosticians. Without hesitation, I rate it, to date, the most important work in the field."

– **Rachelle K. Sheely PhD,** *President RDI*

"Lived experiences, professional expertise, and research are carefully woven together in *Is This Autism?* – a must-read for ALL clinicians to enable them to recognize and better serve the often unseen and unheard autistic clients that come into their offices."

– **Kim Clairy, OTR/L,** *autistic occupational therapist*

"*Is This Autism?* presents current autism research and relevant clinical guidance within an affirming, easy-to-understand framework."

– **Jeremy Sharp, PhD**, *licensed psychologist and host of* The Testing Psychologist *podcast*

"This amazing book is an indispensable tool for helping clinicians and parents understand and identify the less obvious presentations of autism. It is filled with practical wisdom rooted in the authors' personal and clinical experience, as well as their enormous respect for neurodiversity. I've learned a ton that will make me a better psychologist!"

– **William Stixrud, PhD**, *clinical neuropsychologist and co-author of* The Self-Driven Child and What Do You Say?

"This groundbreaking book will revolutionize the way we think about autism. Well researched and well organized, Drs. Henderson and Wayland have created a definitive text that specifies and widens the lens through which we understand autism. This should be required reading for all professionals and lay people who want to understand the world of neurodiversity."

– **Dr Rita Eichenstein**, *neuropsychologist and author of* Not What I Expected: Help and Hope for Parents of Atypical Children

"Do you know what autism looks like in your neighbor, teacher, coworker, or aunt? An abundance of quotes and real-life examples bring neurodiversity to life in this exceptional book that does not disappoint."

– **Theresa M. Regan, PhD**, *author of* Understanding Autism in Adults and Aging Adults

"*Is This Autism?* is revolutionary in its empowering messages for clinicians and for individuals with autistic brains, alike. Drs. Henderson and Wayland are clearly changing the conversation about how autism is understood and diagnosed, and the world is a better place for it. If you have any interest in autism (and even if you don't!), this book is truly a must-read! I assure you: You have never read another one like it."

— **Karin Varblow, MD**, *pediatrician*

"*Is This Autism?* takes you on a personally guided tour into the hearts and souls of autistics. With the knowledge that Donna Henderson and Sarah Wayland have harvested from decades of personal and professional work, they convey the many twists and turns of the developmental journey of autistics. One phrase stuck with me in particular: 'A sense of belonging.' This desire to be validated for who we are — no matter how we show up in the world — lies at the deepest core of every human's longing. Henderson and Wayland show us — with compassion and inclusivity — not only how to be *informed* about autistics but also how to be *wise* as well. With solid research, practical suggestions, and moving narratives from the experts who live the neurodivergent journey, we are invited to understand that only by knowing what is on the inside can we — as professionals and family members — help on the outside. This book will become an essential guide for those of us committed to creating a world that adapts to and celebrates the unique experiences of autistics."

— **Rick Silver, MD**, *psychiatrist, founder, and director,*
The THRIVE Center

Is This Autism?

Though our understanding of autism has greatly expanded, many autistic individuals are still missed or misdiagnosed. This highly accessible book clarifies many ways that autism can present, particularly in people who camouflage to hide their autistic traits.

The authors take the reader step by step through the diagnostic criteria, incorporating the latest research as well as quotes from over 100 autistic contributors that bring that research to life. They also describe many aspects of autism that are not included in the current diagnostic criteria, such as autistic strengths and co-occurring disorders. Readers will learn about highly relevant topics, such as different types of empathy, sensory systems that are not well known, neuro-crash and burn out, and relative versus absolute thinking.

This book provides a deep, current, and neurodiversity-affirmative understanding of the less obvious presentations of autism. It is relevant to all healthcare professionals, educators, family members, autistic individuals, and anyone who is curious about autism. A clinical companion guide, *Is This Autism? A Companion Guide for Diagnosing*, is available for clinicians who make mental health diagnoses.

Donna Henderson, PsyD, is a clinical psychologist, specializing in neuropsychological evaluations for children, adolescents, and adults who would like to understand themselves better. She is a sought-after lecturer and provides training and consultation for other healthcare professionals.

Sarah Wayland, PhD, is the founder of Guiding Exceptional Parents, and co-founder of The Behavior Revolution. She provides neurodiversity-affirmative support, education, and community for parents of neurodivergent children.

Jamell White, PhD, LCSW-C, has a background in clinical social work, special education, and human development. She specializes in working with autistic children, adolescents, and adults and has over 20 years of clinical experience.

Is This Autism?

A Guide for Clinicians and Everyone Else

Donna Henderson and
Sarah Wayland, with Jamell White

Routledge
Taylor & Francis Group

NEW YORK AND LONDON

Designed cover image: artwork by Jeremy Sicile-Kira,
www.jeremysvision.com/

First published 2023
by Routledge
605 Third Avenue, New York, NY 10158

and by Routledge
4 Park Square, Milton Park, Abingdon, Oxon, OX14 4RN

Routledge is an imprint of the Taylor & Francis Group, an informa business

Library of Congress Cataloging-in-Publication Data
Names: Henderson, Donna A., author. | Wayland, Sarah C., author. |
White, Jamell, author.
Title: Is this autism? : a guide for clinicians and everyone else /
Donna Henderson, Psy.D., Sarah Wayland, Ph.D. with Jamell White, Ph.D.
Description: New York, NY : Routledge, 2023. |
Includes bibliographical references and index.
Identifiers: LCCN 2022058068 (print) | LCCN 2022058069 (ebook) |
ISBN 9781032150239 (hardback) | ISBN 9781032150222 (paperback) |
ISBN 9781003242130 (ebook)
Subjects: LCSH: Autism—Popular works. |
Autism spectrum disorders—Popular works. | Autism in children.
Classification: LCC RC553.A88 H4615 2023 (print) |
LCC RC553.A88 (ebook) | DDC 616.85/882–dc23/eng/20230203
LC record available at https://lccn.loc.gov/2022058068
LC ebook record available at https://lccn.loc.gov/2022058069

ISBN: 978-1-032-15023-9 (hbk)
ISBN: 978-1-032-15022-2 (pbk)
ISBN: 978-1-003-24213-0 (ebk)

DOI: 10.4324/9781003242130

Typeset in Sabon
by Newgen Publishing UK

To our autistic clients, friends, and family,
Especially those with late diagnoses,
And for those who still feel invisible or misunderstood.
We see you.

To my favorite autists
and that one special ADHDer.
– D.H.

To my patient and good-humored family.
I learn from you every day.
Thank you.
– S.W.

Contents

PART TWO
What else might be part of this presentation?   171

Notes for the reader

Before we begin, we want to orient you to our book and to the reasoning behind some of the decisions we made as we considered how to best communicate with you, our reader.

This book is based on a combination of research, clinical experience, and life experience. Our understanding of autism began at home and extended into our professional lives. Living and working with autistic individuals has given us a deeper understanding than experience alone could have provided. Of course, our experience and this book are informed by the research and we have referenced it whenever possible. Because we are aware that footnotes and in-line citations can be off-putting for many readers, we have attempted to make our book more readable by using the citation convention adopted by publications like *Scientific American*. We refer directly to the authors in the text and list references at the end of each chapter. Other observations are based on our professional experience.

We fully support #nothingaboutuswithoutus. We, the authors, are each neurodivergent but not autistic ourselves, and it is essential to include the perspective of autistics. To that end, well over 100 autistic individuals generously offered to share their lived experience in the form of quotes for this book. We asked each of these individuals to choose the attribution for their quotes. Many of these are real names, some are pseudonyms, and a few are simply one name with no last initial. Each was the choice of the person who is quoted.

Additionally, we include many vignettes throughout this book. They are all true, but of course all identifying information has been changed. We feel honored that so many people have entrusted their stories to us.

Additionally, we have an *autistic advisory board*, who read and provided feedback on each chapter. We aimed to create a board that is diverse in age, gender, race, and ethnic background. There also happen to be several autistic individuals on our *clinician advisory board*.

We present the research on females because that research informs our understanding of autism for individuals of all genders. There is a substantial body of research on the ways in which autistic women and girls present differently from their male counterparts. However, there are also numerous boys and men who are not identified early, if ever. And, of course, the experiences of people who are non-binary, transgender, gender fluid, or otherwise not represented in the current literature also matter. It is our hope that by shedding light on the experiences of *anyone* with previously undiagnosed autism – regardless of gender – all will benefit.

In an attempt to better understand the experiences of people of different cultures, we have included sections on *Connecting Culture,* written by Jamell White, PhD, LCSW-C. Jamell points to the importance of explicitly discussing the intersection of culture and autism, as a person's cultural experience and identity affect every interaction and cannot be parsed out from their broader experience.

It is beyond the scope of this book to review the enormous amount of relevant information regarding cultural awareness, diversity, and sensitivity. However, we will attempt to highlight instances where the issues of cultural humility are particularly relevant and to generally raise clinicians' awareness of the need to continually strive to understand each client within their own individual cultural context.

–Dr. Jamell White

Stories are interwoven throughout the *Connecting Culture* sections in order to illuminate the experience of culture in the journey of life with autism. As one mother beautifully stated, *"The insensitivities are intersectional: race, gender, disability, and developmental differences."*

Overview of this book

In the Introduction, we explain the **WHY**. That is, we explain *why* it is so important for clinicians (and everyone else) to identify and understand this type of autism.

In Part One, we discuss the **WHAT**. We review the many different ways that less obvious autism can present, and we explain exactly what to look for, using the DSM-5-TR criteria as a guide.

In Part Two, we discuss the **WHAT ELSE**. We introduce common co-occurring traits and challenges that are not currently part of the diagnostic criteria. Some of these are widely known, such as anxiety and ADHD, while others are less known but just as important, such as alexithymia, autistic burnout, and a high need for context. The more clinicians know about these challenges, the better they will be at recognizing and understanding their autistic clients. We also offer an overview of autistic strengths.

The **HOW** is covered in *Is This Autism? A Companion Guide for Diagnosing*. In that book, Donna describes her methods for collecting, organizing, and integrating information, and for engaging in collaborative discussions with her clients to make meaning of their experience. This information is crucial, not only because it helps us determine whether or not an individual is autistic but also because it helps us explain the diagnosis to others and make meaningful recommendations. If clinicians do a good job of gathering information and communicating their findings, the diagnosis should be a positive and life-changing moment for their clients.

The words we use

A central aim of this book is to convey our thoughts in a neurodiversity-affirmative manner, and in working toward this end we have found ourselves struggling with language. Determining which words and phrases to use has been a moving target, in part because autistic individuals themselves have varying opinions on these matters, and in part because our collective thinking about this topic is evolving quickly, even as we write. With this in mind, we have made the best choices we could, knowing that inevitably some people would disagree with them. We are also aware that some of our choices, while based on current thinking, will become outdated at some point. We ask the reader to keep this complicated dilemma in mind and know that our intention has been to use language that is as inclusive and respectful as possible. Following is a brief explanation of our decisions about language.

Person-first language versus identity-first language. In the general community of people with medical disabilities, there has been a shift toward identifying an individual as a *person first*, with their disability representing only one aspect of their profile (i.e., a person with diabetes, versus a diabetic person). Person-first language was conceived to ensure that people with disorders or diseases were not defined by their challenges.

However, many autistic people argue that autism is lifelong, integral to who they are, and pervades every aspect of their lives. Their identity cannot be separated from their autism. Moreover, the use of person-first language implies that the descriptor is a disease or disorder, and many autistics argue that autism is neither of these. Thus, they prefer to refer to themselves with their *identity first* (i.e., as an *autistic person*, versus a *person with autism*).

The issue is complicated by the fact that while some autistic people prefer to use identity-first language, there are others who prefer person-first language. We feel strongly that people should get to choose the way in which we refer to them. Based on our interactions with the autistic community, and particularly the type of individuals for whom we are writing this book, we are choosing to use identity-first language. We hope that our readers understand our dilemma; there is no perfect solution.

Similarly, we sometimes use the word *autistic* as a noun (instead of writing *autistic person*). Because we were unsure how this would be taken, we did online polls with two autistic communities. Both clearly indicated to us that the vast majority of participants were comfortable or agnostic regarding this usage.

Referring to people who are not autistic. Many people use the word *neurotypical* to refer to non-autistic people. However, there are many individuals who are not autistic but also do not have typical neurology (if such a thing even exists). Dividing people into *autistic* and *neurotypical* categories does not take into account the countless individuals who have non-autistic types of neurodiversity, such as ADHDers, dyslexics, and so on. While the term *allistic* means non-autistic, we find that many people are not familiar with this term. For these reasons, we have chosen to refer to non-autistic individuals simply as *non-autistic individuals*. Some of the people we quote use the term *neurotypical* to mean *non-autistic*; we have preserved their wording within their quotes.

Avoidance of functioning labels (e.g., high functioning and low functioning). In the autism literature, *high functioning* is an outdated term that typically refers to autistic people who do not have an intellectual disability; it does not take into account the countless ways in which these people may nonetheless struggle and require support. Similarly, *low functioning* is an outdated term that often refers to low intellectual functioning and/or profound autistic traits, without reflecting the many ways in which those individuals may be using their strengths to function well in their lives. Moreover, *functioning* is not static; our functional level varies from day to day and context to context. Indeed, many autistics argue that environments designed by and for non-autistics is what makes it hard for them to function. Finally, labeling a person as *high* or *low* functioning is a subjective judgment made by one person about another person, often without regard for the individual's lived experience. For all of these reasons, we avoid these terms.

Referring to females. Throughout Part One of this book, we highlight ways that autistic females can present differently from autistic males. We have titled these sections *What we've learned from the girls*, though clearly we have learned about this phenotype from *women* as well. We have used the word *girls* in this context for brevity and readability, and we hope our female readers will not be offended by this choice.

From the experts: Their words about the words they use

> I was "somewhere on the spectrum" or "had autistic traits" or "was not neurotypical." It was a big step for me to say "I

am autistic" instead of putting any qualifications or modifiers on to it.

–Drew R.

I feel like I'm only "high functioning" in other people's eyes and they're missing all the very strenuous work I'm doing under the surface. You could meet me at a party and never even be able to tell I'm on the spectrum, but what you don't know is that I had to have lots of alone time to pump myself up for the party, and then lots of wind down time afterwards to recover. And even though I've never been described as "low functioning," I get mad when some of my friends are described that way, because I feel like it discounts how well they're doing considering all of the difficult things they're dealing with on a daily basis.

–Zoe M.

Many autistics, myself included, see it as a key part of who we are, akin to things like race and gender.

–Zachary M.

Reference

Henderson, D. (in press). *Is this autism? A companion guide for diagnosing*. Routledge.

Foreword

Dena Gassner, MSW, PhD

Anyone who is a part of the world of autism has read many books. In fact, when I teach about autism in adulthood, my class begins by reading a first-person account of life with autism from one of my many autistic friends or colleagues. I always wished I had a book that would combine these lived experiences with the research. In fact, that is precisely how I teach.

Any of us who have operated as parents of our own beloveds have not only read these autobiographical accounts but also many parent accounts of navigating systems and finding our way. And as professionals, hopefully you too have a rich library of these lived experiences as we serve as systems navigators, diagnosticians, or as therapeutic and educational providers. But in all of my 25 years in the field, consuming millions of words about autism, I have never found anything that combines these three worlds, in the same book. I have one now.

Is This Autism? A Guide for Clinicians and Everyone Else by Donna Henderson and Sarah Wayland has so very much to offer! Without compromise, this book provides the research-based perception of autism through the medical model that is utilized by most systems, while also pointing to transformation – the evolution – of a neurodiversity framework for considering autism.

There is truth-telling in calling out the limitations of the available research on autistic adults. For example, these authors immediately acknowledge the reality that the explicit gender fluidity of autistic persons is not in alignment with the gendered literature. Noting the reality of the binary thinking related to autism, they then go on to challenge that idea. They acknowledge that many males and gender non-binary people may present in a more nuanced, internalized way. Similarly, there are females who present in an externalized manner, closer to the more outwardly notable stereotype of autism. And there are others who are a combination of both. This book provides a reporting of the current research, provided with caveats that touch the true realities.

The strength of the book comes from the fact that the authors sought explicit feedback, collaborating deeply with multiple autistic contributors, who guided the direction of the book. Storytelling vignettes provide case examples that offer insight. And then segments close out with beautiful quotes from the many autistic contributors, bringing real lived experience into the process.

This is a significant strength, as many books do not utilize such an extensive process for attribution. In the true spirit of community participatory efforts, this creative gift gave autistic contributors substantive input into the content, feedback, and shared experiences that informed every chapter. This form of writing also firmly grounds what autism is in a manner that seeks to benefit autistic individuals, family members, healthcare professionals, and educators. The ebb and flow of research, vignettes, and lived experience keeps the reader engaged and acutely aware of the insights each chapter brings.

For me, as one of those multi-hat-wearing autistic/parent of an autistic/researcher/educator/provider, I found this book spoke informatively to all of these identities. It is creative, insightful, and meaningful in painting a globally valuable image of what autism is for the *lost generations* of autistics for whom a diagnosis was not available and, in turn, for whom services were denied (Lai & Baron-Cohen, 2015, p. 1013). It also seeks to close the gap in understanding created by the dichotomous presentation of autism for those who experience pressure to internalize their features. Finally, our shared experiences are elevated to a space where their capacity to teach professionals, family members, peers, and everyone else is celebrated and maximized.

Reference

Lai, M.-C., & Baron-Cohen, S. (2015). Identifying the lost generation of adults with autism spectrum conditions. *The Lancet Psychiatry*, 2(11), 1013–1027. https://doi.org/10.1016/S2215-0366(15)00277-1

Foreword

Meng-Chuan Lai, MD, PhD

*Child and Youth Mental Health Collaborative at the Centre
for Addiction and Mental Health, The Hospital for Sick Children,
and Department of Psychiatry, Temerty Faculty of Medicine,
University of Toronto, Toronto, Ontario, Canada.*

I remember vividly the first autistic person I met. It was the first week of my four-month child rotation in psychiatry residency training. My mentor and I were in the clinic waiting for the first family. A boy suddenly opened the door, went straight to the window and looked outside without talking or looking at either of us, flapped his hands a few times, stayed there for half a minute, then walked straight back to the door and out of the room – no hesitancy, no eye contact, no talking. I was not even sure if he paid any attention to us. My mentor looked at me encouragingly, "What do you think his diagnosis might be?" I had not read Leo Kanner or Hans Asperger then, not to mention Grunya Sukhareva. I felt stupid that I could not tell by that glimpse.

Then it was my child psychiatry fellowship. I was more confident about using the DSM-IV-TR and ICD-10. I knew how to diagnose and make differential diagnoses. I was finally able to connect with the lovely teenager who always brought me his school notebook with his favorite space shuttle drawings. I worried a lot about him though; he talked at me, close to my face, and would frequently and abruptly reach out to touch my hair. I could tell he was autistic, as could his peers at school. He was protected by some and bullied by more.

Later I met many autistic women through their participation in my research. I found myself confused. I could not tell whether they were autistic as quickly as I had before, because some of them "did not look autistic" based on the clinical gestalt in my mind formed by my six years of clinical training. These women made eye contact, were socially engaged, and they did not show the midline hand-washing movement that I saw in young girls with Rett syndrome. These autistic women and their parents were patient with me. They generously shared their long and sometimes painful life stories, so I learned what the autistic characteristics in their early life looked like (yes, they all "met the ADI-R criteria"). They may or may not have "met the ADOS criteria" but there was always something that stood out during the session – sometimes our interaction just did not "sync" despite advanced language and the presence of many communication skills; other times they were just so polite, too perfectly aligned with what was expected of them socially.

The more I spoke with these women and their families, analyzed the quantitative data from the standardized measures, read the autistic autobiographical literature, and gathered insights from other clinicians, the more the clinical gestalt of autism evolved in my mind. I learned about the subtleties and could make sense of the commonalities across the spectrum. Over time, I realized how culture and gendered experiences could in fact shape autistic behaviors, thinking, and experience. I gathered that there isn't a "male" versus "female" phenotype of autism – instead, the presentations are distributed along the axis of typicality, from classic to subtle, building on what Lorna Wing unveiled for us over 40 years ago. The shifts and continuity in my conceptualization of autism came from pondering the lived experiences of autistic people and their families, and the research and clinical encounters that I was lucky enough to be part of. My experiences may be seen as a micro-representation of the "epistemic iteration" in scientific progression – the successive steps toward a better approximation of reality (Kendler, 2009, p. 1939).

I believe many clinicians share similar experiences. The DSM-5-TR and ICD-11 are an important foundation, as they provide a conceptual consensus of autism as a clinical entity and offer common language to describe it. They also give essential guidance about common behavioral characteristics. Further, clinicians who have been trained to use standardized instruments (such as the ADI-R, ADOS, DISCO, 3Di, CARS, etc.) learn to integrate more specific, detailed inquiries and observations into their assessment repertoire. Seasoned diagnosticians will have many opportunities for diagnostic encounters, formulations, and reflections before they learn to appreciate both the fuzziness and value of clinical diagnostic practices. It would be a dream come true if there was an easy and efficient, but comprehensive, way to learn all these during our clinical training, so the field could have more clinicians who are able to serve the under-served.

Now the dream comes true. *Is This Autism? A Guide for Clinicians and Everyone Else*, and the companion volume, *Is This Autism? A Companion Guide for Diagnosing*, offer exactly this. The clear illustration of diagnostic conceptualization, open and reflective discussion (and harmonization, when possible) of paradigms and perspectives, honest and pluralistic presentation of opinions, masterful synthesis of research findings, clinical expertise and autistic lived experiences, and the organic depiction of the nuances of autism – from typicality to subtlety – make it the book that I will turn to whenever I am puzzled clinically about autism diagnostics (which is common). Reading these two volumes is like being supervised simultaneously by several master clinicians and a community of autistic people who know autism inside out. They are super-accessible, completely down-to-earth, and full of clinical pearls. In my view, the two volumes of *Is This Autism?* are essential reading for anyone who works in the fields of autism, psychology, psychiatry, neurology, pediatrics, child and youth development, education, speech and language therapy, occupational therapy, and mental health.

The purpose of a diagnosis is to understand and help. Understanding autistic people, including recognizing them as autistic, is not about what a clinician can tell from first sight. It is about detailed and compassionate observation and appreciation of the person's developmental journey in the context of their environments – by integrating developmental history, collateral information, behavioral observations, cognitive and medical assessments if indicated, and an empathic understanding of the person's inner experiences in various contexts. Only with this level of understanding can the formulation be useful for guiding support. Clinicians should be given the resources and training to understand autism and feel comfortable serving all autistic people across developmental levels, support needs, intellectual capabilities, ethnicity, sex, gender, and on the dimension from typicality to subtlety. This is not an easy learning process for any single one of us, but we are so lucky that Donna, Sarah, Jamell, and the many contributors to these books, autistic or non-autistic, have now paved the way for us all.

References

Henderson, D. (in press). *Is this autism? A companion guide for diagnosing.* Routledge.

Kendler, K. S. (2009). An historical framework for psychiatric nosology. *Psychological Medicine, 39*(12), 1935–1941. https://doi.org/10.1017/S0033291709005753

Wing, L. (1981). Asperger's syndrome: A clinical account. *Psychological Medicine, 11*(1), 115–129. https://doi.org/10.1017/S0033291700053332

Acknowledgments

Donna and Sarah

This book was a labor of love. When we started, we could not have imagined how many friends, colleagues, and even strangers would labor along with us, and words seem inadequate to convey the tremendous gratitude we feel to each of these individuals. We hope they know how deeply we have been moved by their generosity.

First, we want to thank each and every one of our autistic clients, and those who love them, for generously sharing their lived experience.

The members of our *autistic advisory board* have spent countless hours reading every chapter, providing invaluable feedback, calling us out when we drifted into ableism, and helping us think through the many complexities of explaining the experience of one neurotype to another. We are deeply indebted to Carol Blymire, Yael Clark, Taylor Menetski, Eric Olsen, Drew Rae, Charlotte Riggle, Allie Segal, and Leen Vermeersch.

We are also indebted to the many other autistic individuals who engaged with us in person, online, and in social media, including Andrew Komarow, Asiatu Lawoyin, Audrian Flory, Emily Gerson, Angelina Lu, Zachary McGinley, Lauren Ober, everyone in our Slack group, and the many individuals who engaged with us in various Reddit and Facebook groups.

We were lucky to have a *clinical advisory board* whose comments made us work harder, think more deeply, and write more precisely. We are deeply grateful to Amara Brook, Audrey Brumback, Kathy Dow-Burger, Lara Doyle, Jennie Green, Carol Stock Kranowitz,

Julie Kovac Ray, Melissa Schwartz, Karin Varblow, and Monica Adler Werner.

We offer special thanks to our friends and colleagues Patty Eyster, Katia Fredriksen, and Cathy Marchese. It is not hyperbole to say that this book would not exist without Patty, who provided more types of support, insight, and inspiration than we can count. Katia is a well-respected psychologist with a superpower in copyediting, and she took our adequate writing and consistently improved it. Cathy is a remarkable graduate student who provided invaluable research support.

In addition to contributing to the book directly, Meng-Chuan Lai, Dena Gassner, and Jamell White each provided much-appreciated encouragement, support, and feedback.

We are grateful to the following clinicians who shared their knowledge and wisdom with us along the way: Kira Armstrong, Jesse Brand, Kim Clairy, Yael Clark, Meaghan Doyle, Wendy Law, Kelly Mahler, Elisa Nebolsine, Megan Anna Neff, Steven Vobach, and Bonnie Zucker.

We are also indebted to friends and family who provided all manner of support, from giving us space to work in to providing administrative support to offering their wisdom to cheering us on when we thought we'd never finish. These include: the Auptimists (Judy Bass, Caron Starobin, and Jamell White), Kelly Carney, Jeanine Cogan, Laurie Friedman, Stephanie Hicks, Bob Wayland, Salya Namazi, and Bill Stixrud.

Last, but certainly not least, we thank our husbands, who had no idea what they were signing up for when they first said, "Sure, write a book!"

Jamell

A special thank you to all of the wonderful individuals, families, and professionals who were willing to trust me with their personal journey living, loving, and supporting autism. I hope their stories (and the many others shared with me throughout my career) bring us all to a greater place of cultural *humility* as we *lean in* to understand and appreciate how autism *uniquely* informs experiences.

I would like to particularly thank Serene Habayeb, Joette James, Yetta Myrick, Salya Namazi, and Allysa Ware.

To the amazing authors, Donna and Sarah, thank you for inviting me to join you in this endeavor of bringing the experiences of autistic people to the forefront, while giving the (often overlooked) cultural aspects a spotlight.

May the words and expertise of those shared in this book remind us to not assume and to *simply ask*!

Introduction

I have spent my lifetime feeling shame and punishing myself for something I should be owning as my truth as simply being neurodivergent.

–Sherry W.

Why did we write this book?

If you are confused, intrigued, or curious about autism, you are not alone. Our understanding of autism has evolved tremendously in the past few decades, and it's been hard to keep up! Many people have stereotyped and outdated ideas about autism – including many healthcare professionals and educators.

This is problematic because there are countless autistic people who do not fit the stereotypical, "classical" presentation of autism. Many of these individuals happen to be female, but this problem exists for people of all genders, as well as all ages, cultural, educational, and professional backgrounds.

Unidentified autistic individuals can spend their lifetime with a persistent sense of not fitting in. They frequently struggle with both physical and mental health challenges and are often burdened with guilt and shame for "not living up to their potential." All too frequently, they are given diagnoses that don't seem to fit and interventions that don't seem to help. These individuals may wonder:

- Why is the world such a hard place for me?

- Why do I feel like I'm different from other people?

DOI: 10.4324/9781003242130-1

- Why do I feel so alone?

- Why do I have such persistent anxiety or depression?

- Am I just not trying hard enough?

- What's wrong with me?

Of course, these individuals are not the only ones affected by this problem. Their parents, partners, siblings, friends, and others who love them may feel helpless, invalidated, or unsupported themselves. Moreover, countless healthcare professionals, educators, employers, coworkers, and others who interact with these individuals may feel confused or frustrated. It's hard to imagine an individual who has not been in a personal or professional relationship with an autistic person (whether or not they knew it).

We wrote this book because we want to help people update their understanding of autism. At first, our intended audience was mental health professionals, the individuals who are most likely to identify autistic people. Mental health professionals have widely varied educational and clinical backgrounds and just as varied perceptions of autism.

Dr. Murphy is a psychiatrist who works with adult clients. He had little training in autism, in part because he was trained several decades ago, and in part because his training did not address disorders that begin in childhood. When Dr. Murphy thinks of autism, he thinks of someone who flaps, is minimally verbal, and requires full-time care and supervision. Dr. Murphy is not aware that his knowledge of autism is outdated, and he never considers autism in the process of differential diagnosis with his clients.

Dr. Billings is a licensed psychologist. She received some training about autism, but it was never a strong interest for her, and she has always felt vaguely intimidated by it. Now that she has been a psychologist for 20 years, Dr. Billings is secretly embarrassed that she does not fully understand autism. She rarely considers it in the differential for her clients, and, when she does, she simply refers them to another professional.

Marci Grey is a masters-level psychotherapist. Marci is aware that some of her clients are undiagnosed autistics, but she is unsure of what to do about it. Even though she is licensed to diagnose in her state, Marci feels that she should not diagnose autism because she does not do formal assessments.

We have met countless clinicians who confide that they are confused and intimidated by autism. There is now research to support this observation, suggesting that many therapists have misconceptions about autism, have received significantly less education about autism than other diagnoses, and often do not feel competent to work with autistic clients.

These studies are consistent with reports from autistic adults, who describe difficulty accessing diagnosis and treatment. They report that the most frequent reason mental health professionals decline to take them as clients is the professionals' lack of knowledge about autism. Autistic adults also report that mental health professionals have difficulty understanding that their physical and mental health challenges are often related to their autism. In short, *autistic individuals do not have the same access to care as non-autistic individuals*, and healthcare professionals feel uncertain, ill-equipped, and, we believe, secretly embarrassed about this weakness in their professional expertise.

This was why we set out to write a book about autism for mental health clinicians.

As we wrote, however, we quickly realized that *all* healthcare professionals have autistic clients (whether or not they know it) and need to understand how these individuals may present. This includes not only pediatricians and neurologists, but adult primary care providers, GI specialists, sleep doctors, occupational therapists, speech/language pathologists, and many more. Then we realized that educators of all types – teachers, school counselors, paraprofessionals, and administrators – also need to recognize and understand their less obviously autistic students.

Then, family members of autistics told us that they, too, need this understanding. We were surprised at how many non-healthcare, non-educators showed interest in this topic, whether it was to better understand their child, their partner, another loved one, or themselves.

Thus, while we initially wrote this book with clinicians in mind, eventually we realized that we were writing this book for everyone who is autistic, may be autistic, has an autistic friend or family member, works with an autistic person, or teaches or supports an autistic person. In short, we wrote this book for *everyone*.

What is autism?

This is a challenging question to answer because our understanding of autism keeps evolving.

If you had asked us 40 years ago, when we were in high school, what autism was, we likely would not have heard of it.

If you had asked us 30 years ago, when we were in graduate school, we probably would have talked about something along the lines of Dustin Hoffman's portrayal of Raymond in *Rain Man*. At that point, when many people, including healthcare providers and educators, thought of autism, they probably thought of White males with overtly odd behaviors who avoided eye contact and needed almost constant care and supervision, even if they had some special abilities. Sadly, some people in the general population still have this limited perception of autism, though awareness that other ways of being autistic are possible does seem to be growing.

Our understanding of autism has, in fact, steadily expanded, and if you had asked us 20 years ago, we would have mentioned Asperger's, which included people who were autistic and also had average to well-above-average intelligence and less obvious (or perhaps less disabling) autistic traits. We probably still would have thought of a White male who was overtly quirky, if not downright odd, kind of like Sheldon from *Big Bang Theory*. While a bit more inclusive, this perception of autism is still held by countless people, including many healthcare professionals and educators. Thankfully, by the late 1990s, researchers and clinicians understood autism as a neurological difference that is largely genetic, rather than a psychological disorder caused by uncaring parents or so-called *refrigerator mothers*.

Our understanding of autism has continued to expand rapidly in recent years. If you had asked us a few years ago, we would have added the so-called *female phenotype of autism*, which is less externally obvious. These individuals do not fit our stereotypical idea of autism but are nevertheless autistic.

The idea of the *female phenotype* of autism taught us about the concept of *camouflaging*, sometimes called *masking* or *passing as non-autistic*. In recent years, a burst of research has focused on autistic females presenting in different, generally less obvious, ways than autistic males, and many autistic females shared their lived experience not only of being autistic but also of their incredible difficulty getting an accurate diagnosis. From them, we learned that some autistics actively mask their autism (e.g., by effortfully making eye contact or by hiding their repetitive behaviors), and that we needed to look under the surface to "see" the autism. Autistic girls and women taught us about autistics who mask so well that they blend in, which makes it even harder for them to access diagnoses and support.

However, even as we wrote this book, the concept of the female phenotype of autism became somewhat outdated for two important reasons. First, many males have a less obvious presentation of autism, and many females have a more traditional presentation. Second, we now understand that gender is not a binary construct. By referring to a *female phenotype*, we are excluding the many individuals who are gender non-binary, gender fluid, or otherwise do not relate to the social construct of gender. A significant number of autistic individuals fall into one of these groups.

Thus, rather than a female phenotype of autism, we discuss less obvious presentations of autism, modulated by demographic and/or cultural factors. This often, but not always, is observed in those assigned female at birth, and, throughout this book, we will highlight *what we've learned from the girls* as we discuss the less obvious presentations of autism.

Recently, our thinking has expanded again, to include the idea that autism is a natural form of human variation, rather than a genetic "mistake." This is referred to as the *neurodiversity paradigm*.

Who is "right"?

Pat (they/their) is a healthcare professional with an advanced degree who identifies as autistic and feels strongly that this is a trait, not a diagnosis or a disorder. Pat feels offended that autism is even included in the DSM and feels marginalized by people who think of autism as undesirable or problematic in any way. Pat also feels marginalized by people who suggest that their autism isn't legitimate by saying, "but you don't look autistic!"

Andrew (he/his) is a highly accomplished finance professional who identifies as autistic. He feels that having an autistic brain confers both strengths and challenges, and he is comfortable with autism being seen as a diagnosis. Andrew feels invalidated by people who feel that he is too successful to be truly autistic. At the same time, Andrew feels that he has been shamed for preferring the phrase "person with autism" instead of "autistic person." Andrew feels stuck in the middle.

Josie (she/her) is a 6-year-old with tremendous academic, social, emotional, and behavioral challenges related to being autistic. Josie's parents feel overwhelmed as they try to support her and manage her behavior. They also often feel exhausted, angry, isolated, and guilty. Josie's mother recently read an article about neurodiversity, which stated that autism is simply a form of biodiversity and should not be considered a medical problem. Josie's parents feel marginalized and invalidated by the idea of neurodiversity.

There is no single truth in this complex matter. Each person and family needs to find their own way through, while honoring different points of view.

The neurodiversity model holds that autism, like other biological variants, is simply part of human biodiversity. To explain this, we'll use the example of being left-handed, though we are not suggesting that left-handedness is as consequential an experience as being autistic.

There was a time when being left-handed was pathologized. It was considered to be a defect or a sin (the word "sinister" actually means *left* in Latin). Lefties were shamed, blamed, inconvenienced, and *forced to go against their natural physiology, for the sole reason that they were different*. At times, this was abusive. For example, some lefties had their left hand tied behind their back throughout the school day. Eventually, the medical community, educators, and the general public realized that being left-handed is not inherently bad; it is simply part of biodiversity. Now, lefties are not shamed, blamed, or made to struggle against their own bodies (though it can still be more stressful to be a lefty in a right-handed world).

The term *neurodiversity* was first used by Judy Singer, an autistic social scientist, in the late 1990s. We find it helpful to compare the neurodiversity paradigm to the traditional medical model (see Table 0.1).

Table 0.1 Medical model versus neurodiversity paradigm

	Medical model	*Neurodiversity paradigm*
Core assumption	There is a *normal* way of being, and anything significantly different from that is inherently bad – a flaw that requires correction.	There is no *normal*. Brains come in many varieties; no two brains are alike; and there is no better or worse. Moreover, neurodiversity confers a competitive advantage to our species.
Conceptualization of autism	Autism is a disease or disorder. It is undesirable and categorically bad.	Autism is part of human biodiversity and on an individual level is an inherent part of a person's identity.
Conceptualization of disability	Disability is a defect *within* a person.	Disability results from a poor fit between a person and their environment. The lack of environmental support or flexibility is disabling.

(continued)

Table 0.1 Cont.

	Medical model	*Neurodiversity paradigm*
Language used	Deficit based, ignores strengths.	Difference based, includes strengths.
Goals of treatment	The goal is to make the autistic person look less autistic or to find a cure.	The goal is to help the autistic person be their authentic self in a way that is functional in their life. Treatment should effect change in the environment to shift negative perceptions and better support the autistic person.
Ideal outcome	To prevent or cure autism.	To change the cultural narrative about autism (and other forms of biodiversity that have been pathologized).

As Elizabeth Pellicano and Jacquiline den Houting have stated, in the medical model, "autistic people and their families are regularly presented with the message that being autistic is a tragic fate, with an autism diagnosis presumed to prompt grief and mourning." In addition to the obvious implications for autistics and their families, *we are concerned about the effect this model has on clinicians.* Presumably, if a clinician thinks of autism as tragic, they will be disinclined to look for it, diagnose it, and openly discuss it with their clients. And when these clinicians do discuss autism, it will be with trepidation, anxiety, and pity. How else does one present bad news?

However, if we take the point of view of neurodiversity, then autism is not a disorder, much as being left-handed is not viewed as a disorder. We don't diagnose people whose profiles vary in ways that are a regular part of the human experience. However, if someone is struggling, even though the struggle results from a mismatch between their body and their environment, a diagnosis can serve many purposes. It can change the narrative – for the individual, their family, school, and so on – and eliminate labels that are inaccurate and/or judgmental. A diagnosis can also confer legal rights, such as accommodations and support, and it can guide appropriate intervention and support. A diagnosis, however, should not mean to convey that something is wrong *within* this person. Instead, it leads to an understanding that the person was born with a different type of nervous system, and it is incumbent on us to acknowledge that. In doing so, we can then discuss tools and strategies for living an authentic life as an autistic person in what we know is a non-autistic world.

With these additional gains in our knowledge about autism, the spectrum is now understood to be much wider and more varied than previously believed. While our focus in this book is on people who have less obvious presentations of autism, of course there are many autistic people whose presentation is more consistent with what we knew about autism in the early days, that is, with low intellectual functioning, significantly impacted language skills, and/or high support needs.

Different experiences: All valid

As we were writing this book, the world population reached 8 billion people. At the current prevalence estimate of over 2%, that means there may be more than 160 million autistic people in the world. Any group this large inevitably represents tremendous diversity. One autistic person or group does not speak for all autistic people (and we certainly don't speak for any of them). And the neurodiversity approach feels right and appropriate for some but not all autistic people.

In this book, we do not focus at all on people who are easily recognized as autistic, who have very high support needs, who may require significant care and supervision throughout their lives, and who are more likely to receive early diagnoses. We do not want in any way to invalidate the experience of these individuals, or the experiences of those who love and support them. They are just not the focus of this particular book.

We encourage everyone in the autistic, autism, and healthcare communities to continue to engage in thoughtful and respectful dialogue as we all grapple with these complex issues. We have a common goal; to improve the lives of **all** autistic people.

As our understanding of the autism spectrum has grown more complex, it has become increasingly difficult to come up with a single definition that can account for such a huge and heterogeneous group of people (as noted, probably over 2% of the world's population, so over 160 million people). *Autism has countless variations.*

With that in mind, and focusing on verbal individuals with a less obvious presentation of autism, we know that:

- Being autistic, at its core, means having a different type of nervous system.

- People who have this different kind of nervous system *experience*, *process*, and *respond* to the world differently from non-autistics in a number of ways. This can include differences in their experience of external sensations (e.g., noise, textures), their experience of internal sensations (e.g., hunger, thirst, pain), their movement patterns (e.g., stimming (self-stimulating), dyspraxia), communication (e.g., having and preferring a more direct communication style), and information processing (e.g., being more detail-oriented and less context-driven).

- These differences change over time but are lifelong and pervasive.

That is the core of autism, but there is also more to it than that. Depending on the severity of the presentation (again, this book focuses on people with a less obvious presentation), having an autistic nervous system is not necessarily a problem per se, except that autistics have to live in a world that is designed for and largely by non-autistics. This can be incredibly stressful. Simply stated, the problem is not that something is inherently wrong *with* autistics, it's that they must cope with the *mismatch* between their nervous system and a world that was not designed for them.

This mismatch causes many problems for autistics, which can very generally be categorized as *overwhelm* and *misunderstanding/being misunderstood*. These two challenges – frequent overwhelm and miscommunication – often result in social problems and anxiety, which is what non-autistics routinely see. People see the *visible, behavioral manifestations of autism*, so they think that's what autism is, like seeing the part of the island on top of the water and thinking that the island is a flat, floating land mass with nothing underneath. However, the social problems are the *result* of being autistic (in a world built for non-autistics), not the *core* of it. When we understand this, we can see why some autistic people do not look as autistic as others. The *behavioral manifestations*, that is, the social challenges, are a *result* of the autism, not the autism itself.

Let's try a thought experiment to illustrate this. Pretend that I'm taking you to the land of Flurb. Let's say that in this culture, as in most cultures, most of the social rules are not explicit (i.e., they aren't explicitly taught but need to be intuited by each individual), but we'll tell you a few just to help out. Eye contact is considered to be rude. Every time you say the word *the*, you are expected to touch your shoulder. Be careful not to smile when you greet or meet someone or when you say goodbye, but be sure to smile during conversation. Additionally, the Flurbians have different sensory needs than we do. They strongly prefer to have very loud music blaring all the time, and their preferred room temperature is about 102 degrees Fahrenheit. Let's pretend that you are in Flurb, and throughout your day, during every interaction and task, you have to cope with all of this.

- Would you be distracted? Stressed out? Physically uncomfortable?

- Would you have difficulty hearing others?

- Would your attention, energy, and social motivation suffer?

- Would you be easily able to connect with others? Impress them, convince them, self-advocate?

- Would you be able to be your authentic self?

By the way, we helped you out by listing some of the rules explicitly for you. In real life, autistics have to figure out these *implicit* rules, which frequently change in different situations, for example, how much eye contact to make, how close to stand, and how much to self-disclose are all context- and relationship-dependent.

Do you think you would accidentally make eye contact or forget to touch your shoulder? If so, **you would be considered rude, disrespectful, or weird.** And you'd want to say, "Hey! I'm new here! I'm just trying to figure out what I'm supposed to be doing to fit in! And I have a headache from the music and the heat!" But you might not be able to say any of that, and, if you did, people would find you odd. You would not be meeting the (arbitrary) social expectations, so you would be **misunderstood, invalidated, and rejected.**

But wait, there's more! When there is a mismatch like this, the pressure is entirely on the people in the minority to change and adapt. In our world, autistic people are the minority. When there is an awkward interaction between an autistic person and a non-autistic person, only the autistic person is faulted or blamed. This paradigm is referred to as *ableism.* Autistic people are blamed by others, and they often then **internalize and blame themselves.**

> *I've sort of learned to think about it as a cultural difference, that when I'm communicating with someone who is neurotypical, we're engaged in intercultural communication. I might as well be talking to someone from Portugal or Brazil or India, and the differences between us are really grounded in a very different kind of worldview, orientation, and experience.*
>
> –Pat G.

We are certain that our understanding of autism will continue to evolve, but there are four constants we know for sure:

- Being autistic affects every aspect of an individual's experience – not just social but also sensory, information processing, communication, physical health, emotional experience, etc.

- The manifestation of nervous system differences presents differently in each person; there are endless variations.

- Autistic people have both strengths and challenges.

- There are people who do not look like the stereotypical picture of autism, but they are nevertheless autistic.

If the external presentation is so subtle, what's the big deal?

> Mitch is paraplegic; he is able to use his arms well but not his legs, so he uses a wheelchair to get around. One day, Mitch arrives for an important meeting only to realize that he needs to climb a flight of stairs to enter. There is no other way into the building. Because he has no other options, Mitch leaves his wheelchair and slowly, effortfully climbs the stairs, using his arms to drag his body. Mitch eventually gets to the top, but he is exhausted, embarrassed, and unable to progress into the building without his wheelchair.
>
> On your way to the same meeting, you easily breeze up the stairs. When you encounter Mitch, and he tells you what he had to go through, would you say to Mitch, "What's the big deal? You got here, didn't you? So, there's no problem."

One of the most common questions we are asked is: "If these individuals can blend in and present themselves as non-autistic, then they aren't really autistic, are they? What's the problem?" This question takes the point of view that autism merely consists of *the behaviors that others can see*, and it does not account for the tremendous effort, exhaustion, and stress that is going on *behind the scenes*. For example, someone may seem to be "good at making eye contact." However, if doing so is effortful, forced, distracting, or uncomfortable for them, that is a problem!

The research clearly shows that being autistic leads to a much higher risk for anxiety, depression, sleep disorders, eating disorders, and suicide (ideation and action). Autistic individuals are also at higher risk for many other co-occurring conditions, such as cardiovascular disease, gastrointestinal disorders, asthma, allergies, autoimmune diseases, thyroid disease, diabetes – the list is too long to include here (see, e.g., the work of Lisa Croen and her colleagues for more detail). We review many, but not all, of these in Part Two of this book.

For now, we'd like to highlight some of the many ways that being autistic can be incredibly hard, even when, or *especially* when, the autistic person is able to blend in.

- **Compensatory techniques do not mean that a person has social intuition:** These strategies are what an individual has figured out will help them to fit in. The individual uses compensatory techniques, such as smiling back at a smiling person, because they often seem to work – not because the individual understands other people's intentions or can anticipate other people's reactions.

- **Compensatory techniques only work in some situations:** Inevitably, the individual will encounter situations in which their methods do not work. They must then develop new strategies, often with no guidance or support (e.g., when they get their first job or have their first romantic relationship).

- **Even when they work, compensatory techniques require significant cognitive, emotional, and sensory resources.** Remember the thought experiment from the land of Flurb?

- **Autistics are chronically misunderstood.** The camouflaging that these individuals must do can leave them feeling misunderstood and isolated. All too often, autistic traits and behaviors are interpreted by non-autistics as character flaws. Even worse, the autistic individual often internalizes this judgment, which then fuels their depression and poor self-image.

- **Pretending to be someone else most of the time doesn't allow a person to figure out who they really are.** Thus, autistics are at a huge disadvantage when trying to develop a sense of self, understanding who they might connect with, choosing a career, self-advocating, etc.

- **Camouflaging makes it much harder to get an accurate diagnosis.** Countless autistics who camouflage well, even when they themselves identify as autistic, are told by healthcare professionals that they cannot be autistic, simply because the clinician does not "see" the autism. It is important to be aware that interactions with clinicians are the best-case scenario for camouflaging. These interactions occur on a one-on-one basis, with few, if any, expectations of reciprocity. Moreover, they are highly structured and take place in environments that tend to be sensory-controlled (i.e., quiet and comfortable). This is one of the reasons why we are cautious about autism measures that rely solely on brief snapshots of an individual's overt behavior. We rely on information gleaned from multiple sources, such as history and an individual's inner experience.

- **Invalidation is chronic.** Even when these individuals do get a proper diagnosis of autism, they need to fight both internal and external perceptions that it's not "real autism" because they don't "look autistic." This chronic invalidation can lead to a variety of emotional responses, including self-doubt, anxiety, frustration, etc.

- **Autistics can easily be misdiagnosed.** When their autism is not recognized, they can be given other diagnoses instead. While some of these diagnoses are indeed co-occurring challenges (such as anxiety and ADHD), others may be inappropriate and even damaging. There is a long history of misdiagnosing unrecognized autistics. As Jessica Wright wrote in 2015, "In the 1950s and 1960s, thousands of children who had autism were either completely missed or were saddled with the wrong label." Subsequent studies have borne this out. As Theresa Regan noted in her book about autism in adulthood, "K. Takara and colleagues (2015) reported five mental health conditions that were highlighted as misdiagnosed psychiatric conditions or '*responsible for unrecognized [autism]*' (italics added). These diagnoses included schizophrenia, psychotic disorder, bipolar disorder, major depressive disorder, and personality disorder." These misdiagnoses can lead to interventions and medications that are at best ineffective and at worst harmful.

Remember, **being able to compensate for a challenge is *not* the same as not having that challenge.** The act of compensating comes at great cost to the individual's emotional well-being, cognition, ability to develop a sense of self, and general functional ability. Autistics who camouflage are at risk for anxiety and depression, and all too often they are lonely, victimized, and utterly drained, with little true sense of identity, negligible (socially acceptable) tools to self-regulate and self-advocate, and few, if any, opportunities for validation, support, accommodation, or intervention. It IS a big deal.

From the experts: Reflections on having a hidden disability

In what other context does compensating for something mean that thing disappears? Someone with a broken ankle that uses a boot so they can continue to walk around still has a broken ankle. Making it about what you [an observer] are seeing/perceiving, instead of about what we are experiencing/ living, is really invalidating. [There is] vulnerability behind the camouflage. The burnout, the headaches, the crying, the disassociation, the pain, the exhaustion. For many of us, I think that vulnerability is a deeply intimate and private affair – you will probably never see it. That doesn't make it any less real, any less impactful, or any less valid.

–Ralph G.

When my partner used to pick me up from work and I'd slump into the car exhausted, I'd describe it as having had to play Tetris non-stop all day, on top of doing my actual job. I worked 13 hours a week, and those 13 hours consumed my life. I spent the days after work recovering from a 7-hour masking session, and the days before in an anxious haze over doing it again.

–Jess O.

If a schizophrenic person doesn't tell you that they're hallucinating, and manages to behave "normally" while you're interacting with them, are they not schizophrenic? You don't see us after the interaction, or during the mental and physical breakdown that is burnout, or when we push ourselves/get pushed a bit too far and melt down. We're autistic. We hide it for survival – until we can't.

–Lexa G.

The cost of camouflaging is mostly the exhaustion. Life is like the music is blasting all day long, it reeks of perfume wherever I go, I am pushed and shoved in a crowd, and everything is in bright psychedelic colors. And while my senses are under assault, I have to look pleasant, not irritated, trying to read social cues and follow a conversation, but my brain is busy taking care of all the other stuff. At the end of the day, I often just shut down and can't even answer the most basic questions. The other cost is that I found my relationships – the few I have had – were very unfulfilling. Of course they were! I hid a huge part of who I was! My social self is basically a mix of sitcom characters and a mental checklist of what I should and shouldn't do during a social interaction. Absolutely exhausting!

–Marie T.

Not even my parents know that I will excuse myself to my room or the bathroom and cry and hit and scratch myself. I'll bang my head on the wall and want to die over very simple interactions or events.

–Katie R.

Key points

As you read this book, please bear the following in mind.

Autism is far more prevalent than previously believed. As our understanding of autism has evolved, prevalence rates have dramatically increased. The first estimate of the prevalence of autism was about 1 in every 2,222 children in 1966. That number has steadily increased through the following decades: 1 in 667 in 1979, 1 in 150 in 2000, 1 in 59 in 2014, 1 in 54 in 2016, and the most recent survey from 2018 found 1 in 44! And other research suggests that even this may be an underestimate.

Autism affects as many adults as children. Historically, prevalence studies focused on children, but we now know that the prevalence of autism in adults is comparable. This makes sense, as autism does not simply disappear when children grow up (though the behavioral manifestations may become less noticeable to others).

Meng-Chuan Lai and Simon Baron-Cohen's phrase, *the lost generation of autistic adults*, refers to the countless adults who are only now recognizing autism in themselves, often after their children have been diagnosed. As Johan Nyrenius and his colleagues noted, autistic individuals born prior to the mid-1990s are far less likely to have received a diagnosis before the age of 18, compared to those born after the year 2000. Traolach Brugha and colleagues found that while the rate of autism was steady across age groups, the rate of diagnosis was not. And as John Elder Robison observed about that study, "the older the study participant, the less likely they were to have been previously diagnosed with autism." Robison's interpretation of the data led him to suggest that only 3–10% of autistic adults are actually diagnosed as such.

This problem persists at least in part because so many healthcare professionals who work with adults have not been trained to recognize autism. For instance, in Ousseny Zerbo and colleagues' survey of almost 1,000 adult healthcare providers, most (over 86%) reported that they lacked the knowledge and skills to treat autistic adults, and many were not even aware that they had autistic patients. By the time someone reaches adulthood, there are simply fewer opportunities for proper diagnosis, not to mention the increased misdiagnosis of conditions like personality disorders.

Undiagnosed autism is even more prevalent in clinical populations. Recent research shows that the prevalence of autism in clinical populations (especially those with mental health conditions) is higher than in the general population, often about 20% or more! As of this writing, high rates of previously undetected autism have been found in general psychiatric outpatients, as well as those with eating disorders, substance abuse, depression, and those who have died by suicide.

These studies generally found that many, if not most, adults with significant autistic traits in the population in question had never been formally identified as autistic. It is clear that autism is even more prevalent in mental healthcare settings than previously thought.

Diagnosis is empowering! We have known far too many people (including clinicians) who – either overtly or subconsciously – think of autism as categorically bad. This mindset, and the anxiety that comes with it, makes clinicians less likely to diagnose or even consider the possibility of autism. In our experience, getting a proper diagnosis of autism, particularly when it is conveyed in a neurodiversity-affirmative manner, is a very positive and even life-changing experience. Some of the benefits are concrete, such as having access to supports, accommodations, and appropriate intervention. Other benefits are less tangible but can be even more powerful. These include protection from inaccurate or pejorative labels (e.g., "difficult," "overly sensitive," personality disorder diagnoses), a sense of community with other people who share the neurotype, and greater understanding from their family, educators, and healthcare professionals.

In our opinion, the most powerful benefit of proper diagnosis of autism is the gift of *nonjudgmental self-understanding*. Only accurate and neurodiversity-affirmative self-understanding can free an individual from a lifetime of self-blame and shame. Countless autistic individuals have beautifully expressed the freedom and validation they felt when they were finally recognized as autistic. For many, understanding themselves through this lens has enabled them to experience less emotional distress, engage in better self-care, feel a sense of community, and advocate more effectively for their needs. As Elizabeth Pellicano and Jacquiline den Houting noted, "a positive sense of autistic identity is also associated with better mental health."

From the experts: Reflections on being diagnosed

> *I cried from relief when she said autism. I never thought I could be autistic, but I knew I was different from others and wasn't sure why or how to articulate that. It made a lot of sense to me.*
>
> –DJ Chopstick

> *I am a lot more aware of my own needs, and how to address them, now that I know that I am autistic. I am also much more forgiving of myself, now that I know that the things that I had always blamed myself for and felt shame over not being able to*

control are not flaws but are a result of my neurodivergence, which is not something that I should be ashamed of. I like myself a lot more and I feel like I know who I am a lot better. I am much more comfortable with the person that I am and the things that I do. Overall, I am much, much happier and much more aware of myself, my brain, my emotions, and my body; much more capable of taking care of myself and my needs; and I like myself much more.

–Annie R.

Autism cannot and should not be ruled out solely because an individual demonstrates some "non-autistic" behaviors. In our experience, many otherwise well-trained clinicians not only miss less obvious autistic traits but they may also erroneously rule out autism when they observe what they consider to be "non-autistic" traits or behaviors. Countless autistics have been denied a diagnosis because they have typical eye contact, use basic social niceties, have friends, are socially engaging, or enjoy sarcasm. We have also encountered clinicians who rule out autism simply because an individual is happily married, a loving parent, or successful in their field. *These are not reasons to rule out autism.*

We are *not* "all a little bit autistic." A more accurate statement is that many people have one or more traits in common with autistics. For example, many ADHDers have sensory processing differences, some people with social anxiety have low eye contact, and people may also have difficulty with change or transitions. Having one or two traits is not the same as being "a little bit autistic." As our (autistic) friend Andrew says, "You can have swollen ankles and not be pregnant!"

We need to do better. Having undiagnosed autism is not a rare phenomenon; current data suggest that nearly one-fifth of people who present in a mental health clinical setting may have autism, which may be contributing to their presenting concerns. These individuals are at particularly high risk for co-occurring challenges, and they are regularly misunderstood, misdiagnosed, and marginalized. Recognition of their autism is central to, if not essential for, their well-being.

It is not reasonable to send all of these clients to autism specialists or clinics for diagnosis. These specialists are expensive and/or have long waiting lists (months to years). This makes identification and intervention even less accessible. It is also questionable for providers to categorically refer this minority group out of their practice.

Over the past decade, we have encountered countless undiagnosed autistic individuals. These individuals have appeared in our offices and in our lives. They are all ages, genders, and cultural backgrounds, with diverse levels of education, careers, and life circumstances. The common denominator has been the suffering they have endured due to being unrecognized, invalidated, and unsupported. It is for (and with) these people that we wrote this book.

References and related reading

Atladottir, H. O., Gyllenberg, D., Langridge, A., Sandin, S., Hansen, S. N., Leonard, H., Gissler, ... & Parner, E. T. (2015). The increasing prevalence of reported diagnoses of childhood psychiatric disorders: A descriptive multinational comparison. *European Child & Adolescent Psychiatry*, 24(2), 173–183.

Autism Science Foundation. (2021, December 2). *Autism Science Foundation comments on today's CDC data indicating 1 in 44 children diagnosed with autism*. Autism Science Foundation. https://autismsc iencefoundation.org/about-asf/media-center/press-releases/cdc-autism-prevalence-data-2021/

Bargiela, S., Steward, R., & Mandy, W. (2016). The experiences of late-diagnosed women with autism spectrum conditions: An investigation of the female autism phenotype. *Journal of Autism and Developmental Disorders*, 46(10), 3281–3294. https://doi.org/10.1007/s10 803-016-2872-8

Barnard, J., Harvey, V., Potter, D., & National Autistic Society. (2001). *Ignored or ineligible? The reality for adults with autism spectrum disorders*. National Autistic Society.

Baron-Cohen, S. (2019, April 30). The concept of neurodiversity is dividing the autism community. *Scientific American Blog*. https://blogs. scientificamerican.com/observations/the-concept-of-neurodiversity-is-dividing-the-autism-community/

Brugha, T. S., Spiers, N., Bankart, J., Cooper, S.-A., McManus, S., Scott, F. J., Smith, J., & Tyrer, F. (2016). Epidemiology of autism in adults across age groups and ability levels. *The British Journal of Psychiatry: The Journal of Mental Science, 209*(6), 498–503. https://doi.org/10.1192/bjp.bp.115.174649

Cassidy, S., Au-Yeung, S., Robertson, A., Cogger-Ward, H., Richards, G., Allison, C., Bradley, L., ... & Baron-Cohen, S. (2022). Autism and autistic traits in those who died by suicide in England. *The British Journal of Psychiatry*, February 15, 1–9. https://doi.org/10.1192/bjp.2022.21

Croen, L. A., Zerbo, O., Qian, Y., Massolo, M. L., Rich, S., Sidney, S., & Kripke, C. (2015). The health status of adults on the autism spectrum. *Autism, 19*(7), 814–823. https://doi.org/10.1177/1362361315577517

de Leeuw, A., Happé, F., & Hoekstra, R. A. (2020). A conceptual framework for understanding the cultural and contextual factors on autism across the globe. *Autism Research, 13*(7), 1029–1050. https://doi.org/10.1002/aur.2276

den Houting, J. (2019). Neurodiversity: An insider's perspective. *Autism, 23*(2), 271–273. https://doi.org/10.1177/1362361318820762

Hull, L., Petrides, K. V., Allison, C., Smith, P., Baron-Cohen, S., Lai, M.-C., & Mandy, W. (2017). "Putting on my best normal": Social camouflaging in adults with autism spectrum conditions. *Journal of Autism and Developmental Disorders, 47*(8), 2519–2534. https://doi.org/10.1007/s10803-017-3166-5

Huke, V., Turk, J., Saeidi, S., Kent, A., & Morgan, J. F. (2013). Autism spectrum disorders in eating disorder populations: A systematic review. *European Eating Disorders Review: The Journal of the Eating Disorders Association, 21*(5), 345–351. https://doi.org/10.1002/erv.2244

Kim, Y. S., Leventhal, B. L., Koh, Y.-J., Fombonne, E., Laska, E., Lim, E.-C., Cheon, K.-A., ... & Grinker, R. R. (2011). Prevalence of autism spectrum disorders in a total population sample. *American Journal of Psychiatry, 168*(9), 904–912. https://doi.org/10.1176/appi.ajp.2011.10101532

Lai, M.-C., & Baron-Cohen, S. (2015). Identifying the lost generation of adults with autism spectrum conditions. *The Lancet Psychiatry, 2*(11), 1013–1027. https://doi.org/10.1016/S2215-0366(15)00277-1

Lipinski, S., Boegl, K., Blanke, E. S., Suenkel, U., & Dziobek, I. (2022). A blind spot in mental healthcare? Psychotherapists lack education and expertise for the support of adults on the autism spectrum. *Autism, 26*(6), 1509–1521. https://doi.org/10.1177/13623613211057973

Livingston, L. A., Shah, P., & Happé, F. (2019). Compensatory strategies below the behavioural surface in autism: A qualitative study. *The Lancet Psychiatry*, 6(9), 766–777. https://doi.org/10.1016/S2215-0366(19)30224-X

McKowen, J., Woodward, D., Yule, A. M., DiSalvo, M., Rao, V., Greenbaum, J., Joshi, G., & Wilens, T. E. (2022). Characterizing autistic traits in treatment-seeking young adults with substance use disorders. *The American Journal on Addictions*, 31(2), 108–114. https://doi.org/10.1111/ajad.13247

Nyrenius, J., Eberhard, J., Ghaziuddin, M., Gillberg, C., & Billstedt, E. (2022). Prevalence of autism spectrum disorders in adult outpatient psychiatry. *Journal of Autism and Developmental Disorders*, 52(9), 3769–3779. https://doi.org/10.1007/s10803-021-05411-z

Pearson, A., & Rose, K. (2021). A conceptual analysis of autistic masking: Understanding the narrative of stigma and the illusion of choice. *Autism in Adulthood*, 3(1), 52–60. https://doi.org/10.1089/aut.2020.0043

Pellicano, E., & den Houting, J. (n.d.). Annual research review: Shifting from "normal science" to neurodiversity in autism science. *Journal of Child Psychology and Psychiatry*, n/a(n/a). https://doi.org/10.1111/jcpp.13534

Regan, T. (2021). *Understanding autism in adults and aging adults: Updated in 2021 with new insights for improving diagnosis and quality of life* (2nd ed.). IndieGo Publishing.

Robison, J. E. (2019). Autism prevalence and outcomes in older adults. *Autism Research*, 12(3), 370–374. https://doi.org/10.1002/aur.2080

Russo, F. (2018, February 21). The costs of camouflaging autism. *Spectrum | Autism Research News*. www.spectrumnews.org/features/deep-dive/costs-camouflaging-autism/

Takara, K., & Kondo, T. (2014). Autism spectrum disorder among first-visit depressed adult patients: Diagnostic clues from backgrounds and past history. *General Hospital Psychiatry*, 36(6), 737–742. https://doi.org/10.1016/j.genhosppsych.2014.08.004

Wright, J. (2015, December 10). Autism's lost generation. *The Atlantic*. www.theatlantic.com/health/archive/2015/12/the-lost-adults-with-autism/419511/

Zerbo, O., Massolo, M. L., Qian, Y., & Croen, L. A. (2015). A study of physician knowledge and experience with autism in adults in a large integrated healthcare system. *Journal of Autism and Developmental Disorders*, 45(12), 4002–4014. https://doi.org/10.1007/s10803-015-2579-2

Part One

What can autism actually look like?

In the chapters that follow, we will take you point by point through the criteria for autism. For each criterion, we will describe what many people *think* it means and we will then describe other ways in which it can present.

We will also cover the ways in which females may present differently from males. Over the past decade, there has been a great deal of research highlighting the under-diagnosis of autism in females as well as the different ways that they might present. We now understand that (1) males can also have a less obvious presentation and can be missed or misdiagnosed, and (2) gender is not a binary and there are many autistics (and non-autistics) who do not identify as exclusively male or female. Still, the research on autistic females is useful because it sheds light on some of the possible presentations of autism, particularly in those who camouflage.

Included in this section are the following chapters:

1. Our framework: The current diagnostic criteria

2. Reciprocity

3. Nonverbal communication

4. Relationships

5. Repetitive or idiosyncratic behavior

6. Flexibility

7. Intense or atypical interests

8. Sensory differences

DOI: 10.4324/9781003242130-2

Our framework

The current diagnostic criteria

Before we dive into our discussion, we want to orient you, the reader, to the diagnostic criteria as written in the *Diagnostic and Statistical Manual of Mental Disorders* (DSM-5-TR, 2022) and in the *International Classification of Diseases* (ICD-11, 2019).

> We want to emphasize that we are aware that these diagnostic criteria represent the perspective that non-autistic ways of communicating and responding to the world are *correct* or *appropriate* and that autistic ways of communicating and responding are *incorrect, impaired, inferior, abnormal, inappropriate,* or represent *failure.* **We disagree with the use of these words,** and in subsequent chapters, as we explain each criterion in detail, **we strive to offer wording that is more neurodiversity affirmative** and, we feel, more appropriate.
>
> For this chapter alone, however, **we are presenting the criteria exactly as written in the DSM-5-TR and in the ICD-11.** We hope our readers understand this context, and understand that words like *deficit* and *symptom* are reported below as they are used in the published criteria.

A few things to keep in mind:

• The DSM-5-TR and the ICD-11 no longer distinguish between autism and Asperger's. Instead, they collapse autistic disorder, Asperger's, and pervasive developmental disorder – not

DOI: 10.4324/9781003242130-3

otherwise specified (PDD-NOS) – into a single diagnosis: "autism spectrum disorder." Nonetheless, there continue to be individuals who identify strongly with "Asperger's," and we encourage clinicians to use language that feels right for each of their clients.

- The features do not need to be current; they can be *either* current *or* by history. This is important because some of the criteria (e.g., sensory challenges) are often more evident when people are very young. While parents and some clinicians may think that those features should not contribute to the diagnosis if the child has outgrown them, they still count. In contrast, some criteria might not have been evident early in life but may have become more clear as the child has matured; this is particularly true for autistic females.

- When working with children or adolescents, it is essential to remember that young autistic people often interact quite nicely with supportive adults (such as therapists) and that they can also do well with children who are a couple of years older or younger. When assessing their social skills, it is more important to particularly consider their interactions with same-aged peers, more so than their interactions with people who are significantly older or younger.

The criteria are divided into two major groups: (1) Social and communication challenges, and (2) Repetitive and restricted behaviors (RRBs).

Social and communication challenges

For clinicians using the DSM-5-TR, there are three criteria in this category, and an individual must experience difficulty in all three areas, either currently or historically, in order to qualify for a diagnosis.

1. Social/emotional reciprocity

2. Nonverbal communication

3. Relationship management

For clinicians using the ICD-11, there generally need to be "persistent deficits in the ability to initiate and to sustain reciprocal social interaction and social communication."

Repetitive and restricted behaviors

The DSM-5-TR lists four repetitive and restricted behaviors, and individuals only need to meet criteria for two of the four, either currently or by history, in order to qualify for diagnosis. Clinicians using the ICD-11 need to show that there is "a range of restricted, repetitive, and inflexible patterns of behaviour and interests." Either way, it is quite possible to be autistic without having repetitive behaviors, or to be autistic without having restricted interests, etc. To meet the DSM-5-TR criteria for repetitive and restricted behaviors, only two of the following four criteria must be met.

1. Repetitive or idiosyncratic behavior

2. Difficulty with flexibility

3. Restricted interests that are intense or atypical

4. Sensory differences

In the following chapters, we describe each of these criteria in detail and how they can present in people with less obvious presentations of autism. Please note that non-autistic people may experience *some* of these differences without meeting sufficient criteria for a diagnosis.

Additional Criteria

Three more criteria must be considered.

First, **symptoms must be traced back to childhood.** The DSM-5 states that "symptoms must be present in the early developmental period," and the ICD-11 states that "the onset of the disorder occurs during the developmental period, typically in early childhood." However, they both also state that symptoms may not fully manifest until later, "when social demands exceed limited capacities." The DSM-5 also adds that symptoms may not be seen at times because they "may be masked by learned strategies." This all highlights the fact that autism is not something that can begin in adolescence or adulthood. It is important to determine whether the issues were present but manageable early in life. Be careful to avoid assuming that a symptom wasn't present when the person may have been hiding it from others (masking/camouflaging) or when their environment (such as their parents) was helping them compensate.

Second, a diagnosis of autism spectrum disorder requires evidence of **clinically significant impairment** in social, occupational, or other important areas of current functioning. This can also include emotional impairment, such as anxiety, depression, or being exhausted when forced to camouflage, with a significant need for recovery time alone. It is common for the presentation to differ depending on context, holding it together when in public and breaking down once at home. Other areas that may be impacted include burnout, school or work avoidance, difficulty launching into adulthood, etc. Clearly, individuals who are seeking either an evaluation or therapy do have clinically significant challenges.

Finally, the DSM-5-TR specifies that the presentation is "not better explained by intellectual developmental disorder (intellectual disability) or global developmental delay."

DSM-5-TR and ICD-11 similarities

- Autism, Asperger's, and PDD-NOS have been collapsed into a single diagnosis: autism spectrum disorder (ASD).

- Two categories of criteria: social/communication challenges and restricted/repetitive behaviors.

- Both state that autism is present from early in the individual's development but that symptoms may not fully manifest until later.

- Both the DSM and the ICD specify that symptoms cause clinically significant impairment, which can be in any area of functioning (e.g., social, educational, vocational, emotional, etc.).

- Neither includes language impairment as a criterion.

- Both have been updated to include sensory issues as part of the criteria.

DSM-5-TR and ICD-11 differences

- The DSM specifies a minimum number of symptoms in each category – i.e., that all three social/communication criteria and two of the four restricted/repetitive criteria – must be met. In contrast, the ICD does not require a specific threshold of symptoms. Instead, it requires "persistent deficits" in the social/communication and the repetitive/restricted domains.

- The DSM specifiers include some co-occurring disorders (e.g., "with or without accompanying intellectual impairment" and "with or without accompanying language impairment"). In contrast, the ICD has different diagnostic codes for ASD, depending on such factors as the presence or absence of intellectual disability and/or functional language.

- The DSM does not include regression as a symptom or basis for diagnosis, while the ICD specifies that "loss of previously acquired skills" can be used as a basis for diagnosis.

We refer you to the DSM-5-TR for the full diagnostic criteria, and invite you to read on to learn the ways in which these criteria can be met.

References and related reading

American Psychiatric Association. (2022). *Diagnostic and statistical manual of mental disorders* (5th ed., text rev.). https://doi.org/10.1176/appi.books.9780890425787

World Health Organization. (2019). *International statistical classification of diseases and related health problems* (11th ed.). https://icd.who.int/

Chapter 2

Reciprocity

I often feel like I am in a box made of myself. Every wall is my own reflection and I can't climb out of it to where the other people are. I know I'm not relating like other people. It's like there's no door in the box.

–Nicole R.

What people often think difficulty with reciprocity means

Many clinicians believe this means someone who is entirely disengaged from or lacks empathy for others. Not only is this untrue, but reciprocal interactions also involve much more than engagement and empathy.

What do reciprocal interactions really entail?

Before we can talk about problems with reciprocity, we need to first understand what reciprocal interactions *between non-autistic people* usually require. Non-autistics don't typically think of social interactions as complex because for most of us these interactions are fairly intuitive. For instance, if you are a non-autistic person and you see someone you know, you will have an intuition about how to behave. You may or may not be in the mood for it, and you may or may not enjoy it, but generally you don't have to put any conscious thought into whether or not to greet them and how to do it.

But when you think about it, interactions are actually quite complicated. For instance, we have many different types of greetings, from a formal handshake with a new colleague to a

DOI: 10.4324/9781003242130-4

warm embrace for an old friend. In addition, you have to manage the back-and-forth and flow of the interaction. (Am I talking too much? Am I interrupting? Am I building on what the other person says?) Again, generally speaking, people who do not have autism manage all of this with little conscious thought.

Co-regulation is a key component of reciprocity. Co-regulation refers in part to the adaptations you make to sustain a social interaction. For example, if you are talking to someone, and they suddenly look annoyed, you will try to figure out what you said that annoyed them, and you will then try to address it by apologizing or correcting a mistaken impression. One goal with co-regulation is to keep the interaction going, and going well.

Building on what the other person says is another core aspect of reciprocity. If I "drop a social breadcrumb," non-autistic people will typically pick it up. For example, if I say, "Something funny happened to me last night," my conversational partner might say, "Oh! What happened?" That's how we build a conversation *together*. If your conversation partner doesn't respond in a way that builds on what you have said, there's a lack of typical reciprocity.

Another way that people establish reciprocity is by **sharing experiences**. Let's say you make a new friend. You have lunch every week or two for a few months. After a while you realize that she never brings up anything about herself. You don't know anything about her family, her job, her last vacation, or the books she has read. Would you feel close to her? Probably not. To connect with others, we have to share about ourselves.

One day, 16-year-old Ethan said to his mom, "Can you give me a ride to school tonight?"

His mom said, "Sure, but why?"

Ethan said, "Because there's a film festival I'm going to go to."

His mom replied, "Oh! I didn't know you had any interest in film. It's totally fine, I'm just curious, where is this coming from?"

Ethan said, "Well, my teacher wants me to go."

"Why does your teacher want you to go?"

"I don't know, I think it's because I won an award."

If Ethan had not needed a ride, it would have never occurred to him to tell his mom that he had submitted a video and won an award.

Another side of non-autistic reciprocity is **to show curiosity about the other person,** to wonder about what is going on with them. If you made a new friend and had lunch with them every few weeks for a few months, would you feel close to them if they never once followed up on something you had shared ("Oh, your kids were sick; how are they feeling?" or "You were stressed out at work; how's that going?" or "I can't wait to hear about your big trip!")? Probably not. Sharing your own experiences and being curious about the other person's experiences are critical to reciprocal interactions.

Reciprocity also involves **the ability to see the world from the other person's point of view.** Because most of us do this all the time, we don't realize how intuitive it is, but it is absolutely essential. For example, Donna's 15-year-old approached her a few nights ago while she was doing something and said, "I'm having trouble concentrating." Donna had to understand her child's point of view to grasp that what she really meant was, "Please stop what you're doing and listen to me because I'm upset."

We sometimes help people understand reciprocal conversation by thinking of it as a ping pong game. To play ping pong, we have to hit a ball back and forth to each other. If you keep hitting balls to me, but I never even try to send them back to you, we are not really playing together. If I hit the ball to you, you need to at least try to send it right back to me. Also, if I'm hitting one ball, and you're hitting a different ball, even if we are at the same table, we aren't really playing together. When we are hitting the same ball back and forth, we are playing a game together!

So, what might this look like in someone with a less obvious presentation of autism?

Autistic individuals can have different social/communication preferences and styles, which can present in a variety of ways and can often be misinterpreted as an undesirable or off-putting personality trait. Remember, autistics can struggle with any number of the examples below, but not necessarily with all of them. As Drew R. reminded us, "there is no right or wrong way to have a conversation."

Areas of difficulty can include:

Difficulty greeting or responding to greetings: Some autistic people do not spontaneously greet others or intuitively know how to respond to greetings. This can sometimes be misinterpreted as shyness. If an individual seems self-assured, this can also be misinterpreted as arrogance or rudeness.

Low level of interpersonal interest: Some autistics have a low level of genuine interest in other people, their perspectives, or their interests (not to be confused with social motivation, which is an interest in connecting with others). Sometimes they "turn off" or disengage when conversations don't interest them, and sometimes they don't ask other people follow-up questions (e.g., How was your vacation? Is your husband feeling better?). People who don't have natural curiosity about others can be misunderstood as selfish or self-centered.

The myth of low empathy

Many people mistakenly believe that autistics have low empathy. To understand this, we need to understand the difference between *cognitive empathy* (the capacity to take the perspective of another person and infer their mental state) and *affective empathy* (which refers to one's emotional response to another person's experience). Additionally, some researchers also describe *compassionate empathy* (when you want to take action to help someone else). Many autistics struggle with cognitive empathy but have typical (or even tremendous) affective empathy. That is, *when they are aware* of another person's (or animal's) pain, they may be deeply concerned. This feeling may or may not be reflected in their behavior.

The concept of *empathic disequilibrium* is also relevant here. This idea, proposed by Ido Shalev and Florina Uzefovsky, proposes that some autistics have an *imbalance between their cognitive and affective empathy*. This is consistent with our clinical experience.

Difficulty feigning interest, knowing that they are expected to feign interest, or understanding why: Autistic people can often easily engage in conversation pertaining to a topic they enjoy. Sarah heard an anecdote from a colleague about a child he initially misdiagnosed because they shared the same intense interest. He mistakenly thought the child was reciprocal, but the reciprocity was only evident when they talked about a shared interest. However, when the topic changes to something they are not interested in, they may disengage. This violates an implicit social expectation, that is, showing curiosity about the experiences of others, and it can seem very rude.

A tendency to not share personal information, experiences, or emotions: Some autistics are happy to talk about topics of interest, facts, or information but do not spontaneously share more personal information (e.g., what they did this weekend, something funny that happened to them this morning, etc.). This lack of sharing can lead to a vague feeling that someone may be pleasant, yet we can't quite connect with them.

Difficulty initiating interactions: Sometimes autistic children or adults want to initiate an interaction with others (teachers, peers, a romantic interest, etc.) but are unsure how to do so. They may try in an unusual manner, try in a manner that is ultimately successful but ends up depleting their social energy, or they may give up and not try at all. For autistics with unmet social needs, this can lead to loneliness, frustration, and/or self-blame.

Difficulty with the back-and-forth flow of interactions: For many autistics, the turn-taking in interactions with non-autistic conversation partners is not intuitive. For instance, they may take up too much "air time" or talk *at* people instead of *with* them. This can make them appear self-centered. Alternatively, some autistics put a lot of thought and energy into the back-and-forth flow of conversation; while this may result in a richer and more satisfying conversation for the non-autistics involved, it involves camouflaging and can be exhausting and/or stressful for the autistic individual.

Difficulty building a conversation that feels reciprocal to non-autistic partners: This has more to do with the *content* of conversations, rather than the flow itself. Many autistic people have difficulty intuitively building on what other people say in conversation. This may manifest in failure to respond at all (e.g., "I'm so mad at my math teacher!" being met with silence), or in a disjointed attempt at conversation ("I'm so mad at my math teacher!" being met with, "Tomorrow's my birthday!"). This can sometimes be misinterpreted as lack of interest/caring or of attention (and sometimes poor attention is *part* of the problem).

Having an unusually direct communication style: Many autistic people have a very direct communication style that can be experienced as overly blunt by non-autistic people. This can inadvertently make them appear to be unkind or disrespectful.

Giving an unexpected amount of context to the listener: If an autistic person does not intuitively understand another person's point of view, they may not realize that the other person does not have all of the information that they themselves have. This can lead them to tell stories without giving any context, which can be confusing or frustrating for others, giving the wrongful impression that the person with autism is flighty or ditzy. Alternatively, they may give too much context, that is, they may include far too many details for their listener.

Difficulty engaging with a group: Many autistics can do well one-on-one but have significant difficulty joining and then interacting successfully in a large or even a small group. This is another situation where they can be labeled as shy or stand-offish.

Difficulty seeing a comment or situation from the other person's point of view: This is often a core issue for autistic individuals. If someone is not able to understand how another person may feel in response to what they are saying, they will not be aware of how their words affect the other person. This can lead to the autistic being misperceived as mean, rude, or uncaring.

Kristi was a bright 14-year-old with a same-aged cousin. The families were close and had positive relationships. The cousin had been adopted at birth, but no one ever really thought about that or talked about it. One day, when discussing something related to the family, Kristi said, "Well, except for you, Emily, you're not technically part of the family, since you're adopted." Her mom was (understandably) horrified. She pulled Kristi over and explained, "You can't say that!" Kristi said, "I don't understand why, it's just a fact."

This actually happened again a few months later, even though Kristi's mother had explained to her why it might be hurtful to Emily. Kristi wasn't mean; she simply had no idea how her words would affect her cousin and believed that she was just stating the facts.

Misunderstanding other people's intentions: Some autistic people struggle to understand others' intentions, for instance, which actions are accidental and which are intentional. And if they believe an action is intentional when it was not, they may believe that the other person is deliberately trying to upset them. These can lead to big reactions to minor or benign events and can make a child appear overly sensitive. For example, if one child knocked over another child's toys as he ran past, most children intuitively know that it was an accident. While the child whose toys were knocked over may still get upset, non-autistic kids typically do not think the other child knocked the toys over on purpose. Another frequent misinterpretation involves accidental touching during a sporting event or simply when passing in a hallway. For example, "every time he's playing soccer, if someone just shoulder checks him, he thinks that person is trying to start a fight with him. He takes it personally."

This can cause significant challenges for autistic individuals throughout their lives. For example, as they mature, it may be difficult for them to know whether someone is flirting with them, trying to be helpful, being disrespectful, or is ill-intentioned, just to name a few. Difficulty intuitively understanding others' intentions can make autistic individuals particularly vulnerable to manipulation or victimization.

Overusing one way of interacting with others: Sometimes when an autistic person does not know how to manage interactions with peers, they will find one way that works and then repeat it whether it's appropriate or not. For example, they may tell a joke one day, and if it goes over well, conclude that joking is a good way to interact with others and begin telling jokes all the time (i.e., being the class clown). This limited repertoire of ways to interact with others can create challenges (e.g., joking when the teacher is reprimanding, repeating the same jokes even though others no longer think they are funny).

From the experts: Reflections on some things that make interactions challenging

> **Implicit rules change with context:** "*Sometimes the social rules at play in a situation allow for – even positively encourage – interrupting; it's seen as making for lively, interesting discussions. And other times interrupting is unbearably rude. And I've never figured out how to tell which set of rules is in play.*"
>
> –Charlotte R.

> **Social rules aren't always logical:** "*Learning manners was particularly hard because I wanted to know why we had to do some of these odd things and could never get a logical answer, or the historical reason was outdated and seemed no longer relevant to society.*"
>
> –Taylor M.

> **Slow processing speed gets in the way:** "*The timing thing. OMG the timing thing. Because I tend to process information more slowly than most people, when I'm in a larger group of people, especially if I'm the only neurodivergent person in the group, I'm often just sitting there listening to the others talk since I can't process what everyone's saying fast enough to get a word in before the conversation moves to another topic or someone else has already said what I wanted to say.*"
>
> –Zachary M.

Scripting takes time and doesn't always work: "*I used to have to script everything I was gonna say before I said it. Sometimes it worked but sometimes the conversation moved on and I never got to [use the script].*"

–Mimi

It's hard to know how much is too much: "*I'm in the 'TMI' faction. Basically, I meet strangers and two minutes in I'm telling them about deep dark secrets, such as how my time in prison was and all about my sexual and romantic preferences. I know that's not appropriate. And dangerous. And not helpful in making new contacts/friendships. And every time I tell myself, 'this time you'll listen more than you talk! And when you talk, talk more about benign things!' – and then it's the same as usual.*"

–Elena-María G.

Cognitive attention and effort are being used for coping: "*My brain is working twice as hard in the conversation, taking in and understanding and responding to what everyone is saying, and also thinking about what I said and how everyone reacted, and what I will say next, and thinking about how this is the same or different as other conversations I've had, and if I have it again how would it go. It feels like my brain has to work during conversations.*"

–Mimi

Similarly, Nate B. explained to us that he relies on data to analyze and respond to social interactions, stating, "*I think about things methodically, even in social situations. It's like I have an internal database based on past experiences.*" Nate likens this to AI algorithms in that he makes predictions and uses those data to refine future predictions for conversations.

Misunderstanding other people's intentions hinders interactions: "*There was a time when I flirted with someone. We had romantic dates, like reading poetry to one another. Then one night on my balcony, she asked me if I felt like kissing someone. Dumbass me went on a kinda rant on whom*

I'd like to kiss under what conditions, purely hypothetically speaking. Now it's clear to me she was implicitly asking whether I wanted to kiss HER and she was communicating her interest in doing so."

–Elena-María G.

It's hard to engage when it's neither a topic of interest nor "useful": *"I'm constantly trying to figure out the right thing to say next since there isn't an actual exchange of useful information or ideas taking place. I don't want to be rude or dismissive. I want to be polite and friendly, yet carrying on a conversation about an uninteresting (or arguably non-existent) topic requires a LOT of effort."*

–Jesse P.

Misread signals affect participation: *"I register a vast majority of facial expressions as surprise or confusion. I think this ties into my conversation problem as well. I take these believed expressions as being indicators that I need to talk MORE, and in more detail, to resolve the issue of their being surprised or confused by what I am saying."*

–Eric O.

Sometimes there's awareness but no control: *"My conversational dominance came out when I laid out in detail how Chernobyl happened; then I carried over – without any input from others – to the ExxonMobil accident, and so on. I was so passionate about the topic and felt like I just needed to explain better and kept going until everyone was gone. I feel awful now. I knew they didn't want to hear it – why did I continue?"*

–Elena-María G.

Countless other factors may hinder the ability to engage: *"One of the things that make interactions difficult is that I'm faceblind. If I'm out on a walk and someone waves at me from the other side of the street, I have to figure out if that's a random stranger who is just being friendly, or if it's someone I know well. That has to happen before I can respond appropriately. Which means I have to do an immediate calculation of the possible responses, the time available to respond, and the cost of getting it wrong. The risks and difficulties of this kind of awkwardness in and around the office are even greater. That person I'm passing in the hall – is it the new guy? Someone on another team that I've been working with regularly, in another building, for the past 6 months? My boss's boss?"*

–Charlotte R.

What is camouflaging, anyway?

It is impossible to understand the less obvious presentations of autism without understanding *camouflaging*. To camouflage basically means *to change one's external presentation in order to blend into one's surroundings.* This is sometimes referred to as *masking* (though some people use the term masking to represent only one type of camouflaging), *passing as non-autistic, nuanced presentation,* or *pretending to be normal.*

There are countless ways to camouflage, such as studying and copying other people, following scripts in conversation, reminding yourself to use eye contact, looking at people's foreheads instead of their eyes, consciously using voice intonation or gestures differently from what feels natural, hiding stimming behaviors, ignoring sensory sensitivities, and many more.

All of us – autistic or not – camouflage at times. For example, there are times that we are furious with our children but work hard to remain calm as we interact with them. There are times when we have distractions, such as a headache, hunger, or a personal problem, but we do not let that show when we are interacting with our clients. However, many autistic individuals camouflage far more frequently, for longer periods of time, and it is highly effortful for them to do so.

Using this verb – *camouflaging* – implies that the act is a *choice.* However, as autistic social psychologist Dr. Devon Price points out, this is less a conscious decision and more a burden that is forced upon autistics by the expectations of those around them. Whether conscious or unconscious, camouflaging requires effort and energy. Moreover, when the individual is trying to present as a member of the dominant culture, there is an element of shame involved, which increases the resulting stress and exhaustion. As Dr. Price noted when interviewed on the *Uniquely Human* podcast, "You have to be hypervigilant all the time to try to avoid detection, and you've even internalized that shame and blame."

The effort of camouflaging often begins before the interaction, while the individual is still alone and can plan how to greet others, practice facial expressions and gestures, memorize topics for conversation, and many other aspects of interactions that most of us do not carefully plan or even consciously think about. Similarly, the effects of camouflaging can last long after the individual has left a situation; autistics who camouflage regularly report extreme fatigue and the need for long recovery periods afterward.

> *I very consciously practiced how to express different emotions so that other people understood me better. I remember especially practicing being nervous and shy in the "right way." I wasn't even always nervous, I just thought this is a nervous type of situation or I should be a bit shy now or things like that, so I tried to fit my body language to this, based on how I saw other people behave in that situation. I've also consciously copied having a fight with someone, not only words but also tone of voice, and when is it okay to leave, how to leave and make a point out of it, and so on.*
>
> —Miko

Camouflaging is neither categorically *good* nor *bad*. The primary advantage of camouflaging is blending in and not calling negative or unwanted attention to oneself. (However, it doesn't always work. For instance, we can't plan for novel or unusual situations.) That said, if someone feels forced to camouflage much or most of the time, even with close friends and family, it will lead to anxiety, a high stress level, exhaustion, a sense of not truly being understood by others, and/or difficulty developing a sense of one's true identity (i.e., you can't figure out who you are if you are constantly pretending to be someone else). Thus, the goal with autistics is not to teach them to camouflage more or to camouflage less but to gain awareness about their camouflaging and to find a balance between using that as a tool to be functional in their lives while still being able to "drop the mask" and be themselves.

Recent research suggests that autistic females may camouflage more, more frequently, and/or more successfully than autistic males. However, autistics of any gender may camouflage to the extent that their autism is less obvious, which can lead to serious consequences, such as stress and exhaustion. Clinicians and others need to understand how much a client is camouflaging and to what extent that is causing them distress (and clinicians also need to consider the possibility that their clients are camouflaging during therapy or testing).

From the experts: Reflections on camouflaging

Camouflaging is like speaking a second language. Even if you speak it fairly well, it will never be your first language and it will always be harder than speaking your first language.

–Matthew G.

Analyzing social situations takes so much energy and attention, which means I have less energy and attention to devote to the content of the conversation or the task I'm trying to do.

–Grace O.

It hurts a lot when people say "you don't seem autistic." Masking has been ingrained in me by society and has become a habit. It's taxing and it hides who I am. So, when people tell me I don't seem autistic, it points out that they don't see me. They don't see the hours I spend decompressing from the day. They don't see the struggle to communicate and the worry that I will say something offensively blunt or tactless. Society has told me that who I am is wrong, and that hurts. I mask because I don't want to be alone.

–Sarah K.

I have camouflaged my entire life by not doing things (like rocking) that other people objected to. I wasn't given alternatives – it didn't occur to anyone that these behaviors were meeting a need. They just weren't appropriate, and I wasn't allowed to do them.

–Charlotte R.

Reciprocity: What we've learned from the girls

Autistic girls often present differently than autistic boys. This is in part because **autistic girls are more likely to follow the implicit non-autistic norm of reciprocity** than autistic boys. (The *ableist* way to put this is that autistic girls have better functional conversational skills than autistic boys do.) They are more likely to use functional conversational skills by greeting others, asking others about themselves, and sharing personal information. They understand the basics of non-autistic reciprocal communication. Donna was talking about this one day with a group of her colleagues, including a young associate, Eric, who has run many social skills groups and was excited by this idea. He said, "Every time we start a new group, by the end of the first session, I always know why the boys are there. It's always obvious. Sometimes it's subtle, but I can always tell why they are there in the group. And sometimes I can tell with the girls as well, but there are always some girls ... we get through the first session, the second session, the third session ... and I don't know what they're doing there. I start thinking this is a mistake, she shouldn't be here. What's going on?" Eric continued, "But sooner or later, I always see it. I always see why the girls are there, it just takes longer because they camouflage so well."

Eric's observations are absolutely consistent with the research. Many autistic girls demonstrate typical (i.e., non-autistic) basic social interaction skills. To determine whether they struggle with this, it is essential to understand their inner experience. For most of us, engaging in social niceties can be pleasant, sometimes boring if we're not in the mood, sometimes anxiety-provoking, but it rarely requires conscious effort. In contrast, autistic women have been telling us for years that **they can be reciprocal, but that it takes work and is incredibly exhausting and stressful.** This is because they are determining how to navigate the social niceties using their prefrontal cortex, while the rest of us don't have to do that. It's like doing math in your head all day long! No wonder it's exhausting. And when you are using all of your executive functioning skills to navigate social interactions, your prefrontal lobe has no additional resources to devote to planning and organizing, staying on task, and other executive functioning skills.

Mr. and Mrs. Parker and their three children frequently hiked. Over time, Mrs. Parker noticed that the younger two children always greeted other hikers. Typically, when you're hiking in a remote area and you pass somebody, you say hello, or you at least nod and make eye contact. She noticed that her older daughter, Erica, didn't do that, so she coached her: "The rule is, when no one else is around and you pass someone on the trail, you greet them."

One day, when Erica was in 8th grade, she and her mom were walking into the supermarket. They passed a family that had a same-aged daughter. They knew this family pretty well but hadn't seen them in about a year. Mrs. Parker stopped to chat, but Erica just kept walking into the supermarket. When her mom caught up, she said, "Why didn't you say hello to Abby?" Erica replied, "I don't really know Abby." Mrs. Parker said, "Can you picture her kitchen? Has she played with our dog? Were you in the same girl scout troop?" "Yes." "Well, all of those things mean that you know her. The rule is, if you know someone, you stop and say hello, even if you haven't seen them in a long time. Especially if you haven't seen them in a long time."

By this time, the mother and daughter were in the supermarket. Erica thought about what her mother had said and asked, "So do I say hello to everyone in the supermarket? Is it like the hiking trail?" Mrs. Parker replied, "No, that'd be weird!" Erica, who was a very bright, straight A student, burst into tears and exclaimed, "There are so many secret rules! How does everyone learn all of the secret rules?"

Non-autistic people generally do not need to put conscious thought into following the social "rules," they just intuitively know whether or not to say hello to someone. In contrast, **autistics who have learned to camouflage need to think through every interaction, even simple ones.** This is, understandably, exhausting.

Connecting culture

The social rules around communication, reciprocity, turn-taking, interrupting, and humor are culture-bound. For example,

Donna grew up in New York and New Jersey, where sarcasm is a regular part of conversations. When she went to graduate school in Ohio, she quickly learned that sarcasm was less integral to daily conversations. There are endless variations to cultural differences, and there is no way for clinicians to know all of them, so we recommend that clinicians proactively ask their clients about their cultural background and communication norms.

Clinicians often consider the nature of play and parent–child interactions in social cognition assessments. In the United States, the benchmarks for "acceptable" or "desired" play skills (and, thus, related interventions) are often based on Euro-American behavioral norms. Adults often teach or encourage exploratory play, physical play, pretend play, cause-and-effect play, toy play, and goal-oriented or constructive play (like building blocks, doing puzzles, drawing). Clinicians encourage parents to play with their child to model "appropriate" social behaviors. While these skills can be developmentally helpful, it is essential to *ask* about the norms and practices that are important to the client's personal, family, and cultural background. Not all cultures define or value these concepts in the same way. Components of reciprocity where cross-cultural differences may be particularly relevant include topics of conversation, rules around turn-taking and interrupting, use of humor, and type of play partner (e.g., adult versus peer; familiar versus unfamiliar).

Even *within* racial groups (e.g., White, Black, Asian, Middle Eastern, Latin, etc.), there are cultural subgroups, each with their own variability in social norms and experience. For example, we recently heard an episode of the *Hidden Brain* podcast with Batia Mesquita, a Dutch psychologist married to an American. Dr. Mesquita explained that, in her country of origin, if someone you are close with does something for you – say, cooks you dinner – the act of kindness is part of the closeness of that relationship and thanking them would be considered rude. In contrast, in the United States it is considered rude *not* to thank someone for doing something kind, regardless of your relationship with them. There are countless variations on these types of cultural differences, even within larger cultural groups. The only way to truly understand an individual's personal and cultural (and subcultural) experience is to ask them.

Race, gender, and ethnic/societal/cultural expectations are intertwined with the act of masking. People camouflage in many different situations, and not just to hide autistic traits. An example of this can be seen with the behavior of *code switching*: the act of changing your tone of voice and mannerisms to match or fit in with certain audiences. In Black culture, code switching is often equated to "talking White." For many, this necessary and often fluent ability to code switch is something learned early in life. However, for a Black autistic person, code switching can be quite complicated. They have to: (1) be *aware* enough of their environment/audience to *recognize* the need to code switch; and (2) *quickly and repeatedly shift* their behavior/language/manner to optimize their interactions with a particular person or group. Thus, autistics from certain cultural backgrounds may have to *double camouflage* in some situations.

Romantic interests and attempts at dating are uniquely precarious for autistic people of color (POC). For example, autistic males of color are at risk of being perceived as *aggressively stalking* when they pursue a romantic relationship.

Awkwardness, clumsiness, and misreading of social cues (and especially of the other party's level of interest) may be seen as much more aggressive and intimidating than they would be in a White autistic male. Moreover, there are studies that have shown that if the two people involved are from different cultures, the pursuing behavior may be interpreted as even more threatening.

Additionally, while all autistic females are at elevated risk for victimization, this risk may be even higher for some minority groups. For instance, young Black females have historically been oversexualized in American culture (e.g., see the work of Shirley Anne Tate, as well as Rebecca Epstein and her colleagues). They have been viewed as promiscuous and more sexually mature at younger ages than their White counterparts, which could place them at risk of being taken advantage of or blamed for sexual promiscuity, when perhaps they simply misunderstood the intentions of a sexual partner and did not know how to navigate the delicate (or threatening) situation.

Frequently asked questions

- If someone initiates interactions with an unusual behavior, would it qualify here or in a different category? This is a great example of how one behavior can seem to satisfy different criteria. For instance, if a child licks people to say hello, the clinician should determine if the point of the licking is to greet (in which case it belongs in this category), or if the licking is primarily to taste/explore/enjoy (in which case it belongs in the sensory category).

- I don't like small talk. Does that make me autistic? No. Many people don't enjoy small talk, which is different from a situation where even basic conversations are incredibly effortful and exhausting. Additionally, there are people who aren't particularly socially skilled but are not autistic.

References and related reading

Ai, W., Cunningham, W. A., & Lai, M.-C. (2022). Reconsidering autistic 'camouflaging' as transactional impression management. *Trends in Cognitive Sciences*. https://doi.org/10.1016/j.tics.2022.05.002

Amalia, R. P. (2018, September). Teaching children with autism by implementing Floor Time method at elementary schools in Situbondo. International Seminar on Language and Culture, Universitas Negeri Malang. http://repository.unars.ac.id/id/eprint/208/

American Psychiatric Association. (2022). *Diagnostic and statistical manual of mental disorders* (5th ed., text rev.). https://doi.org/10.1176/appi.books.9780890425787

Baldwin, S., & Costley, D. (2016). The experiences and needs of female adults with high-functioning autism spectrum disorder. *Autism: The International Journal of Research and Practice, 20*(4), 483–495. https://doi.org/10.1177/1362361315590805

Bargiela, S., Steward, R., & Mandy, W. (2016). The experiences of late-diagnosed women with autism spectrum conditions: An investigation of the female autism phenotype. *Journal of Autism and Developmental Disorders, 46*(10), 3281–3294. https://doi.org/10.1007/s10803-016-2872-8

Bell, E. L. (1992). Myths, stereotypes, and realities of Black women: A personal reflection. *The Journal of Applied Behavioral Science, 28*(3), 363–376. https://doi.org/10.1177/0021886392283003

Burkett, C. (2020, January 21). 'Autistic while Black': How autism amplifies stereotypes. *Spectrum | Autism Research News.* www.spect rumnews.org/opinion/viewpoint/autistic-while-black-how-autism-amplifies-stereotypes/

Candido, M. R., & Feres, J. (2019). Representation and stereotypes of Black women in Brazilian film. *Revista Estudos Feministas, 27*. https://doi.org/10.1590/1806-9584-2019v27n254549

Carter, J. A., Lees, J. A., Murira, G. M., Gona, J., Neville, B. G. R., & Newton, C. R. J. C. (2005). Issues in the development of cross-cultural assessments of speech and language for children. *International Journal of Language & Communication Disorders, 40*(4), 385–401. https://doi.org/10.1080/13682820500057301

Colombi, C., Narzisi, A., Ruta, L., Cigala, V., Gagliano, A., Pioggia, G., Siracusano, R., ... & Muratori, F. (2018). Implementation of the Early Start Denver Model in an Italian community. *Autism, 22*(2), 126–133. https://doi.org/10.1177/1362361316665792

Dean, M., Harwood, R., & Kasari, C. (2017). The art of camouflage: Gender differences in the social behaviors of girls and boys with autism spectrum disorder. *Autism, 21*(6), 678–689. https://doi.org/10.1177/1362361316671845

Dickens, D. D., & Chavez, E. L. (2018). Navigating the workplace: The costs and benefits of shifting identities at work among early career U.S. Black women. *Sex Roles, 78*(11), 760–774. https://doi.org/10.1007/s11199-017-0844-x

Duvall, S., Armstrong, K., Shahabuddin, A., Grantz, C., Fein, D., & Lord, C. (2021). A road map for identifying autism spectrum disorder: Recognizing and evaluating characteristics that should raise red or "pink" flags to guide accurate differential diagnosis. *The Clinical Neuropsychologist, 36*(5), 1–36. https://doi.org/10.1080/13854046.2021.1921276

Dworzynski, K., Ronald, A., Bolton, P., & Happé, F. (2012). How different are girls and boys above and below the diagnostic threshold for autism spectrum disorders? *Journal of the American Academy of Child and Adolescent Psychiatry, 51*(8), 788–797. https://doi.org/10.1016/j.jaac.2012.05.018

Epstein, R., Blake, J., & González, T. (2017). Girlhood interrupted: The erasure of Black girls' childhood (SSRN Scholarly Paper No. 3000695). Social Science Research Network. https://doi.org/10.2139/ssrn.3000695

Farver, J. M., & Howes, C. (1993). Cultural differences in American and Mexican mother–child pretend play. *Merrill-Palmer Quarterly*, *39*(3), 344–358.

Fitzgerald, M., & Yip, J. (2017). *Autism: Paradigms, recent research and clinical applications*. InTech Limited.

Geelhand, P., Bernard, P., Klein, O., van Tiel, B., & Kissine, M. (2019). The role of gender in the perception of autism symptom severity and future behavioral development. *Molecular Autism*, *10*(1), 16. https://doi.org/10.1186/s13229-019-0266-4

Green, R. M., Travers, A. M., Howe, Y., & McDougle, C. J. (2019). Women and autism spectrum disorder: Diagnosis and implications for treatment of adolescents and adults. *Current Psychiatry Reports*, *21*(4), 22. https://doi.org/10.1007/s11920-019-1006-3

Hester, N., & Gray, K. (2018). For Black men, being tall increases threat stereotyping and police stops. *Proceedings of the National Academy of Sciences*, *115*(11), 2711–2715. https://doi.org/10.1073/pnas.1714454115

Hiller, R. M., Young, R. L., & Weber, N. (2014). Sex differences in autism spectrum disorder based on DSM-5 criteria: Evidence from clinician and teacher reporting. *Journal of Abnormal Child Psychology*, *42*(8), 1381–1393. https://doi.org/10.1007/s10802-014-9881-x

Hull, L., Lai, M.-C., Baron-Cohen, S., Allison, C., Smith, P., Petrides, K. V., & Mandy, W. (2020). Gender differences in self-reported camouflaging in autistic and non-autistic adults. *Autism: The International Journal of Research and Practice*, *24*(2), 352–363. https://doi.org/10.1177/1362361319864804

Hull, L., Mandy, W., & Petrides, K. V. (2017). Behavioral and cognitive sex/gender differences in autism spectrum condition and typically developing males and females. *Autism: The International Journal of Research and Practice*, *21*(6), 706–727. https://doi.org/10.1177/1362361316669087

Hull, L., Petrides, K. V., & Mandy, W. (2020). The female autism phenotype and camouflaging: A narrative review. *Review Journal of Autism and Developmental Disorders*, *7*(4), 306–317. https://doi.org/10.1007/s40489-020-00197-9

Hull, L., Petrides, K. V., Allison, C., Smith, P., Baron-Cohen, S., Lai, M.-C., & Mandy, W. (2017). "Putting on my best normal": Social camouflaging in adults with autism spectrum conditions. *Journal of Autism and Developmental Disorders*, *47*(8), 2519–2534. https://doi.org/10.1007/s10803-017-3166-5

Kang-Yi, C. D., Grinker, R. R., & Mandell, D. S. (2013). Korean culture and autism spectrum disorders. *Journal of Autism and Developmental Disorders*, *43*(3), 503–520. https://doi.org/10.1007/s10803-012-1570-4

Kirkovski, M., Enticott, P. G., & Fitzgerald, P. B. (2013). A review of the role of female gender in autism spectrum disorders. *Journal of Autism and Developmental Disorders*, *43*(11), 2584–2603. https://doi.org/10.1007/s10803-013-1811-1

Kopp, S., & Gillberg, C. (1992). Girls with social deficits and learning problems: Autism, atypical Asperger syndrome or a variant of these conditions. *European Child & Adolescent Psychiatry*, *1*(2), 89–99. https://doi.org/10.1007/BF02091791

Lai, M.-C., & Baron-Cohen, S. (2015). Identifying the lost generation of adults with autism spectrum conditions. *The Lancet. Psychiatry*, *2*(11), 1013–1027. https://doi.org/10.1016/S2215-0366(15)00277-1

Lai, M.-C., & Szatmari, P. (2020). Sex and gender impacts on the behavioural presentation and recognition of autism. *Current Opinion in Psychiatry*, *33*(2), 117–123. https://doi.org/10.1097/YCO.0000000000000575

Lai, M.-C., Lin, H.-Y., & Ameis, S.H. (2022). Towards equitable diagnoses for autism and attention-deficit/hyperactivity disorder across sexes and genders. *Current Opinion in Psychiatry*, *35*(2), 90–100. https://doi.org/10.1097/YCO.0000000000000770

Lai, M.-C., Lombardo, M. V., Pasco, G., Ruigrok, A. N. V., Wheelwright, S. J., Sadek, S. A., Chakrabarti, B., MRC AIMS Consortium, & Baron-Cohen, S. (2011). A behavioral comparison of male and female adults with high functioning autism spectrum conditions. *PloS One*, *6*(6), e20835. https://doi.org/10.1371/journal.pone.0020835

Lancy, D. F. (2007). Accounting for variability in mother–child play. *American Anthropologist*, *109*(2), 273–284. https://doi.org/10.1525/aa.2007.109.2.273

Leung, C., Tsang, S., Heung, K., & Yiu, I. (2009). Effectiveness of Parent–Child Interaction Therapy (PCIT) among Chinese families. *Research on Social Work Practice*, *19*(3), 304–313. https://doi.org/10.1177/1049731508321713

Liao, Y., Dillenburger, K., & Buchanan, I. (2018). Does culture matter in ABA-based autism interventions? Parent and professional experiences in the UK and China. *European Journal of Behavior Analysis*, *19*(1), 11–29. https://doi.org/10.1080/15021149.2017.1399657

Mandy, W., Chilvers, R., Chowdhury, U., Salter, G., Seigal, A., & Skuse, D. (2012). Sex differences in autism spectrum disorder: Evidence from a large sample of children and adolescents. *Journal of Autism and Developmental Disorders*, 42(7), 1304–1313. https://doi.org/10.1007/s10803-011-1356-0

McCabe, K. M., Yeh, M., Garland, A. F., Lau, A. S., & Chavez, G. (2005). The GANA Program: A tailoring approach to adapting parent–child interaction therapy for Mexican Americans. *Education and Treatment of Children*, 28(2), 111–129.

McNeil, C. B., & Hembree-Kigin, T. L. (2010). PCIT around the world. In C. B. McNeil & T. L. Hembree-Kigin (Eds.), *Parent–child interaction therapy* (2nd ed., pp. 421–427). Springer US. https://doi.org/10.1007/978-0-387-88639-8_24

Moses, H. (2020, October 20). Oversexualization of Black girls, women must stop. *Marquette Wire*. https://marquettewire.org/4041391/featured/moses-oversexualization-of-black-girls-women-must-stop/

Niec, L. N., Abrahamse, M. E., Egan, R., Coelman, F. J. G., & Heiner, W. D. (2018). Global dissemination of parent–child interaction therapy: The perspectives of Dutch trainees. *Children and Youth Services Review*, 94, 485–492. https://doi.org/10.1016/j.childyouth.2018.08.019

Pearson, A., & Rose, K. (2021). A conceptual analysis of autistic masking: Understanding the narrative of stigma and the illusion of choice. *Autism in Adulthood*, 3(1), 52–60. https://doi.org/10.1089/aut.2020.0043

Pilgrim, D. (2000, November). The brute caricature – Jim Crow Museum. Ferris State University. www.ferris.edu/HTMLS/news/jimcrow/brute/homepage.htm

Prizant, B. & Finch, D. (Host). (2022, April 15). Unmasking autism: A discussion with Dr. Devon Price (No. 49) [Audio podcast episode]. In *Uniquely human: The podcast*. Elevated Studio. https://uniquelyhuman.com/2022/04/15/ep49/

Russo, F. (2018, February 21). The costs of camouflaging autism. *Spectrum | Autism Research News*. www.spectrumnews.org/features/deep-dive/costs-camouflaging-autism/

Sedgewick, F., Hill, V., Yates, R., Pickering, L., & Pellicano, E. (2016). Gender differences in the social motivation and friendship experiences of autistic and non-autistic adolescents. *Journal of Autism and Developmental Disorders*, 46(4), 1297–1306. https://doi.org/10.1007/s10803-015-2669-1

Shalev, I., & Uzefovsky, F. (2020). Empathic disequilibrium in two different measures of empathy predicts autism traits in neurotypical population. *Molecular Autism*, 11(1), 59. https://doi.org/10.1186/s13229-020-00362-1

Shalev, I., Warrier, V., Greenberg, D. M., Smith, P., Allison, C., Baron-Cohen, S., Eran, A., & Uzefovsky, F. (2021). *Reexamining empathy in autism: The role of empathic disequilibrium in autism and autistic traits* [Preprint]. In Review. https://doi.org/10.21203/rs.3.rs-1064950/v1

Sharpe, P., Mascia-Lees, F. E., & Cohen, C. B. (1990). White women and Black men: Differential responses to reading Black women's texts. *College English*, 52(2), 142–153. https://doi.org/10.2307/377441

Shulman, C., Rice, C. E., Morrier, M. J., & Esler, A. (2020). The role of diagnostic instruments in dual and differential diagnosis in autism spectrum disorder across the lifespan. *Child and Adolescent Psychiatric Clinics of North America*, 29(2), 275–299. https://doi.org/10.1016/j.chc.2020.01.002

Song, A., Cola, M., Plate, S., Petrulla, V., Yankowitz, L., Pandey, J., Schultz, R. T., & Parish-Morris, J. (2021). Natural language markers of social phenotype in girls with autism. *Journal of Child Psychology and Psychiatry, and Allied Disciplines*, 62(8), 949–960. https://doi.org/10.1111/jcpp.13348

Tate, S. A. (2015). *Black women's bodies and the nation*. Palgrave Macmillan. https://doi.org/10.1057/9781137355287

Tubío-Fungueiriño, M., Cruz, S., Sampaio, A., Carracedo, A., & Fernández-Prieto, M. (2021). Social camouflaging in females with autism spectrum disorder: A systematic review. *Journal of Autism and Developmental Disorders*, 51(7), 2190–2199. https://doi.org/10.1007/s10803-020-04695-x

Vedantam, S. (Host). (2022, September 12). Decoding emotions. [Audio podcast episode]. In *Hidden Brain*. Hidden Brain Media. https://hiddenbrain.org/podcast/decoding-emotions/

Wilson, J. P., Hugenberg, K., & Rule, N. O. (2017). Racial bias in judgments of physical size and formidability: From size to threat. *Journal of Personality and Social Psychology*, 113(1), 59–80. https://doi.org/10.1037/pspi0000092

Wood-Downie, H., Wong, B., Kovshoff, H., Mandy, W., Hull, L., & Hadwin, J. A. (2021). Sex/gender differences in camouflaging in children and adolescents with autism. *Journal of Autism and Developmental Disorders*, 51(4), 1353–1364. https://doi.org/10.1007/s10803-020-04615-z

Wuensch, K. L., Campbell, M. W., Kesler, F. C., & Moore, C. H. (2002). Racial bias in decisions made by mock jurors evaluating a case of sexual harassment. *The Journal of Social Psychology*, 142(5), 587–600. https://doi.org/10.1080/00224540209603920

Young, H., Oreve, M.-J., & Speranza, M. (2018). Clinical characteristics and problems diagnosing autism spectrum disorder in girls. *Archives de Pédiatrie*, *25*(6), 399–403. https://doi.org/10.1016/j.arc ped.2018.06.008

Young, S., Hollingdale, J., Absoud, M., Bolton, P., Branney, P., Colley, W., ... & Woodhouse, E. (2020). Guidance for identification and treatment of individuals with attention deficit/hyperactivity disorder and autism spectrum disorder based upon expert consensus. *BMC Medicine*, *18*(1), 146. https://doi.org/10.1186/s12916-020-01585-y

Chapter 3

Nonverbal communication

I know I'm supposed to do it, but eyes just creep me out.
−Max R.

What people often think difficulty with nonverbal communication means

Many people, even many clinicians, believe that autistics do not make eye contact. The truth is that while some autistic people don't use eye gaze to manage interactions, others use gaze quite well, although doing so may be uncomfortable, distracting, and/or effortful for them. Moreover, as described below, nonverbal communication involves so much more than eye contact.

What does nonverbal communication really entail, and what might this look like in someone with autism?

We use nonverbal aspects of communication to better understand others, to interpret others' language, and to clarify and augment our own messages to others.

Before we dive into the details of nonverbal communication, however, it is essential to discuss **the double empathy problem.** This phrase was coined by Dr Damian Milton, an autistic researcher and speaker. Dr. Milton, like many others, suggests that it can be helpful to think of autistics and non-autistics as two groups of people from entirely different cultures who experience and respond to the world in fundamentally different ways. As Dr. Milton states, "simply

DOI: 10.4324/9781003242130-5

put, the theory of the double empathy problem suggests that when people with very different experiences of the world interact with one another, they will struggle to empathise with each other."

When there is a breakdown in communication and mutual understanding between people from entirely different cultures, it is often because of a divide between their ways of experiencing, understanding, and responding to the world, *not because there is something inherently wrong with the people in one of the groups.*

If Dr. Milton's hypothesis is accurate, then we would expect (a) autistic people to find it easier to form connections with and understand each other; (b) non-autistic people to find it easier to form connections with and understand each other; and (c) people from each group to have difficulty communicating with, understanding, and empathizing with people in the other group. This is what the research shows.

One of our favorite examples of this was described in a study by Catherine Crompton and her colleagues, who assembled three groups of people: one composed entirely of autistic people, another with only non-autistic people, and a third with members of both neurotypes. They then asked one person in each group to repeat a story to one other person in their group, who repeated the story to the next person, and so on. The authors then scored the accuracy of the final version of the story for each group. Accuracy was much lower in the *mixed* neurotype group than in the groups with members of the *same* neurotype (autistic *or* non-autistic).

As such, the problem is not that there is something inherently "wrong" with autistic people. Instead, because they are a minority, autistics may be seen as wrong, impaired, or lacking empathy when there is a disconnect between them and their majority (i.e., non-autistic) peers. The general perception of non-autistic people is that their way of communicating is "right," and when autistic individuals do not conform to non-autistic norms, they may be blamed, shamed, and/or labeled as "impaired."

"One could say that many autistic people have indeed gained a greater level of insight into [non-autistic] society and mores than vice versa, perhaps due to the need to survive and potentially thrive in a [non-autistic] culture. Conversely, the [non-autistic] person has no pertinent personal requirement to understand the mind of the 'autistic person' unless closely related socially in some way," Milton explains.

It is particularly essential to remember the double empathy problem when discussing nonverbal communication. It is a mistake to use language that implies the presence of deficits or impairment (e.g., "eye contact is impaired," "she showed inappropriate facial expressions," "her ability to read other people is impaired"). Rather, our thinking needs to reflect an understanding that these behaviors and skills are different in autistic and non-autistic people, and that *it is this difference, not an inherent "malfunction," that creates challenges*, for instance, "Eye contact is uncomfortable for Amy," rather than "Amy doesn't make appropriate eye contact."

With that clarification, we can now discuss the many components of nonverbal communication, which require simultaneous attention to and integration of countless behaviors.

Body positioning: Many people have an intuitive sense of their body's position in space and time and of their body's movements. This is referred to as proprioception and includes an intuitive sense of how to coordinate their body with other people's bodies, depending on context. For instance, we may position our head and body so that we are facing others during interactions, except perhaps if we are angry or bored. Likewise, we may lean in if we are interested in what they are saying. These are just a couple of examples; there are countless scenarios in which we intuitively and unconsciously position our bodies in space to interact effectively with others. Body positioning becomes even more complex when people are moving together while communicating. For instance, when we walk alongside a friend, we need to match their pace, turn toward them slightly to indicate we are listening, but still face forward to see where we are walking.

In autistics, we may notice overtly or vaguely awkward body positioning and movement. As the individual matures and learns cultural norms, this may be less noticeable. We often see evidence of a difference in this area when people are younger, for example, in preschool report cards. There may be notes such as, "Manny is working on listening with his whole body," or "Johnny is working on looking the right way during circle time." Those are clues that, as children, they were not positioning their bodies in the same ways as their peers. There are many possible reasons for these differences, such as sensory/proprioception challenges, inattention, hyperactivity, and low muscle tone, and it is essential to consider these other factors when assessing body positioning and movement as nonverbal communication differences.

From the experts: Reflections about body positioning

I have hundreds of conversations in my head about how to stand: is this stance right? Should I try something else?

–Elle J.

Much of daily discomfort arises from being hyper-aware of my body. I find I must manually 'put everything in the right place.' The eyes should be focused, the hands should be still, and the body should look relaxed; none of it is automatic, and it's always distractingly uncomfortable.

–Fabian B.

Personal space: Non-autistic people generally develop a basic awareness of where our body ends and another person's body begins, and how to manage that space in interactions. For instance, if we want to flirt, we move closer, but if we want to convey respect or dislike, we may keep some distance. (Actually, using the same positioning for different reasons is a great example of how arbitrary and confusing these "rules" can be!) There are countless implicit rules about distance in different types of relationships; we can stand very close to our spouse or our children but not to a coworker. To make matters even more confusing, context can change these implicit rules. For example, we can stand very close to a coworker if we are in an elevator together or if we are in a crowded restaurant waiting for a table. There are also cultural considerations; people in some cultures rarely touch, whereas other cultures encourage physical contact (for example, greeting a friend with a kiss on each cheek). Violating the expectations of that culture can have profound negative repercussions.

It is even more complicated to manage both body position and personal space, as we do when we are moving with other people. When we walk alongside others, we need to attend to both of these at once, in addition to the conversation. One of our favorite questions to ask parents is, "how does your child do when they're walking with you?" If this is an area of difficulty, the parents will likely respond, "It's so funny that you ask that, because we would not have thought to bring it up. She is always 10 feet ahead of us, 10 feet behind us, or bumping into us!" We've heard this many times. Other clues suggesting a history of difficulty understanding or managing personal space would be a preschool report that mentions something like, "Maria is learning that other children need more space."

Eye contact and gaze: This includes making eye contact, using eye contact, and emotional responses to eye contact. Many autistics can learn to look directly at someone's eyes, or at least to look close enough to the eyes to meet non-autistics' social needs. Many autistics compensate by looking *near* people's eyes but not directly at them, such as looking at their nose, their forehead, or something just behind them. This is noticeable if people are conversing at close range but may otherwise be missed.

It is also important to consider the individual's use of eye gaze to manage interactions. This is a much more complex skill. For instance, if I am talking to you and I quickly glance at the clock a few times, you will instinctively know that you have to pick up the pace and end the conversation. Likewise, if I suddenly turn my head to look out the window at something, you may also look out the window to see what had grabbed my attention. Or, you may make eye contact to check in with a trusted person when you are unsure about something. There are countless examples like these.

Additionally, many autistic individuals have a different *emotional response* to eye contact than non-autistics. As far as we can tell, most non-autistic people have a neutral to positive reaction to eye contact. Most of the time, they are not even conscious of it; it just sort of happens, though they likely find it uncomfortable in specific situations, such as when they are feeling shy or ashamed. In contrast, autistic individuals may find eye contact pointless or useless, or, even worse, distracting, uncomfortable, anxiety-provoking, or downright disturbing.

Eye contact is easier in some situations than in others. It may be easier when conversing with a trusted or familiar person, when discussing topics of interest, and in one-on-one situations. It may be more challenging when talking with strangers, speaking about non-preferred or anxiety-provoking topics, and/or in groups. These differences exist for both autistics and non-autistics but may be more pronounced for autistics.

From the experts: Reflections about eye contact

I just have no instinct regarding eye contact. With that, I have no clue when I should or shouldn't.

–Rob L.

I do eye contact fairly well, but I count myself in and out and consciously tell myself to do it.

–Katie Anne

I think I don't really look people much in the face, it feels like a waste of time because I don't really see much there anyway.

–Miko

Sometimes I'm so busy stressing about the eye contact that I can't follow the conversation anymore.

–Leen V.

I am a communications and PR exec who focuses on body language of executives in crisis situations. One piece of common knowledge is that if someone looks away or doesn't make eye contact, it's assumed they are lying. Once I was diagnosed and began reading the literature about traits and identifiers, I went on an emotional rollercoaster of all the times I was accused by my parents or teachers of lying when, really, eye contact made me incredibly uncomfortable. Over time, I learned to mask so that I could make eye contact – which was excruciating! Too much time in person and having to make eye contact is a big shutdown trigger for me, and I can sleep for up to 18 hours after too much of it.

–Carol B.

I've repeatedly been told that I am not making eye contact
even when I think that I am. So now I have no idea what is
normal, or even what is comfortable for myself. I just try to
make as much eye contact as I think I am supposed to, and
adjust up or down if I don't seem to be getting it right.

–Drew R.

Volume: Most of us constantly and intuitively adjust our vocal volume based on the relationship and the context. For example, with our children we may raise our voice to get their attention, but we would not do this with our boss. In addition, we usually speak more loudly to emphasize an important point or to convey a strong feeling, while we may speak more softly to convey a different message, such as sharing a secret or indicating embarrassment. Most of us also adjust our volume based on the ambient noise level. For example, we talk more loudly in a crowded restaurant and more softly in a quiet room. Non-autistics do all of this intuitively, with little conscious awareness or effort.

In contrast, many autistic individuals have difficulty *intuitively* managing their volume. Some may persistently be too loud, others may persistently be too soft, and some can be too loud at times and too soft at other times. Of course, there are other reasons for poor volume control; for instance, if a girl speaks softly, she may just be sensitive or shy. However, if she even speaks too softly for her parents to hear, and they have to persistently ask her to speak up, then that is probably not due to shyness. Physiological reasons for difficulty with volume should not be ruled out. For instance, motor issues like dyspraxia can also make it hard for people to control speaking volume, and individuals with hearing problems may have trouble determining what the appropriate volume should be. It is all the more important in these cases to look at other aspects of nonverbal processing when considering whether someone meets criteria in this category.

From the experts: Reflections about volume

I truly have no concept of how loud I am. I had a teammate
in college who would always put her hands over her ears when
I really got going talking and I thought she was joking. But it

turns out, I am so damn loud! When I hear the words come out of my mouth, sometimes I feel like I can barely hear them, but in reality, I'm talking way louder than everyone around me. It's definitely a joke now and I get that I'm crazy loud. But it does make me embarrassed, especially because I have no idea – as it's happening.

–Lauren O.

My husband often tells me that I'm "mumbling," but sometimes he tells me there's no need to shout too.

–Leen V.

Prosody: Prosody refers to "the melody and rhythm of language." It provides important clues about the emotional intent of the speaker (think about how someone sounds when they are excited versus when they are sad), the meaning behind spoken words (e.g., sarcasm is often conveyed with different prosodic patterns), and the grammatical structure of a sentence. For example, "I DON'T think he said that" is different from "I don't think HE said that." If you think about how a robot from a bad 1960s science fiction movie might speak, with no melody to their output, you will get an idea of what spoken language would sound like without prosody.

Autistic individuals can have any combination of the following atypicalities with prosody. They may use less inflection, more inflection, no inflection, unusual inflection, unusual pauses, and/or have difficulty using *other people's* inflection and pauses to aid in their understanding of what others are saying.

From the experts: Reflections about tone of voice

My mother often tells me my voice is monotone, but I just don't know what I do or how to make it acceptable, which is why, although I'm a clinical professional, I have to work in private practice and be absolutely explicit with clients about my neurodivergent traits, so that there are no misunderstandings if I give off the "wrong" (facial) expression.

–Elinor R.

When I want to convey a particular emotion, it seems like I need to be deliberately three times as expressive as I actually feel to convey the right level of emotion. Otherwise, I just sound flat.

–Drew R.

I work in a retail job and have gotten the right facial expressions and tone of voice down for basic greetings but I have a harder time when trying to joke or be serious. I often sound very serious when I am trying to joke, and sarcastic when I am trying to be serious. I generally have to follow up with a verbal explanation of my intentions so that people don't get angry or misunderstand me.

–Allie S.

Rate of speech: When we speak to another person, our goal is for them to understand us. Some people process spoken language very quickly; for others speech needs to be slower. However, if it's too slow, that can be distracting and make the message harder to process. If the goal is for your communication partner to understand what you are saying, you will intuitively adjust your rate of speech so that you are understood. There are cultural differences, too, about what constitutes a comfortable rate of speech. For example, Sarah grew up in New Mexico, and when she moved to Boston for graduate school, she initially found it very hard to keep up with how quickly some of her colleagues spoke. Some autistic individuals speak at a rate that feels comfortable to the listener, while others may speak extremely rapidly or quite slowly. Autistics may or may not be aware of how their rate (whether too fast or too slow) affects their listeners.

From the experts: Reflections about rate of speech

I've previously had someone refer to me as manic because I was talking so fast.

–Katie A.

People are always interrupting me, or finishing my sentences for me. It makes it really hard for me to express myself if other people don't take the time to listen to what I have to say.

–Namik T.

Facial expressions: Faces convey a lot about what a person is feeling and thinking. A wrinkled brow, a raised eyebrow, eyes opened wide, downturned corners of the mouth, head tilted to the side, looking up and to the right – these (and countless other details) are all important clues as to what a person is thinking. To make it even more complicated, expressions constantly change, providing information that is both complex and dynamic. This information is a critical part of communicating.

As with the other aspects of nonverbal communication, differences in managing facial expressions can be receptive and/or expressive. That is, autistic individuals can have difficulty noticing and/or interpreting other people's facial expressions. Separately, autistic individuals may not express their emotions via facial expressions. They may have a limited range of facial expressions, may have facial expressions that don't match the content of the conversation or the context, or may have unusual facial expressions at times. These can all lead to miscommunication and hurt or angry feelings, without either party understanding what went awry.

From the experts: Reflections about our own facial expressions

I feel like I have to consciously and uncomfortably move my face so neurotypicals can "read" me.

–Angela P.

I worked with a colleague who would complain about my face – I never understood what her problem was with my face, but it would make her so angry.

–Elinor R.

Something I struggle with is that nurses tell me I "don't look like" I'm in pain even in literal life or death situations, so I have been ignored or put at a lower priority than people who make a big show of it.

–Jessica P.

I really hate getting gifts that require me to open them in front of the giver. I often ask if I can open it later by myself when I have more time to absorb the generosity. But, in reality, I cannot stand having to figure out how to organize my face and general body language if I DON'T like the gift. I feel like I am the worst at faking it and I worry that I am going to be found out. Like the gift giver is going to know with absolute certainty that I hate what they got me. And then they are going to feel terrible. And then I'm going to feel terrible and everything will feel interminably awkward.

–Lauren O.

My husband never used to know when I was upset or being serious because I would look and sound the same. Now I tell him things on a scale of 1–10 so he knows, because he says it's really hard to tell if I'm serious or upset or just normal.

–Katie A.

I'm trying to be respectful and look attentive, listen, not interrupt, figure out how to apply the assertive person posture and head tilt or the subordinate workhorse chin tuck and head nod, get something that looks like eye contact going at opportune times (even though that's actually usually me looking at their mouth or hair), and then I can't process what they're saying, so I'm taking notes, and I find with all of that going on that my eyebrows are raised as high as I can get them, so I keep reminding myself to put my eyebrows down ... like they're a weapon or something. "Drop the eyebrows!"

–Jesse P.

Gestures: These motions with hands, arms, shoulders, and head are used to emphasize what we are saying. Both the position and the quality of the motion are important. Meng-Chuan Lai and his colleagues describe *conventional* gestures (e.g., waving goodbye), *descriptive* gestures (e.g., indicating the size of something), and *emphatic* gestures (e.g., repeatedly jabbing your finger at the listener). The quality of the gesture communicates emotional intent – if you are feeling intensely about something, your gestures may be quick and emphatic, whereas your gestures may be slower and more relaxed if you are feeling dreamy and thoughtful. Gestures can also serve to cue speech production; some research shows that people who use gestures with their speech become less verbal when they are not allowed to use their hands. Dr Lai and his colleagues note that even when autistics use gestures, they may do so in different ways from non-autistics (e.g., their gestures may not seem integrated with the spoken words).

From the experts: Reflections about gesturing

I never know what I'm supposed to be doing with my arms ... it feels weird when my arms aren't doing anything. If I'm talking to people, I like to at least be holding a drink or a pen or something, because if they're just hanging there doing nothing, it feels awkward and I'll be thinking about it and wondering what to do with them.

–Cindy B.

Same on the arms! I like to cross my arms – but people think I'm stand-offish or uninterested – or put my hands in my pockets. I don't know how people just have their hands out all the time and know what to do with them.

–Jessica P.

Every aspect of nonverbal communication requires flexibility and adaptability: Facial expressions are not exactly the same from person to person. They are also not the same in one person from situation to situation. So, learning "a surprised face," "a happy face," or "my girlfriend's angry face" will not only be effortful but also it will only work some of the time. Moreover, we do not take in each type of nonverbal cue separately; rather, understanding what someone is saying involves continuously integrating auditory and visual nonverbal channels with the words that are being spoken and also with the context. There is no such thing as "figuring it out" in the moment, because the moment is constantly evolving.

From the experts: Reflections about context

I usually try to guess what people are feeling from what their energy is and what they are saying. I know main expressions

*like happy, sad, angry, shocked, but I don't know nuances.
I mostly just guess from the context and hope it's right! There's
a lot of deduction going on.*

–Miko

*If people are acting or looking in a different way than I'm used
to when I speak to them, I often don't know if it means the
same emotion or something I don't already know. Like when
I meet a new person with a different body language, I have
maybe practiced to recognize happy and interested in one way,
and then I'm confused when the new person expresses this in
a slightly different way.*

–Miko

A world without nonverbal communication?

Texting (without emojis) gives us a way to imagine a
world where there is only verbal communication, with no eye
contact, body language, facial expressions, or voice intonation
to assist the interaction. Think about the times when you
were not sure how to interpret a comment, or when your own
comments were misinterpreted. Humor can get missed, anger
can be construed when there is only annoyance, and so many
other possible miscommunications can occur.

Now imagine if the real world were just like texting. You
see a friend for the first time in years, and they stand perfectly
still and say in a monotone, "It's nice to see you." Or, you
give a lovely gift to your spouse and they respond, "Thank
you," with no eye contact or smile. Or, your doctor breaks
bad news to you while standing across the room, in a loud
volume, not pausing at all for the news to sink in or for you to
respond. And neither Sarah nor Donna can imagine a world
without the voice inflection necessary for sarcasm! Nonverbal
communication gives color, context, and meaning to our
interactions. It has an enormous impact on communication,
similar to the difference between looking at a picture of the
beach and actually hearing the waves, smelling the salt, and
feeling the warm sand between our toes.

Nonverbal communication is both receptive and expressive: Autistic people can have difficulty reading non-autistic nonverbal cues (i.e., receptive difficulty) and/or their own nonverbal cues can be confusing to non-autistics (i.e., expressive difference). Some autistics (particularly females) have eye contact, facial expressions, and body language that do not appear to be different from the norm, but they may have significant difficulty reading those cues in other people. Alternatively, some autistics can read other people fairly well but do not give off their own cues in ways that make sense to non-autistics (e.g., their affect may be "flat" – that is, they may have a persistently neutral facial expression). And, of course, some can have differences in both receptive and expressive aspects of nonverbal communication.

Assessing an autistic person's ability to read other people's cues is challenging in part because many autistics are exquisitely sensitive to general emotional tone. For example, if there is a negative feel in the room, they are often the first ones to detect it. That sensitivity can fool others (parents, spouses, healthcare providers, etc.) into thinking that the autistic person can accurately read nuanced social cues. But what they often can't do is intuit *the reason underlying* the feel in the room, or the specific emotion. Is it anger or just annoyance? Sadness? Disappointment? Fatigue? Jealousy? They may not be able to differentiate between these negative emotions and may, for instance, always conclude that people are mad at them. Simply being sensitive to general emotional tone does not mean that one can fully read social cues. Moreover, being *overly sensitive* to emotional tone can cause one to actively misread others and/or to have unexpectedly strong emotional reactions.

From the experts: Reflections about reading other people

I find it hard to tell if someone is either tired, angry, upset, or something else, so I end up walking on eggshells for no reason.

–Katie A.

I can SEE the looks! I just don't know what they mean!
                                                    –Cindy B.

I have no idea if my partner is sad, sleepy, stressed or angry. I notice an energy shift, I notice his tone of voice and something with his body, but I have absolutely no idea what it means.
                                                    –Miko

I can never tell whether or not someone is flirting with me. I need to have a friend with me, telling me – privately – if someone is or is not flirting.
                                                    –Grace D.

I tend to see people's faces as expressing 'confusion' unless they are extremely exaggerated and obviously some other emotion, which causes me to constantly ask what the other person is thinking about to make sure I am not missing an emotion – but also causing quite a bit of annoyance!
                                                    –Eric O.

We have to figure out how to express ourselves clearly using nonverbal cues: For example, we adjust our voice intonation, eye contact, facial expressions, and movement so the nonverbal information accurately conveys and augments what we are saying, while also adjusting to the situation. This is something most of us do intuitively that can be effortful or confusing for autistics.

I've insulted people by saying the right WORDS but with a tone that was responding to the thought I was having before they walked into the room, or with a facial expression that has more to do with the lighting or someone else's perfume than it does with the conversation I'm having. And the more exhausted I am, the less expressive I get, so by the end of a long day people think I disagree with them or something, but really my tone is just flat because I no longer have the energy to put any texture into it.
                                                    –Marie U.

Some autistics show little affect and/or their affect does not change depending on the situation and what they are saying. These individuals are sometimes described as "incredibly even-keeled."

This is frequently seen as a strength, and in some ways it *is* a strength, though it's important to remember that what presents on the outside may not reflect the person's actual emotions.

Charlie was a very responsible 8th grader. He always followed rules and particularly tried to be on time for all classes and appointments. However, he was continually late for his math class, because he had to go from one end of the school all the way to the other. No matter how hard he tried, he always walked into math a few minutes late. Whenever his teacher communicated her displeasure about this – either verbally or nonverbally– Charlie did not respond in any way. He did not move more quickly to his seat, change his facial expression, or use body language in any way to communicate the fact that he was aware that he was late and was trying his best. His teacher interpreted this flat affect as a lack of caring, and she kept assigning Charlie detention for his lateness. Had he been able to change his affect and body posture, his teacher might have been more understanding. This is one reason that having a clear diagnosis is so important – autistics are chronically misunderstood in countless ways.

Restricted or flat affect can lead to significant repercussions: The possibilities are endless, but we'd like to highlight three that we've frequently heard. First, numerous autistics have told us that giving and receiving gifts can be stressful. They often feel pressure to "have an excited face" when they open a gift and have felt others' disappointment when they didn't show "the right face." Second, many autistic individuals have told us that others frequently think they are sad or angry when they are feeling just fine. As one recently said to Donna, "I have to constantly tell people, 'This is just my face.'" Sometimes, these individuals are seen as depressed when they are not (because clinicians and others often associate flat affect with depression).

A third, more serious and potentially dangerous, consequence of flat affect is that the autistic person may not be taken seriously by their healthcare professionals. When an autistic person *verbally* conveys physical or emotional pain to a healthcare practitioner without pairing their words with the expected facial expressions, body language, and voice intonation, the healthcare practitioner is less likely to take the complaints seriously or even to believe them. It is literally a matter of life and death for healthcare professionals to understand that some people do not show the typical signs of physical or emotional pain and that those people need to be taken seriously based on their verbal report alone. This is another reason why it is so essential for autistics to be armed with a proper diagnosis and education, so they can learn to effectively self-advocate with their practitioners.

From the experts: The repercussions of not showing emotions

I have actually lost incredibly close friends because I didn't 'look right' when opening their gifts and they called me ungrateful. I received these long letters from them which were so heartbreaking ... from them becoming so incredibly upset about the way "I looked."

–Elinor R.

I've run into a lot of troubles over the years in healthcare, when I am sharing, for instance, that I'm doing very poorly but it simply doesn't register. It just gets ignored. It happened just a half year ago after telling my psychologist that I was struggling with suicidal thoughts non-stop, and I really couldn't bear the thought of having to live like this any longer. He said, okay so let's make a new appointment for over 6 weeks. I've come to understand that this happens because I don't show the emotions that come with the story. But these days – and I feel bad about it – if I wake up poorly and I have an appointment I sort of let myself sink into it, so I can cry in front of them, because then suddenly they do open their ears and take me seriously – this worked with the same psychologist. I find this very distressing .... So, what I would really like is for people to just listen to what we say and not just go by their own habitual intuition.

–Lucia K.

I now pretend to show discomfort because so many times I've been dismissed because I don't "look" in pain. I had sepsis dismissed until I insisted on blood tests, and they admitted me for a week and put me straight on a drip. Once I said I couldn't breathe properly, and they said I was probably anxious and said I looked like I was breathing fine. They did some test and were like, "shit, sit down, your heart is 160 and you have really low blood pressure." Turned out I had a pulmonary embolism on my lung. Another time I passed out, but they wouldn't listen to me when I told them I couldn't stand. They thought I was putting it on until I collapsed. Even when I try to make it look like I don't feel well, they don't believe me because I don't look how they would expect. When I had gallstones, they first said I had wind because I didn't look in pain. The doc actually said I would be doubled over. So I went back to hospital a day later and pretended to double over so they would listen, and it turned out I had to have my gallbladder out.

–Katie A.

Nonverbal communication: What we've learned from the girls

Autistic girls tend to have more expressive nonverbal communication than autistic boys. While females are not necessarily better than males at *receptive* nonverbals (i.e., understanding others' expressions), recent research, such as that by Rachel Hiller and colleagues, suggests that autistic females tend to be better than autistic males at integrating verbal and nonverbal communication.

In a *Spectrum News* article, "The Lost Girls," Apoorva Mandavilli quotes Francesca Happé, director of the MRC Centre at King's College London, who noted that, "Without their self-report telling you how stressful it is to maintain appearances, you wouldn't really know. They have good imitation, good intonation in their language, body language – surface behavior isn't very useful for a diagnosis, at least for a certain set of women on the spectrum."

In an article in *Scientific American*, titled "Autism: It's different in Girls," Simon Baron-Cohen, a leading researcher in this field, was quoted as saying that, "If you were just judging on the basis of external behavior, you might not notice anything different about [some of] these girls. It relies much more on getting under the surface and listening to the experiences they are having rather than just looking at how they present themselves to the world." We have stated this previously, but it bears repeating: There are autistics of all genders that fit this description.

It isn't only the researchers who have noted this. For years now, autistic women have communicated that their autism-related challenges are more about their inner experience than their outer behavior. Many autistic females can demonstrate typical nonverbals, but it can be incredibly effortful for them. Using typical eye contact, facial expressions, voice intonation, and body movements requires cognitive attention and energy, and can be highly anxiety-provoking. As with all aspects of camouflaging, there is a real cost to hiding one's authentic self.

This is why we feel so strongly that **clinicians must seriously consider and even prioritize the subjective experiences of autistics**, rather than focusing solely on the behavioral observations of those around them.

Connecting culture

The context of one's culture impacts the importance of nonverbal communication. For instance, high-context cultures place greater emphasis on facial expressions, gestures and body language, tone of voice and inflection, volume, and speech rate. The *tone* of the message is as important as the words themselves. In contrast, low-context cultures place greater emphasis on the words and how they are used.

One's culture can impact other aspects of nonverbal communication as well, including eye contact, touch/physical contact, physical distance, and physical appearance. For instance, Asian Americans may speak more softly, use indirect forms of expression, and not maintain eye contact, as too much eye contact can be considered disrespectful in the context of their cultural background. As DJ Chopstick told us, "*My parents would always tell me when reprimanding me, 'Don't look at me when I am talking to you.' Second generation Asian kids are fine with eye contact, but it is more of a problem with children who recently migrated here or have parents who did not assimilate to their surroundings."*

If a clinician doesn't seek greater understanding, DJ Chopstick's experiences show how intercultural misinterpretation can complicate the diagnostic process. The clinician must discern to what extent their client's low eye contact is related to culture versus possible autism. A lack of eye contact may be construed as "a problem" (low-confidence, rude, lack of interest, etc.) if the evaluator is from a high-context culture.

Remember: When considering the effects of culture, don't assume. *Ask!*

Frequently asked questions

- **Can someone have a difference in either receptive or expressive nonverbals, but not both?** Yes. In fact, it is not uncommon for autistic females, in particular, to express themselves nonverbally in ways that are not noticeably atypical but to still have difficulty accurately interpreting non-autistic people's nonverbal communications. The reverse is also true; autistic people can struggle to use nonverbal communication effectively but can be fairly good at reading it in others.

- **If someone makes good eye contact, does that rule out autism?** Absolutely not. There are plenty of autistic individuals, particularly but not exclusively females, who make excellent eye contact.

- **Where does humor fit into this?** We've said it before, and we know we'll have to say it again: it is a myth that autistics don't have a sense of humor. However, they may sometimes miss a joke because they did not register the tone of voice and/or facial expression that indicated that it was a joke. Additionally, when some autistics attempt humor, the jokes may not "land," because they may not have added the inflection and/or facial expression that would have correctly conveyed the humor of their words.

Other reasons that humor can be problematic for some autistics are noted in the relevant chapters (e.g., inflexibility).

- **What about other interpretations of atypical affect?** Autistics may have flat or atypical affect. Atypical affect can present in a variety of ways, such as having affect that does not match the situation (e.g., always smiling). Based on our personal experience, we find that if a male has unusual affect, clinicians will think of autism as a possibility. However, if a female has unusual affect, clinicians are more likely to think that she is overly dramatic or possibly that she has borderline personality disorder.

- **Are there other possible reasons for unusual nonverbal expression?** Absolutely. For instance, people who are depressed or schizophrenic can have flat affect, and people who are manic can have rapid speech (though this would only occur during manic phases, not all the time), so these are important possibilities to consider.

References and related reading

American Psychiatric Association. (2022). *Diagnostic and statistical manual of mental disorders* (5th ed., text rev.). https://doi.org/10.1176/appi.books.9780890425787

Bargiela, S., Steward, R., & Mandy, W. (2016). The experiences of late-diagnosed women with autism spectrum conditions: An investigation of the female autism phenotype. *Journal of Autism and Developmental Disorders*, *46*(10), 3281–3294. https://doi.org/10.1007/s10803-016-2872-8

Compton, C. J., Ropar, D., Evans-Williams, C. V. M., Flynn, E. G., & Fletcher-Watson, S. (2020). Autistic peer-to-peer information transfer is highly effective. *Autism*, *24*(7), 1704–1712.

Davis, R., & Crompton, C. J. (2021). What do new findings about social interaction in autistic adults mean for neurodevelopmental research? *Perspectives on Psychological Science*, *16*(3), 649–653. https://doi.org/10.1177/1745691620958010

de Leeuw, A., Happé, F., & Hoekstra, R. A. (2020). A conceptual framework for understanding the cultural and contextual factors on autism across the globe. *Autism Research*, *13*(7), 1029–1050. https://doi.org/10.1002/aur.2276

Duvall, S., Armstrong, K., Shahabuddin, A., Grantz, C., Fein, D., & Lord, C. (2021). A road map for identifying autism spectrum disorder: Recognizing and evaluating characteristics that should raise red or "pink" flags to guide accurate differential diagnosis. *The Clinical Neuropsychologist*, 36(5), 1–36. https://doi.org/10.1080/13854046.2021.1921276

Dworzynski, K., Ronald, A., Bolton, P., & Happé, F. (2012). How different are girls and boys above and below the diagnostic threshold for autism spectrum disorders? *Journal of the American Academy of Child and Adolescent Psychiatry*, 51(8), 788–797. https://doi.org/10.1016/j.jaac.2012.05.018

Golson, M. E., Ficklin, E., Haverkamp, C. R., McClain, M. B., & Harris, B. (2022). Cultural differences in social communication and interaction: A gap in autism research. *Autism Research*, 15(2), 208–214. https://doi.org/10.1002/aur.2657

Hall, E. T. (1989). *Beyond Culture*. Anchor Books.

Harrop, C., Jones, D., Zheng, S., Nowell, S., Schultz, R., & Parish-Morris, J. (2019). Visual attention to faces in children with autism spectrum disorder: Are there sex differences? *Molecular Autism*, 10, 28. https://doi.org/10.1186/s13229-019-0276-2

Hiller, R. M., Young, R. L., & Weber, N. (2014). Sex differences in autism spectrum disorder based on DSM-5 criteria: Evidence from clinician and teacher reporting. *Journal of Abnormal Child Psychology*, 42(8), 1381–1393. https://doi.org/10.1007/s10802-014-9881-x

Hull, L., Mandy, W., & Petrides, K. V. (2017). Behavioural and cognitive sex/gender differences in autism spectrum condition and typically developing males and females. *Autism: The International Journal of Research and Practice*, 21(6), 706–727. https://doi.org/10.1177/1362361316669087

Hull, L., Petrides, K. V., Allison, C., Smith, P., Baron-Cohen, S., Lai, M.-C., & Mandy, W. (2017). "Putting on my best normal": Social camouflaging in adults with autism spectrum conditions. *Journal of Autism and Developmental Disorders*, 47(8), 2519–2534. https://doi.org/10.1007/s10803-017-3166-5

Kang-Yi, C. D., Grinker, R. R., & Mandell, D. S. (2013). Korean culture and autism spectrum disorders. *Journal of Autism and Developmental Disorders*, 43(3), 503–520. https://doi.org/10.1007/s10803-012-1570-4

Kim, D., Pan, Y., & Park, H. S. (1998). High-versus low-context culture: A comparison of Chinese, Korean, and American cultures. *Psychology*

& *Marketing*, *15*(6), 507–521. https://doi.org/10.1002/(SICI)1520-6793(199809)15:6<507::AID-MAR2>3.0.CO;2-A

Kirkovski, M., Enticott, P. G., & Fitzgerald, P. B. (2013). A review of the role of female gender in autism spectrum disorders. *Journal of Autism and Developmental Disorders*, *43*(11), 2584–2603. https://doi.org/10.1007/s10803-013-1811-1

Kopp, S., & Gillberg, C. (1992). Girls with social deficits and learning problems: Autism, atypical Asperger syndrome or a variant of these conditions. *European Child & Adolescent Psychiatry*, *1*(2), 89–99. https://doi.org/10.1007/BF02091791

Lai, M.-C., & Szatmari, P. (2020). Sex and gender impacts on the behavioural presentation and recognition of autism. *Current Opinion in Psychiatry*, *33*(2), 117–123. https://doi.org/10.1097/YCO.0000000000000575

Lai, M.-C., Lin, H.-Y., & Ameis, S. H. (2022). Towards equitable diagnoses for autism and attention-deficit/hyperactivity disorder across sexes and genders. *Current Opinion in Psychiatry*, *35*(2), 90–100. https://doi.org/10.1097/YCO.0000000000000770

Mandavilli, A. (2015, October 19). The lost girls. *Spectrum | Autism Research News*. www.spectrumnews.org/features/deep-dive/the-lost-girls/

Mandy, W., Chilvers, R., Chowdhury, U., Salter, G., Seigal, A., & Skuse, D. (2012). Sex differences in autism spectrum disorder: Evidence from a large sample of children and adolescents. *Journal of Autism and Developmental Disorders*, *42*(7), 1304–1313. https://doi.org/10.1007/s10803-011-1356-0

Milton, D. E. M. (2012). On the ontological status of autism: The 'double empathy problem.' *Disability & Society*, *27*(6), 883–887. https://doi.org/10.1080/09687599.2012.710008

Neuliep, J. W. (2020). *Intercultural communication* (8th ed.). SAGE.

Rynkiewicz, A., Schuller, B., Marchi, E., Piana, S., Camurri, A., Lassalle, A., & Baron-Cohen, S. (2016). An investigation of the "female camouflage effect" in autism using a computerized ADOS-2 and a test of sex/gender differences. *Molecular Autism*, *7*, 10. https://doi.org/10.1186/s13229-016-0073-0

Shulman, C., Rice, C. E., Morrier, M. J., & Esler, A. (2020). The role of diagnostic instruments in dual and differential diagnosis in autism spectrum disorder across the lifespan. *Child and Adolescent Psychiatric Clinics of North America*, *29*(2), 275–299. https://doi.org/10.1016/j.chc.2020.01.002

Szalavitz, M. (2016, March 1). Autism: It's different in girls. *Scientific American*. www.scientificamerican.com/article/autism-it-s-different-in-girls/

Young, H., Oreve, M.-J., & Speranza, M. (2018). Clinical characteristics and problems diagnosing autism spectrum disorder in girls. *Archives de Pédiatrie*, *25*(6), 399–403. https://doi.org/10.1016/j.arcped.2018.06.008

Young, S., Hollingdale, J., Absoud, M., Bolton, P., Branney, P., Colley, W., ... & Woodhouse, E. (2020). Guidance for identification and treatment of individuals with attention deficit/hyperactivity disorder and autism spectrum disorder based upon expert consensus. *BMC Medicine*, *18*(1), 146. https://doi.org/10.1186/s12916-020-01585-y

Chapter 4

Relationships

My soul longs for connection, but my body longs for isolation.
I crave community and connection, but my body doesn't hold up
well to them. That is a really core part of the autistic experience
for a lot of people. There's a lot of grief in that, and I think that's
misunderstood by many people, including autistic people.
                        —Autistic psychologist Megan Anna Neff

What people often think difficulty with relationship management means

Many clinicians (and others) assume that this criterion means that autistic people don't have any friends, or they don't want any friends. Not only is this rarely true but also there is so much more to relationship management than simply wanting and having friends.

What does relationship management really entail?

Managing relationships relates to every aspect of understanding, building, and maintaining relationships. As with reciprocal interactions, relationship management is far more complicated than most people realize. So, let's break it down.

Outside of family, friendships and other relationships sustain us through the ups and downs of life. As children learn about relationships, they have to learn many aspects of tending to and caring for their friends. And, because friendships wax and wane, they have to learn how to navigate the changes that are a natural part of the landscape of friendship.

DOI: 10.4324/9781003242130-6

When you move to a new town, start at a new school, change jobs, or simply go to a party where you encounter strangers, making friends is an important skill that can enrich your life and expose you to new perspectives. While many of us may feel awkward when trying to establish a connection with people we don't know, most of us know how to determine whether we have shared interests or common experiences, or we enjoy exploring new things. As we share our experiences with new people and they share their experiences with us, we decide whether we connect and enjoy their company, and whether we want to learn more about them. And as we explore topics of mutual interest, these new people are making similar judgments about us. If the feelings are mutual, there is the possibility of establishing a new friendship.

But just because you have discovered that you want to remain friends with a new person doesn't mean that you will be able to build the friendship into something deep and lasting – the basis for a sense of belonging. This is important because most mental health professionals believe that having a sense of belonging is an important predictor of mental health. As noted by researchers Damian Milton and Tara Sims, this is true for most autistics as well as non-autistics.

Keeping friends requires time and effort. You spend time with your friends so that you have shared experiences, and you show your friends that you care about them in part by showing interest in things that you know are important to them. You may plan fun activities to do together that reflect your shared interests, or you may decide to explore something new together. And, importantly, you help your friends when they are in need. From bringing them food when they are sick, to helping them through tough times, you notice what your friends need and try to support them.

Friendships work differently for kids at different developmental stages. Toddlers are usually content to be near each other playing different games (we call this *parallel play*). As they get older, though, children want to do things with their friends that are unique to that friendship. By late elementary school, most children have a best friend or a small circle of close friends. They enjoy spending time with friends one-on-one and also in groups. A middle- or high-school-aged child can manage the complexity involved in interacting with three or four other kids, and as they get older, most kids start thinking about romance, flirting, and dating. While many kids don't date in high school, most teenagers are thinking about it. They are trying to flirt. They have crushes. They are noticing who they are attracted to and learning how to talk to those people. And then, as they get older, many adults nurture long-term relationships that sustain them through the years. While there are the inevitable ups and downs, and the intensity of a relationship may vary, there are often people who remain part of your life throughout. Likewise, there are new relationships to be made as you explore new social situations – jobs, hobbies, spiritual practices, etc.

Understanding that **different relationships require different kinds of interactions** is another important relationship skill. For example, we treat acquaintances, casual friends, and very close friends differently. Understanding these differences helps us know how to greet others, how intimately to speak with others, who we tell our secrets to, who we are loyal to, what we expect from others, and more. We also need to **understand our place in the social hierarchy**; for instance, children speak in one way to younger children and in another way to peers, and their communication style also varies when talking to different types of adults, such as parents, teachers, principals, and doctors. Understanding these differences guides our behavior and our expectations in all of these relationships.

Social *motivation* is different from social *energy*. It's helpful to think of social energy in the same way as we think of physical energy: some of us have a lot of physical energy while others don't. It's the same thing with social energy. If you have low social energy, you have less energy to use than someone with high social energy. This means that you will have to decide how to ration it wisely so you don't have to suddenly leave in the middle of a social event because you've burnt out.

Some people are energized by being with other people (extroverts) while others are energized after time alone (introverts). Sometimes extroverts will confuse introversion with a lack of social motivation. But introverts enjoy being with friends and socializing, too; it just takes energy, which they need to restore by being alone. This is not due to low social motivation.

In contrast to social energy, social motivation references the *desire* to connect with others. An individual can have any combination of social energy and social motivation; for instance, one can have high social energy and motivation, low social energy and motivation, or high motivation but low energy. We have found that many autistics individuals have a strong desire to connect with others but little energy to do so (which is why we love Dr. Neff's quote at the top of this chapter).

It's also important to distinguish between low social energy or motivation and challenges in actually making and keeping friends. As you can see from the descriptions above, having friends and maintaining relationships is real work. We learn these skills as children because we are motivated to have friends to share our lives with. But making social mistakes, figuring out what we did wrong, and then avoiding making the same mistakes the next time is part of a life-long process. And it takes a lot of social motivation and energy to try again after making a mistake and suffering the consequences.

Successfully interacting with other people also requires social flexibility. By this, we mean intuitively and flexibly adjusting one's behavior to suit different social contexts. For example, if one of your kids is running really late when it's time to leave for school, you may turn into a drill sergeant (speaking loudly, stamping your foot, etc.). But if you are at a speaking engagement and the people organizing the meeting are running late, you would not behave in the same way.

Likewise, it is important to recognize the need to adjust your behavior in order to maintain healthy and happy relationships. For example, if a student notices that her teacher is angry with her, she will need to adjust her behavior to avoid being reprimanded in front of the class or sent to the principal's office.

Another type of social flexibility has to do with how we interact with our friends. Most people can easily adapt to changing social configurations, for example, welcoming newcomers to their circle or having an unusually strong reaction when someone leaves to talk to another friend. Likewise, most people are able to explore different interests and different situations with their friends – they would never expect a friend to do the exact same activity with them every single day. Non-autistic people understand the need to adjust their behavior, and they are able to do so fairly automatically, with little conscious thought or effort.

This brings us to the issue of **how we manage conflict**, which is a critically important skill in our relationships with friends, families, coworkers, and even acquaintances. Anyone who is married can attest to that! When we have a conflict with another person, we need to tell them what they did that upset us, listen to them so we can understand their perspective, and do the hard work of finding a solution so we can both learn and deepen the connection.

So, what might relationship management look like in an autistic person?

Differences with relationship management can present in a variety of ways. Similar to reciprocity and nonverbal communication, autistics may struggle with any number of these but not likely *all* of them. Areas of difficulty can include:

Making friends: Autistic people sometimes have trouble making new friends. For example, Donna was evaluating a 10th grader, and she said to his parents, "Does he have friends?" "Yes." "Nice friends?" "Yes." "Friends you like, long-term friends, real life friends?" "Yes, yes, yes. He's got a really nice group of long-term friends." But when Donna dug deeper, it turned out that his parents had made these friends for him in preschool. The families were close, and they went to the same synagogue, and the boys all went to the same school. Now they are in high school, and they get together once in a while. However, all of the other boys in the group have made other friends, while this boy has not. In fact, he has not made any new friends since preschool, and even those weren't friendships that he formed independently.

Keeping friends: Autistic people may also struggle to maintain friendships. For example, Kate's parents reported that their daughter has always had a variety of really nice friends. But when Donna asked more about this, it turned out that her core stable of friends has changed every six months; as such, Kate has no long-term friends. She is really good at getting out there and meeting new people, but it is harder for her to maintain friendships. Indeed, she has never had a friend for more than a year. This pattern of relationships is unlikely to lead to deep, reciprocal, long-term friendships or lasting romantic relationships.

Relationships not at typical developmental level: Relationships look different at different ages. For instance, many young children consider all acquaintances, such as everyone in their class, to be their friend. By the middle of elementary school, however, children understand that some peers are friends while others are simply classmates or neighbors. As another example, most children have at least one best friend, if not several, throughout childhood and adolescence. If someone has always had friends but never a truly deep, lasting best friend, it is of note. Another example may come in high school or college, where it would be unusual for a person to be entirely uninterested in a romantic partner, or interested but utterly unsuccessful in starting a romantic relationship. Though there are people who are aromantic or asexual, at this time we do not have any data on how many aromantic or asexual people are autistic versus non-autistic.

Understanding and recognizing the nature of relationships: Autistic individuals may have difficulty intuitively understanding the distinctions between different types of relationships. They may interact with all people in generally the same way, for example revealing very personal information to people they don't know well, or treating close family members in a very formal manner. Similarly, some autistic children may misinterpret who is actually their friend, and they may try to be friends with their teachers or with kids who bully or manipulate them.

Some of these kids may hug strangers. Others may speak to adults in the same way they speak to peers or regularly correct their teachers in front of the class. (Sometimes the parents of these kids report, "It's as if he doesn't know he's a child.") Children and adolescents who have this issue may not show a typical fear of authority and can inadvertently come across as rude or disrespectful.

Maddie was a bright 8th grader who entered Donna's office chattering away about her friend in the waiting room. She spoke so enthusiastically that Donna had the impression that she had actually run into a long-term friend during her five-minute wait for her appointment. Donna asked how she knew this friend, and she said, "from your waiting room!" Confused, Donna asked, "How did you originally meet this friend?" Maddie again replied, "I met her in your waiting room, just now." Maddie and Donna then had a long conversation about the difference between acquaintances and friends – she was able to offer beautiful definitions of both, and on a cognitive level she fully understood the difference. However, she still insisted that the other girl was a friend (and Donna later came to find out that this "friend" was only 10 years old). Cognitively, Maddie knew the difference, but she was not able to apply this knowledge in real life.

Social motivation: As we mentioned above, many autistic people have high social motivation and really want friends. But there are some autistics who may not care as much about having friends. They may not initiate interactions, even though they're happy when other kids initiate with them. While these kids may enjoy the company of their friends, they don't see a need to initiate get-togethers. This social motivation, or lack thereof, is different from social energy, so it is important to determine whether the individual needs a lot of down time but wants friends, or if the individual doesn't need more connection than they already have with family members, and genuinely doesn't need more friends to be happy.

While it is true that some autistic people truly do prefer to be alone, many, if not most, autistics want friends and romantic partners, just as non-autistic people do. Sadly, many have given up on this goal after repeated failures. This withdrawal does not result from lack of interest but instead from the laborious and often unsuccessful work required to make and maintain friendships. After failing many times, the autistic person may decide that the pain of trying and failing is simply not worth it. It is important to distinguish between people who prefer to be alone versus those who are alone because it is easier than being in a relationship, as appropriate support and intervention will differ for these two types of individuals.

Social flexibility: Some autistic individuals may not intuitively and flexibly adjust their social presentation to suit different situations. These kids may treat adults the same way they treat peers, which can inadvertently make them look as if they are rude, disrespectful, or lacking in boundaries. Rather than having a variety of ways to flexibly present themselves to the world, these kids tend to be the same all the time. This is often rooted in a poor ability to intuitively understand different types of relationships (as discussed above).

> Ben does not seem to understand how to adjust his behavior to suit different interactions or contexts. For instance, his parents report, "he has never been afraid of a grownup." Similarly, a family friend notes that Ben "will come into a conversation, even between two adults, not realizing that he is intruding." A teacher adds, "he thinks he's an adult."

A different type of social flexibility: If a child doesn't easily adapt to changing social configurations, their actions may be interpreted as exclusionary or rude, when really they simply struggle to navigate the dynamics of groups. For example, if I'm hanging out with Judy, and her friend Caron wants to join us, I have a choice. I may allow Caron to join us. On the other hand, I may want Caron to go away, or I may try to deliberately exclude her from our conversation. This may upset Judy, especially if Caron is her friend, and my behavior may damage my friendship with Judy. Judy may think I'm "glomming onto" and "suffocating" her.

Conflict management: Autistic individuals can have different ways of coping with conflict, including (a) "my way or the highway," (b) "going along to get along" and failing to self-advocate in relationships, or (c) simply leaving the situation or relationship when conflict arises.

Some autistic people expect their friends to do all the compromising. They may have difficulty being flexible and thus may attempt to dictate/control the interactions or play ("it's my way or the highway!"). This can be tiresome and frustrating for others and can have a negative impact on friendships.

Other autistic people will "go along to get along," sometimes at the cost of their own mental health. Because they struggle to understand how they feel, or to tell their friends how they feel, they can find themselves in situations that make them uncomfortable. These folks may look like they are incredibly flexible, or even passive. However, when they reach their limit, they may have a meltdown or shutdown that seems, to their friends, to come from nowhere, when in fact it comes from no longer being able to tolerate their discomfort.

Lastly, there are individuals who protect themselves by avoiding conflict altogether, neither going along with others nor self-advocating. They essentially say, "I'm outta here" when conflict arises. If their friends say something they don't like, these individuals are likely to respond by withdrawing, shutting down, leaving the situation, or ending the relationship entirely.

From the experts: Some things that make relationships challenging

Being dropped without explanation: *"I really love people and want friends but find myself getting ghosted, dropped, or yelled at when I don't know what I did. Usually, I'll make a friend and think it's going okay and suddenly it isn't. Suddenly they are mad and I feel scared and exhausted. I have long-term friends who do care for me and treat me right but they are often older or younger than me by a couple years."*

–Audrian F.

Having to mask – hiding your true self – with friends: *"I don't have an issue making friends, but being myself around them* *and dropping the mask a bit tends to strain relationships of all kinds. I feel like a bad friend sometimes, either completely forgetting about important stuff or having it slip my mind, or not being attentive enough to maintain friendships with NTs [neurotypicals]. I think if I wasn't constantly masking, I would have a much harder time making friends."*

–Emrys J.

Face blindness disrupting the start of new relationships: *"For most of my life, I thought I was a terrible person because people would know me, and I wouldn't know who they were. The only reason I could think of for that was that I didn't care about other people as much as other people cared about me. I might walk right past someone I should have known without speaking to them, and the thing that would have made the most sense to them was that I was aloof or unkind or stuck up. I didn't find out until I was in my late 40s that I'm moderately faceblind. I recognize a small number of people almost always, and a larger number – but still less than most people – when I see them in context, but not out of context and not if they've made a major change to their appearance."*

–Charlotte R.

Being overly trusting: *"Another thing that has been problematic in relationships for me is that my default setting with other people is trust. I believe what you tell me, especially what you tell me about yourself, your feelings, and so on. I mean, it seems beyond rude and presumptuous to question that. With most people, that's a good thing, but with people who are dishonest, or sociopathic, or narcissistic, it's a real problem. It's how I ended up in an abusive marriage for 15 years."*

–Charlotte R.

Not being able to trust: *"My difficulty making friends stems from it taking me a very long time to trust anyone, especially neurotypicals. It doesn't take nearly as long for me to trust other autistics, seeing as we're a lot more likely to show our* *genuine personalities the first time we meet someone, especially someone we know to be a fellow autistic."*

–Zachary M.

More likely to connect with other autistics: *"I tend to make really the best connections with other neurodivergent folks. I find anyone who hyperfocuses and loves immersive and direct conversation very easy to relate to. And people who are more into small talk and don't deep dive into any topics – those folks are just fine for being around but I don't connect with them much and that's the majority of our culture."*

–Debby F.

Emotional dysregulation getting in the way: *"When I was younger and a lot more sensory-sensitive, my fight-or-flight response would usually activate in "fight" mode, which would often manifest itself as me lashing out physically and/or verbally at whatever was causing me to be stressed/overstimulated – thus making other kids, and their parents, not want anything to do with me."*

–Zachary M.

Difficulty understanding the relationship: *"My specific problem with friendships has always been negotiating the type/depth of friendship. I know that there are different levels of friendship, and that different rules apply in the different levels. The closer the friendship, the more permission there is for self-disclosure, asking personal questions, meeting more frequently, calling without prior arrangement, and so on. But, at least in my experience, it's taboo to ask or talk about this. If I'm in a situation where I suspect that there are signals about the friendship that I'm not reading, I only have three choices, none of them good.*

- *I can push on, ignoring my suspicions about the signals. This isn't really an option, because it feels deeply wrong to me to be breaking rules, even if I can't quite see what those rules are.*

- *I can try to have an explicit conversation, telling the other person that I can't read what is happening, and asking for clarity. This hardly ever goes well.*

- *I can do nothing myself to advance the friendship, and just respond directly to the other person. Since friendships are built on reciprocation, and one person can't always take the initiative, this means that the friendship never develops."*

–Drew R.

Social flexibility: *"I am an outwardly very 'subtle' autistic person, but I am absolutely horrified at the idea of mixing people from different [parts of my life]. I try to have a consistent persona from place to place, and I don't have an active catalogue of how the contexts are different, but I absolutely do not want to mix someone I know from grad school with someone I know at work, with a partner from home, or my family. I don't know off the top of my head how those personas differ, but it becomes too much to attempt to mesh them at any given moment and my brain fries – and it's scary, and I want to cry and run and hide ... which you can't do in the middle of a work social event."*

–Jesse P.

Coping with social norms: *"I have no idea how to reciprocate friendship in a way that conforms to neuronormative standards – making reasonable plans to do activities, keeping in touch, having shared experiences – and is not completely exhausting or where I go way overboard. I've traveled to Europe on a lark with people who were basically long-term acquaintances, proposed undying love in college and high school to at least two basically random female acquaintances through long-winded and probably seriously confusing letters, and married the first girl that I went on a date with in college – and subsequently divorced several years later after she revealed she had been cheating on me."*

–Eric O.

Another issue I have is the "management" of friends: how often do you have to contact them? Do you call or text? What should I think when they don't contact me?

—Leen V.

Difficulty with small talk: "*I like having more 'meaningful' conversations, where we discuss specific questions, instead of small talk. But neurotypical people tend to depend on small talk before getting close so I don't have many friends because I want to skip the small talk step.*"

—Noelle B.

Low social energy: "*I do like hanging out with friends but depending on who it is relates to how much social energy I can expend – if it's someone I've known for years and don't have to change how I act around them, I can talk for hours; if it's a new person, it's probably minutes or an hour.*"

—Noelle B.

Accommodating autistic family members (or intolerance in others): "*My social life has been greatly affected by my family's needs. I just don't go where my kids won't be comfortable – where all are neurodivergent. Or where I feel we're being judged.*"

—Elizabeth B.

Relationships on the spectrum: What we've learned from the girls

Autistic girls are more likely to engage in pretend play. This has been noted by researchers, such as Nicole Kresier and Susan White, as well as Rachel Hiller and her colleagues, who also found that autistic girls are often more imaginative in their play than autistic boys. However, the nature of the play can be different than that of their non-autistic counterparts, with more focus on setting up than "being" the characters, or with repeating the same scenarios over and over again.

They are less likely to be loners. As reported by Michelle Dean and her colleagues, autistic girls are more likely to be in close physical proximity to peers than autistic boys, while not necessarily fully integrating. The girls tend to blend in, masking their social difficulty from the adults. If a parent or teacher is watching from the edge of the playground but not actually listening closely to the interactions, they are less likely to notice a child who, at a distance, *seems* to be engaged in reciprocal play but is in actuality only physically close to other children.

Along these lines, autistic boys are more likely to be outright rejected by their peers, while autistic girls are more likely to simply be overlooked. Research suggests that autistic girls are more likely than autistic boys to have one or two close friends. However, while autistic girls are generally more connected than autistic boys, their peer relationships often have atypical patterns. When taking a social history, it is important to learn about the *nature* of the child's friendships. For instance, were the friends always two years younger? Or were they quirky, bossy, or meek? Some autistic girls gravitate to friendships with other kids who need assistance, such as children with obvious physical disabilities. This is not necessarily a reciprocal relationship, as they are often in the helping role.

Autistic girls tend to have higher social motivation than autistic boys. Numerous researchers, such as Lisa Travis, Meng-Chuan Lai, Susanne Duvall, Felicity Sedgewick, Rachel Hiller, and Alexandra Head, and their colleagues, have reported that autistic females tend to have a greater desire to interact and form relationships with others than autistic males. Generally, autistic girls seem to view friendship as challenging, but also more valued and rewarding, than autistic boys.

Autistic girls report higher quality friendships than autistic boys. Felicity Sedgewick and her colleagues found that adolescent autistic girls reported higher friendship quality than autistic boys, and the girls seemed to maintain closer friendships than autistic boys. The authors noted, however, that autistic girls "had fewer of these close friendships than [non-autistic] girls, tending to have one or two intense friendships, because they found them more hard work." As noted by Rachel Hiller and her colleagues, as well as Meng-Chuan Lai and Peter Szatmari, autistic girls are often able to *initiate* relationships but then have significant difficulty *maintaining* them.

Autistic girls may struggle with more and different interpersonal conflict than their male counterparts. For example, Felicity Sedgewick and her colleagues reported that autistic girls may struggle more than autistic boys to identify and cope with interpersonal conflict. The girls were more likely to experience relational conflict and often felt that the conflict was their fault and was unresolvable. In contrast, autistic boys seemed less affected by their conflict with peers, both in terms of their emotional responses and the effect the conflict had on their relationships.

The timeline can be different. As noted by numerous authors, such as William Mandy and his colleagues as well as Marion Rutherford and her colleagues, the autistic traits seen in females can increase during adolescence, an observation that led Meng-Chuan Lai and Peter Szatmari to suggest a possible "adolescent onset" presentation, particularly in females. Specifically, some autistic girls do well throughout much of elementary school (though there generally are, upon closer inspection, signs of difficulty), but they begin to struggle or to struggle more noticeably in late elementary and middle school. There are multiple reasons for this, including:

- **Girl World changes.** When children are young, play and friendships are often based on proximity, for example, who is in your class at school, lives on your street, or is on your soccer team. In late elementary/early middle school, however, interactions and relationships are less proximity-driven and more based on shared interests. They are also based less on physical play and more on verbal interchanges, often focused on personal sharing, talking about relationships, gossiping, etc.

- **Parents become less involved.** When children are young, their parents take the lead in initiating and scaffolding playdates, but as they get older the parents become less involved and children typically begin to do this on their own.

- **Other changes are happening.** In addition to the significant change from elementary to middle school (which usually involves navigating one or two classrooms a day to being in different classes, with different teachers and different kids for each subject), massive changes begin to happen with the onset of puberty. The changes are uncontrollable and can feel somewhat unpredictable, which can be particularly stressful for autistics. They also come with new sensory experiences (e.g., wearing a bra, pads, or tampons, as well as experiencing cramps and also sexual urges). All of this creates more stress, which can result in new social and/or emotional challenges.

For all of these reasons, around the onset of puberty, many of these girls start having problems. The problems may overtly be social in nature (e.g., their friends gravitate away from them or overtly reject them). However, they can also be emotional in nature; the most noticeable issues can be anxiety, depression, an eating disorder, or school avoidance. This can deceive parents, educators, and clinicians, who often think, *"This can't be autism. She was fine through elementary school. The problem just started in middle school so it must just be anxiety."* And sometimes anxiety is indeed the issue. But frequently the anxiety occurs because the girl has hit her ceiling of ability to navigate complex social situations (and the world in general), not to mention the physical changes of adolescence, due to autism.

We cannot stress this point enough. Many autistic girls present with their first clinically significant challenges around the end of elementary school/beginning of middle school. This does not preclude autism! Remember that the DSM specifies that "symptoms must be present in the early developmental period," but it also notes that they "may not become fully manifest until social demands exceed limited capacities...."

Of course, boys and kids who are non-gender-conforming also face significant changes during adolescence, and autism can become more evident with them as well. As with other aspects of autism, the research on girls teaches us about the less obvious presentations of autism and can also apply to people of all genders.

Connecting culture

There are cultural differences in how we interpret the nature, stage, and behaviors associated with our relationships, whether romantic or platonic, and gender, race, religion, and ethnicity intersect with those relationship practices. For example, there are spoken and unspoken rules and norms for dating that may vary across cultures, including expectations around whether or when to marry, whether to date outside of one's race/religion/ethnic background, level of physical intimacy before or outside of marriage, openness to casual dating or multiple partners, accepted behaviors for men versus women, how to choose one's life partner (e.g., arranged marriages), and cohabitation – just to name a few.

> Cindy, a 25-year-old first-generation Cambodian American woman, shared that she is currently dating a White American man (Jack). She has yet to tell her parents that she is dating him because they may not approve of her "American boyfriend." Additionally, though Cindy really likes Jack, they have had arguments because she isn't comfortable with public affection and often asks her girlfriends to join them on their dates. Jack doesn't believe that Cindy is that interested in him because "she doesn't show it." Cindy says she feels caught between the expectations of two worlds.

Cindy is a perfect example of how cultural norms may be misinterpreted if we don't explicitly *ask* for clarification about the meaning behind behavior. Navigating this landscape is challenging for anyone but can be particularly difficult for autistics.

Remember: Don't assume. *Ask!*

Frequently asked questions

- **Do autistic individuals want friends?** Autistic individuals are, well, individuals. Many of them (most, in our experience) do want friends, though some are perfectly content without. Of course, the definition of *friend* matters here. Some autistics enjoy friendships that have little to no contact outside of structured activities or they may prefer online connections.

- **Do online friends count as friends?** This is complicated, especially in a post-COVID pandemic context, when many children (autistic and non-autistic) shifted to connecting with their friends online. Online communities can be a tremendous source of connection, where individuals care for and support each other. We urge you to consider the nature of the friendship within the cultural norms of the child's community.

References and related reading

American Psychiatric Association. (2022). *Diagnostic and statistical manual of mental disorders* (5th ed., text rev.). https://doi.org/10.1176/appi.books.9780890425787

Argyle, M., Henderson, M., Bond, M., Iizuka, Y., & Contarello, A. (1986). Cross-cultural variations in relationship rules. *International Journal of Psychology*, 21(1–4), 287–315. https://doi.org/10.1080/00207598608247591

Bargiela, S., Steward, R., & Mandy, W. (2016). The experiences of late-diagnosed women with autism spectrum conditions: An investigation of the female autism phenotype. *Journal of Autism and Developmental Disorders*, 46(10), 3281–3294. https://doi.org/10.1007/s10803-016-2872-8

Bottema-Beutel, K., Mullins, T. S., Harvey, M. N., Gustafson, J. R., & Carter, E. W. (2016). Avoiding the "brick wall of awkward": Perspectives of youth with autism spectrum disorder on social-focused intervention practices. *Autism*, 20(2), 196–206. https://doi.org/10.1177/1362361315574888

Dean, M., Harwood, R., & Kasari, C. (2017). The art of camouflage: Gender differences in the social behaviors of girls and boys with autism spectrum disorder. *Autism*, 21(6), 678–689. https://doi.org/10.1177/1362361316671845

Duvall, S., Armstrong, K., Shahabuddin, A., Grantz, C., Fein, D., & Lord, C. (2021). A road map for identifying autism spectrum disorder: Recognizing and evaluating characteristics that should raise red or "pink" flags to guide accurate differential diagnosis. *The Clinical Neuropsychologist*, 36(5), 1–36. https://doi.org/10.1080/13854046.2021.1921276

Dworzynski, K., Ronald, A., Bolton, P., & Happé, F. (2012). How different are girls and boys above and below the diagnostic threshold for autism spectrum disorders? *Journal of the American Academy of Child and Adolescent Psychiatry*, 51(8), 788–797. https://doi.org/10.1016/j.jaac.2012.05.018

Goffman, E. (2021). *The presentation of self in everyday life*. Knopf Doubleday.

Hall, M., Williams, R. D., Ford, M. A., Cromeans, E. M., & Bergman, R. J. (2020). Hooking-up, religiosity, and sexting among college students. *Journal of Religion and Health*, 59(1), 484–496. https://doi.org/10.1007/s10943-016-0291-y

Head, A. M., McGillivray, J. A., & Stokes, M. A. (2014). Gender differences in emotionality and sociability in children with autism spectrum disorders. *Molecular Autism*, 5(1), 19. https://doi.org/10.1186/2040-2392-5-19

Hiller, R. M., Young, R. L., & Weber, N. (2014). Sex differences in autism spectrum disorder based on DSM-5 criteria: Evidence from clinician and teacher reporting. *Journal of Abnormal Child Psychology*, 42(8), 1381–1393. https://doi.org/10.1007/s10802-014-9881-x

Hull, L., Mandy, W., & Petrides, K. V. (2017). Behavioral and cognitive sex/gender differences in autism spectrum condition and typically developing males and females. *Autism: The International Journal of Research and Practice*, 21(6), 706–727. https://doi.org/10.1177/1362361316669087

Hull, L., Petrides, K. V., Allison, C., Smith, P., Baron-Cohen, S., Lai, M.-C., & Mandy, W. (2017). "Putting on my best normal": Social camouflaging in adults with autism spectrum conditions. *Journal of Autism and Developmental Disorders*, 47(8), 2519–2534. https://doi.org/10.1007/s10803-017-3166-5

Jackson, P. B., Kleiner, S., Geist, C., & Cebulko, K. (2011). Conventions of courtship: Gender and race differences in the significance of dating rituals. *Journal of Family Issues*, 32(5), 629–652. https://doi.org/10.1177/0192513X10395113

Kirkovski, M., Enticott, P. G., & Fitzgerald, P. B. (2013). A review of the role of female gender in autism spectrum disorders. *Journal of Autism and Developmental Disorders*, 43(11), 2584–2603. https://doi.org/10.1007/s10803-013-1811-1

Kline, S. L., Horton, B., & Zhang, S. (2008). Communicating love: Comparisons between American and East Asian university students. *International Journal of Intercultural Relations*, 32(3), 200–214. https://doi.org/10.1016/j.ijintrel.2008.01.006

Kopp, S., & Gillberg, C. (1992). Girls with social deficits and learning problems: Autism, atypical Asperger syndrome or a variant of these conditions. *European Child & Adolescent Psychiatry*, *1*(2), 89–99. https://doi.org/10.1007/BF02091791

Kreiser, N. L., & White, S. W. (2014). ASD in females: Are we overstating the gender difference in diagnosis? *Clinical Child and Family Psychology Review*, *17*(1), 67–84. https://doi.org/10.1007/s10567-013-0148-9

Lai, M.-C., & Baron-Cohen, S. (2015). Identifying the lost generation of adults with autism spectrum conditions. *The Lancet. Psychiatry*, *2*(11), 1013–1027. https://doi.org/10.1016/S2215-0366(15)00277-1

Lai, M.-C., & Szatmari, P. (2020). Sex and gender impacts on the behavioural presentation and recognition of autism. *Current Opinion in Psychiatry*, *33*(2), 117–123. https://doi.org/10.1097/YCO.00000 00000000575

Lai, M.-C., Lin, H.-Y., & Ameis, S. H. (2022). Towards equitable diagnoses for autism and attention-deficit/hyperactivity disorder across sexes and genders. *Current Opinion in Psychiatry*, *35*(2), 90–100. https://doi.org/10.1097/YCO.0000000000000770

Mandy, W., Chilvers, R., Chowdhury, U., Salter, G., Seigal, A., & Skuse, D. (2012). Sex differences in autism spectrum disorder: Evidence from a large sample of children and adolescents. *Journal of Autism and Developmental Disorders*, *42*(7), 1304–1313. https://doi.org/10.1007/s10803-011-1356-0

Mandy, W., Pellicano, L., St Pourcain, B., Skuse, D., & Heron, J. (2018). The development of autistic social traits across childhood and adolescence in males and females. *Journal of Child Psychology and Psychiatry, and Allied Disciplines*, *59*(11), 1143–1151. https://doi.org/10.1111/jcpp.12913

Milton, D., & Sims, T. (2016). How is a sense of well-being and belonging constructed in the accounts of autistic adults? *Disability & Society*, *31*(4), 520–534. https://doi.org/10.1080/09687599.2016.1186529

Rutherford, M., McKenzie, K., Johnson, T., Catchpole, C., O'Hare, A., McClure, I., ... & Murray, A. (2016). Gender ratio in a clinical population sample, age of diagnosis and duration of assessment in children and adults with autism spectrum disorder. *Autism: The International Journal of Research and Practice*, *20*(5), 628–634. https://doi.org/10.1177/1362361315617879

Sedgewick, F., Hill, V., & Pellicano, E. (2019). 'It's different for girls': Gender differences in the friendships and conflict of autistic and neurotypical adolescents. *Autism*, *23*(5), 1119–1132. https://doi.org/10.1177/1362361318794930

Sedgewick, F., Hill, V., Yates, R., Pickering, L., & Pellicano, E. (2016). Gender differences in the social motivation and friendship experiences of autistic and non-autistic adolescents. *Journal of Autism and*

Developmental Disorders, *46*, 1297–1306. https://doi.org/10.1007/s10803-015-2669-1

Shenhav, S., Campos, B., & Goldberg, W. A. (2017). Dating out is intercultural: Experience and perceived parent disapproval by ethnicity and immigrant generation. *Journal of Social and Personal Relationships*, *34*(3), 397–422. https://doi.org/10.1177/0265407516640387

Shulman, C., Rice, C. E., Morrier, M. J., & Esler, A. (2020). The role of diagnostic instruments in dual and differential diagnosis in autism spectrum disorder across the lifespan. *Child and Adolescent Psychiatric Clinics of North America*, *29*(2), 275–299. https://doi.org/10.1016/j.chc.2020.01.002

Stefanescu, A. (2019, June 19). Dating manners across different cultures. The School of Manners. www.theschoolofmanners.com/blog/datingmannersacrossdifferentcultures

Travis, L., Sigman, M., & Ruskin, E. (2001). Links between social understanding and social behavior in verbally able children with autism. *Journal of Autism and Developmental Disorders*, *31*(2), 119–130. https://doi.org/10.1023/a:1010705912731

Young, H., Oreve, M.-J., & Speranza, M. (2018). Clinical characteristics and problems diagnosing autism spectrum disorder in girls. *Archives de Pédiatrie*, *25*(6), 399–403. https://doi.org/10.1016/j.arcped.2018.06.008

Young, S., Hollingdale, J., Absoud, M., Bolton, P., Branney, P., Colley, W., … & Woodhouse, E. (2020). Guidance for identification and treatment of individuals with attention deficit/hyperactivity disorder and autism spectrum disorder based upon expert consensus. *BMC Medicine*, *18*(1), 146. https://doi.org/10.1186/s12916-020-01585-y

Chapter 5

Repetitive or idiosyncratic behavior

Denying me this would be like telling someone they can't use NSAIDS. It's not an immediate thing for me and sometimes there are workarounds, but it would make my life more painful.
–Esmeralda B.

What people often think repetitive or idiosyncratic behavior means

Many people connect repetitive autistic behaviors with rocking, arm flapping, hand flicking, or repeating words or phrases. This may originate from portrayals of autistic individuals in popular movies or TV shows. For instance, in *Rain Man*, Dustin Hoffman's character, Raymond Babbitt, frequently repeated the phrase, "I'm an excellent driver," regardless of the conversation topic. If Tom Cruise's character said to Raymond, "Do you want to go to dinner now?" Raymond might say, "Dinner now dinner now dinner now." Raymond also flapped his arms and repeatedly hit himself when upset.

Similarly, in *What's Eating Gilbert Grape*, Leonardo DiCaprio's Arnie Grape demonstrated finger flicking, unusual posturing, and echolalia (repeating words and phrases that he just heard). A more recent portrayal of autism is Sam Gardner in *Atypical*. When upset, Sam rocks back and forth, often while repetitively naming types of penguins.

In popular media, these behaviors are typically depicted as obviously out of the norm, often entirely out of the individual's control, and mostly occurring when the individual is distressed. However, behaviors in this category are far more varied.

DOI: 10.4324/9781003242130-7

What do repetitive behaviors really include?

This category refers to any behavior that is *either* repetitive *or* idiosyncratic. This can include motor movements, speech, or use of objects.

Movements in this category can include flapping, flicking of the hands and fingers, swaying, rocking, pacing, or spinning. Toe walking is not uncommon until about age three but is not typical after that. Repetitive skin picking is a fairly common behavior that many people do not associate with autism. For instance, Donna recently met with a 15-year-old whose arms were completely marked up from persistent picking. Most parents and clinicians may assume that persistent skin picking is anxiety-related, and it certainly can be. However, in the context of social challenges, it can also be considered a repetitive motor behavior.

There are other idiosyncratic movements that are patterned, coordinated, and non-reflexive and are performed in exactly the same way with each repetition. An example is playing with your hair in a very particular way that never varies. Another example is rhythmic self-harming, such as repetitive head banging.

From the experts: Common and unique repetitive movements

We asked adult autistics about their repetitive motor movements. Some seem to be more common and likely unsurprising for clinicians, such as the following.

> Rocking (many autistics do this privately so they need to be asked directly about it). *"I hum and rock and flap."*
> –Jesse P.

> Flapping (often privately) or other arm/hand movements.

> Skin picking (sometimes to the point of pain or infection).

> Persistent scratching (often the scalp, sometimes for long periods of time).

> Rubbing toes or fingers together; flicking or wiggling fingers in a particular way.

Other body-based repetitive behaviors, such as *"tapping my collarbone," "twisting my hair,"* or *"rubbing my earlobe, to the point where I have photos of me doing it that other people have taken."*

–Elinor R.

We recently asked autistic adults to tell us their "stims." Fabian B. wrote, *"Tooth tapping is a big stim: you get both percussive sound and tactile vibration; it's a noise you can feel in your head but which nobody else hears."* C.P. added, *"The internal jaw tapping of the teeth to a made-up rhythm is one of my favorites. Plus, I do this one in public a lot as it's not as obvious as my hand scratching/flapping."* Then Aubrian B. chimed in, *"Yes!!! I did this constantly as a child – tapping my teeth to the rhythm of whatever song was stuck in my head."*

This is a great reminder of why we need to ask the client themselves about any type of behavior that might be repetitive, as the behavior may be subtle and unnoticed by others. We have also heard from many clients that they intentionally hide their repetitive behaviors, for fear of being judged by others.

There are also endless numbers of "stims" (self-stimulating behaviors) that are unique to an individual. Here are some real-life examples:

I look around a room in a pattern. I blink hard.

–Jade L.-T.

I will lie down and shake my head side-to-side vigorously.

–Esmeralda B.

I hand-flap and giggle, even jump, but I am sure the stereotype of a giggly girl makes this one easier to overlook.

–Boontarika S.

I tend to move my fingers in a pattern as if I'm pressing keys or playing piano. If my thumb/fingers were labeled as 1–5, I tend to do 1 2 3 4 5 | 5 4 3 2 1 at a whatever beats per minute is soothing at that moment but sometimes I do 1 | 1 2 1 | 1 2 3 2 1 | etc. ...

–Aaliyah B.

Use of objects can be either repetitive or atypical. This can include behaviors like lining up or organizing toys, candy, or other objects, repetitively opening and closing doors or turning lights on and off, taking objects apart (without the desire to understand how they work), or using objects in an unusual way. It can also include reading the same book or watching the same show repeatedly. To be clear, many of us have read our favorite books more than once! Hence, if a child has read a book or watched a show two or three times, we would not consider it to be significant, but if they did it over and over and over again, then that would constitute repetitive behavior. We have also heard from many autistic individuals that they repetitively make lists. These are just some examples; repetitive use of objects can take countless forms.

Marty reports that he makes extensive lists of "things I like and think about." He enthusiastically describes making lists every evening and becomes very excited when discussing and showing me his many lists. Similarly, Maria makes many lists about movies – the ones she loves, the ones she hates, characters, specific plot points, etc.

Throughout 1st grade, Quinn would go to the school counselor's room every day during lunch and "would write on hundreds of sticky notes, letters or words or math, one by one, and plaster them on the white board. It calmed him down, laying them out in a pattern, talking to himself."

Repetitive/idiosyncratic list making can also take the form of spreadsheets. For instance, one young woman we know de-stresses by creating incredibly detailed spreadsheets about specific aspects of plays about medieval kings.

Speech or language can also be either idiosyncratic or repetitive. Idiosyncratic language can include features like pronoun reversal (confusing he/she/it or you/I), unusual use of words, or a quirky or imaginative way of saying things. It can also manifest as unusually formal language (e.g., saying "mother" instead of "mom" or being "a little professor"). It is important to look carefully for these linguistic features, which can come across as being clever or witty, particularly in individuals with above-average verbal skills, amazing vocabularies, and very sophisticated language use. If someone makes a cute pun here and there, it is not out of the ordinary at all; what is more of note is a child who *repeatedly* makes up or uses idiosyncratic words. Even if they are amusing and enjoyable, it still counts.

> George sometimes had a difficult time coming up with the right word. His family loved his creativity and adopted his vocabulary as their own, saying things like, "stay-in-room-store" for "hotel."

> Noah was a very bright 7th grader with a vocabulary far better than most adults. Noah was enjoying the testing process, though he did not like to be timed. After completing a timed test, Noah was told that the next test was not timed, and he replied with relief, "I'm so glad it's not a time ticking contest!"

> Chase was an adorable 4th grader who had an intense interest in dogs. While playing together with plastic dinosaurs, Chase insisted on calling the baby dinosaurs "puppersaurs."

Repetitive speech includes echolalia (repeating words or phrases just heard) or palilalia (repeating one's own words), but more subtly it can manifest as repeatedly including favorite words or phrases in conversations. It is important to differentiate this from stuttering, which involves repeating oneself when attempting to correctly say something after a dysfluency. If clients or parents report a history of stuttering, it is important to make sure it was actual stuttering; many people confuse echolalia or palilalia with stuttering.

Repetitive vocalizations that are not language (i.e., do not include words) also fall into this category. For example, we often hear about a student humming or making other noises in class. Teachers and clinicians tend to assume that this occurs due to the poor impulse control associated with ADHD (sort of like "hyperactivity of the mouth"), and sometimes it does. If there is a young student with a new diagnosis of ADHD who is making noises in class, then that may be the right conclusion. However, if the ADHD is well-treated, and the child is now in 9th grade and still making noises in class, then it may be more likely to be an instance of repetitive or unusual speech.

Examples of repetitive speech and language

- Humming or making other noises, such as "this quiet throat sound that's hard to describe," "a sound in the back of my throat like sucking but fully at the back of the mouth," "animal noises," or "sometimes I screech."

- Repeating words, songs, or parts of songs.

- Singing the same three songs for decades.

- Listening to audiobooks and chanting particular words or phrases along with the narrator.

- Asking the same question or saying the same phrase over and over.

- Repeating lines or dialogue from movies.

- Reciting verbatim a passage from a book or article in response to a particular question. This often occurs when a child has been taught a script for navigating social situations.

- Repeating verbatim a statement or question that was spontaneous the first time. This sometimes happens when the autistic person felt a strong connection with their conversation partner the first time they asked the question, and they want to experience that feeling of connection again by repeating the conversation. In this case, family members may report that the person asks the same question over and over, even though the question has been fully and completely answered previously.

From the experts: The many purposes of repetitive behaviors

Repetitive behaviors are sometimes characterized as undesirable, and treatment is all too frequently targeted at reducing these behaviors, not because they bother the individual, but because they bother the non-autistics around the individual. Like camouflaging, repetitive behaviors can be helpful, problematic, or neutral, depending on the situation. As can be seen from the quotes above, **autistic individuals very often experience the repetition as comforting, calming, or enjoyable.** At times, though, they can get stuck in a "loop" and have difficulty stopping the behavior. This tendency to "get stuck" is another common characteristic of autism, and is discussed in Chapter 6.

For now, we'd like to highlight some of the benefits of repetitive behaviors. The adult autistics we surveyed had great clarity on the many purposes and benefits of these behaviors, most of which can generally be understood as helping to self-regulate thoughts and/or emotions and cope with feeling overwhelmed. For example,

> **Stress relief:** *"They relieve stress and help me not focus on my anxious thoughts."*
>
> –Rachel W.

> **Calming:** *"It's intense, but then deeply calming. I treat this like painkillers: I don't use it much – even when I need it – because it carries some risk, but it's really helpful when I do."*
>
> –Esmeralda B.

> **Promotes focus:** *"It helps with focus, self-regulation, feeling present in my body, able to sit with people."*
>
> –Boontarika S.

Helps with overwhelm: "*The only time I stim is when I'm in 'too muchiness.'*"

–Holly G.

Release of emotion: "*It's calming, lets out excess energy, expressing emotions – many people note that 'happy stims' are often different from 'stressed or sad stims.'*"

–Miko

Just because: Finally, some people report that they do it "for no reason at all." As Elle J. told us, "*I do it because I do it.*"

From the experts: Repercussions when autistics are forced to stop

When autistic individuals are prevented from engaging in their repetitive or idiosyncratic behaviors (including times when they prevent themselves from engaging in order to meet social expectations), they report that it results in negative emotions, which can range from vaguely uncomfortable to anxious/stressed/irritable to complete meltdown. Here are some quotes from adult autistics:

It is like my skin is crawling.

–Rachel W.

It's like being restrained from movement or someone sitting on your chest to keep you from fully breathing. It can get maddening.

–Jade L.-T.

Makes me feel invalidated, sad, ashamed, negatively different, and misunderstood.

–Asiatu Lawoyin

Just NO! It will stress me out to the point that it will cause a meltdown. I mean a major meltdown episode lasting over 20 minutes, then a shutdown cycle.

–Holly G.

It feels like being frozen, like I'm imprisoned in my own body. All my body is tense or distant and I don't feel

I belong in it anymore. Also all my thoughts disappear, I feel empty-like.

–Miko

If I'm stuck in the environment and unwilling to openly stim we might risk a breakdown. Escape is a must.

–Jesse P.

For me, it's a craving that's very hard to resist. When I was in grade school, I realized not everyone stimmed and felt I should try to not do it. What happened was, over time, I developed stims that are imperceptible to others, like the throat sound I make – it's very subtle – or singing songs in my head.

–Ellen J.

We highly recommend asking each individual about the impact of avoiding their repetitive behaviors. We also recommend specifically asking about repetitive behaviors earlier in life, as many autistics learn to stop their preferred behaviors because of negative feedback. As Juston J. told us, "*I adjusted mine over time to be more socially acceptable. I used to flap and chew on my shirts, but now I open and close my fist rapidly at my sides or pluck an eyebrow hair.*"

Repetitive behavior: What we've learned from the girls

The research is clear: girls meet this criterion in more subtle ways. In our experience, girls and their parents rarely bring up these subtle repetitive behaviors spontaneously, and girls typically do not engage in these behaviors during structured and time-limited interactions, such as class, therapy, or testing sessions. Thus, it is extremely important to ask the individual about this possibility, rather than simply asking those around them or trying to observe repetitive behaviors during sessions.

Common examples of repetitive movement in girls are pacing back and forth, walking the perimeter of the playground or yard, walking repeatedly around the kitchen island or the sofa, or a repetitive body movement that can seem like dancing. These are not the kind of behaviors, like flapping, that parents will think to bring up during an interview, because they just do not stand out in the same way. Yet they can be repetitive behaviors. As Josefina E. tells us, *"I'm a pacer. I just walk around my kitchen for three hours straight. I just walk around it and walk around it and walk around it [the island] for hours."*

Frequently asked questions

- **Are repetitive behaviors bad?** Generally, no. As mentioned above, repetitive behaviors can be helpful, problematic, or neutral, depending on the situation. As can be seen from the quotes above, autistic individuals very often experience the repetition as comforting, calming, or enjoyable. At times, though, they can get stuck in a "loop" and have difficulty stopping the behavior. As mentioned earlier in this chapter, this tendency to "get stuck" is characteristic of some presentations of autism; we will cover this feature in more detail in Chapter 6.

  That said, even though the behaviors aren't bad, they can have social repercussions, especially if other people do not understand why the person is repeating things or behaving in a way that they view as unexpected. Many autistic people report that they have been told that their repetitive behaviors are weird or inappropriate, and that they were teased if they engaged in the behaviors in public. Diminishing these behaviors is often a focus of intervention, without regard to the mental health repercussions to the individual.

- **Are these the same as stereotypies or stereotyped behaviors?** Yes, but for many people both on and off the spectrum, the word *stereotyped* implies behavior that is "socially undesirable" or "lacks purpose." We suggest that this term is pejorative, outdated, and inaccurate and prefer to simply say *repetitive behavior*.

- **Are repetitive behaviors the same as "stimming"?** Stimming is an informal term that people use in different ways, but it generally refers to autistic ways of self-regulating. Most examples of stimming that we have heard would fall under the categories of either repetitive behaviors or sensory craving, as will be discussed in Chapter 8. There are also non-stimming ways of self-regulating, such as meditation, deep breathing, self-talk, and many more.

- **When is a repetitive or idiosyncratic behavior merely quirky and when does it qualify as diagnosable?** This depends on several factors: how frequently it occurs; whether the behavior is developmentally typical (e.g., toddlers often rock); if there is a purpose (or purposes) to the behavior (such as it being calming); and whether there is a negative consequence to stopping the behavior.

- **Sometimes scripted language is really an attempt to communicate or connect, so why is it here and not in the chapter on reciprocal interactions?** We include scripted language here because it is an example of repetitive language that is idiosyncratic. That said, it's also an example of how autistic people reciprocate, but in a way that can interfere with the feeling of reciprocity if the conversation partner doesn't understand what is going on. If the individual is using specific scripts repeatedly, we would include it here. If the individual has a larger pattern of using various scripts as spontaneous conversation, we would include it in the reciprocity domain.

- **What's the difference between autistic repetitive behaviors, tics, and compulsions?** Sometimes it's hard to tell, but here are some general guidelines:

A **tic** is a sudden movement or vocalization. It is typically repetitive but nonrhythmic. Common examples of simple motor tics are eye blinking, shoulder shrugging, or neck jerking, while common vocal tics are repetitive throat clearing, sniffing, grunting, or coughing.

A **complex tic** is, well, a bit more complex. These are generally coordinated movements that involve more than one muscle group. Examples of complex tics include facial grimacing, repeating words or phrases out of context, echoing what someone else said, tongue movements, neck stretching, or clapping.

A **compulsion** is always fueled by anxiety. The sole purpose is to lower a feeling of anxiety or tension. A compulsion is part of obsessive-compulsive disorder when it is connected to unwanted, intrusive thoughts (though younger children are often not able to vocalize the obsessive thoughts), for example, excessive hand washing related to a fear of germs.

So, how are tics, compulsions, and autistic repetitive behaviors similar? They are all behaviors that are repetitive and can include movements, words, or sounds. They can all occur more when the individual is stressed and can be controlled to varying degrees with effort.

How are they different? Often a tic is a smaller movement involving one side of the body, whereas autistic repetitive behaviors tend to be larger, bilateral movements. People report that before they experience a tic, they often have an unpleasant premonition or sensation that vanishes afterwards (similar to the sensation you might feel if I told you not to blink). Tics are generally not rhythmic or patterned, whereas repetitive behaviors can be. A tic is never described as relaxing or enjoyable, while an autistic repetitive behavior can be both of these.

It is typically helpful to consider the *function* of the behavior by asking the individual what it means to them and what purpose it serves. Does the individual like engaging in the behavior or do they just do it because it feels wrong if they don't? Would their life be better if they didn't have to do it? Or worse if they couldn't do it? Autistic individuals generally report enjoying their repetitive behaviors and feel their lives would be worse if they couldn't engage in them.

Compulsions in the context of OCD are *unwanted* behaviors that have the *sole* function of relieving anxiety. Repetitive behaviors can certainly relieve anxiety as well, but they can also be relaxing or enjoyable. Tics don't really have a purpose; they are more of a reflex.

Of course, one individual can certainly have a combination of tics, compulsions, and autistic behaviors; they are not mutually exclusive.

- **How do I tell the difference between a behavior that is repetitive and a behavior that is sensory craving?** It may not be possible to differentiate sensory craving behavior from behavior that is either repetitive or idiosyncratic. Ideally, you can ask the person what function the behavior serves. If they talk about it fulfilling a sensory need, it would be classified as a sensory difference. If instead the focus is on a desire or need to repeat the action because it feels right, or if they do not identify a sensory aspect, you would classify it as a repetitive behavior.

References and related reading

American Psychiatric Association. (2022). *Diagnostic and statistical manual of mental disorders* (5th ed., text rev.). https://doi.org/10.1176/appi.books.9780890425787

Duvall, S., Armstrong, K., Shahabuddin, A., Grantz, C., Fein, D., & Lord, C. (2021). A road map for identifying autism spectrum disorder: Recognizing and evaluating characteristics that should raise red or "pink" flags to guide accurate differential diagnosis. *The Clinical Neuropsychologist*, 36(5), 1–36. https://doi.org/10.1080/13854046.2021.1921276

Duvekot, J., van der Ende, J., Verhulst, F. C., Slappendel, G., van Daalen, E., Maras, A., & Greaves-Lord, K. (2017). Factors influencing the probability of a diagnosis of autism spectrum disorder in girls versus boys. *Autism: The International Journal of Research and Practice*, 21(6), 646–658. https://doi.org/10.1177/1362361316672178

Dworzynski, K., Ronald, A., Bolton, P., & Happé, F. (2012). How different are girls and boys above and below the diagnostic threshold for autism spectrum disorders? *Journal of the American Academy of Child and Adolescent Psychiatry*, 51(8), 788–797. https://doi.org/10.1016/j.jaac.2012.05.018

Hallström, L. (Dir.), & Blomquist, A. C. (Prod.) (1993). *What's Eating Gilbert Grape* [Film]. USA: Paramount Pictures.

Hull, L., Mandy, W., & Petrides, K. V. (2017). Behavioral and cognitive sex/gender differences in autism spectrum condition and typically developing males and females. *Autism: The International Journal of Research and Practice*, 21(6), 706–727. https://doi.org/10.1177/1362361316669087

Hull, L., Petrides, K. V., Allison, C., Smith, P., Baron-Cohen, S., Lai, M.-C., & Mandy, W. (2017). "Putting on my best normal": Social camouflaging in adults with autism spectrum conditions. *Journal of Autism and Developmental Disorders*, 47(8), 2519–2534. https://doi.org/10.1007/s10803-017-3166-5

Kaat, A. J., Shui, A. M., Ghods, S. S., Farmer, C. A., Esler, A. N., Thurm, A., ... & Bishop, S. L. (2021). Sex differences in scores on standardized measures of autism symptoms: A multisite integrative data analysis. *Journal of Child Psychology and Psychiatry*, 62(1), 97–106. https://doi.org/10.1111/jcpp.13242

Kirkovski, M., Enticott, P. G., & Fitzgerald, P. B. (2013). A review of the role of female gender in autism spectrum disorders. *Journal of Autism and Developmental Disorders*, 43(11), 2584–2603. https://doi.org/10.1007/s10803-013-1811-1

Kopp, S., & Gillberg, C. (1992). Girls with social deficits and learning problems: Autism, atypical Asperger syndrome or a variant of these conditions. *European Child & Adolescent Psychiatry*, 1(2), 89–99. https://doi.org/10.1007/BF02091791

Kreiser, N. L., & White, S. W. (2014). ASD in females: Are we overstating the gender difference in diagnosis? *Clinical Child and Family Psychology Review*, 17(1), 67–84. https://doi.org/10.1007/s10567-013-0148-9

Lai, M.-C., Lin, H.-Y., & Ameis, S.H. (2022). Towards equitable diagnoses for autism and attention-deficit/hyperactivity disorder across sexes and genders. *Current Opinion in Psychiatry*, 35(2), 90-100. https://doi.org/10.1097/YCO.0000000000000770

Lai, M.-C., & Szatmari, P. (2020). Sex and gender impacts on the behavioural presentation and recognition of autism. *Current Opinion in Psychiatry*, 33(2), 117–123. https://doi.org/10.1097/YCO.0000000000000575

Levinson, B. (Dir.), Guber, P., Peters, C., & Peters, J. (Prods). (1988). *Rain Man* [Film]. United Artists.

Mandy, W., Chilvers, R., Chowdhury, U., Salter, G., Seigal, A., & Skuse, D. (2012). Sex differences in autism spectrum disorder: Evidence from a large sample of children and adolescents. *Journal of Autism and Developmental Disorders*, 42(7), 1304–1313. https://doi.org/10.1007/s10803-011-1356-0

McFayden, T. C., Antezana, L., Albright, J., Muskett, A., & Scarpa, A. (2020). Sex differences in an autism spectrum disorder diagnosis: Are restricted repetitive behaviors and interests the key? *Review Journal of Autism and Developmental Disorders*, 7(2), 119–126. https://doi.org/10.1007/s40489-019-00183-w

Saville, J., & King, T. (Prods.). (2017–2021). *Atypical* [Television series]. Netflix.

Singer, H. S. (2013). Motor control, habits, complex motor stereotypies, and Tourette syndrome. *Annals of the New York Academy of Sciences*, 1304, 22–31. https://doi.org/10.1111/nyas.12281

Stephenson, K. G., Norris, M., & Butter, E. M. (2021). Sex-based differences in autism symptoms in a large, clinically referred sample of preschool-aged children with ASD. *Journal of Autism and Developmental Disorders.* https://doi.org/10.1007/s10803-020-04836-2

Tager-Flusberg, H., Rogers, S., Cooper, J., Landa, R., Lord, C., Paul, R., ... & Yoder, P. (2009). Defining spoken language benchmarks and selecting measures of expressive language development for young children with autism spectrum disorders. *Journal of Speech, Language, and Hearing Research, 52*(3), 643–652. https://doi.org/10.1044/1092-4388(2009/08-0136)

Tsirgiotis, J., Young, R., & Weber, N. (2021). Sex/gender differences in CARS2 and GARS-3 item scores: Evidence of phenotypic differences between males and females with ASD. *Journal of Autism and Developmental Disorders.* https://doi.org/10.1007/s10803-021-05286-0

Uljarević, M., Frazier, T. W., Jo, B., Billingham, W. D., Cooper, M. N., Youngstrom, E. A., Scahill, L., & Hardan, A. Y. (2022). Big data approach to characterize restricted and repetitive behaviors in autism. *Journal of the American Academy of Child & Adolescent Psychiatry, 61*(3), 446–457. https://doi.org/10.1016/j.jaac.2021.08.006

Walkup, J., Shaffer, D., Lee, F., & Singer, H. (2013). Motor control, habits, complex motor stereotypies, and Tourette syndrome. *Annals of the New York Academy of Sciences, 1304.* https://doi.org/10.1111/nyas.12281

Young, H., Oreve, M.-J., & Speranza, M. (2018). Clinical characteristics and problems diagnosing autism spectrum disorder in girls. *Archives de Pédiatrie, 25*(6), 399–403. https://doi.org/10.1016/j.arcped.2018.06.008

Young, S., Hollingdale, J., Absoud, M., Bolton, P., Branney, P., Colley, W., ... & Woodhouse, E. (2020). Guidance for identification and treatment of individuals with attention deficit/hyperactivity disorder and autism spectrum disorder based upon expert consensus. *BMC Medicine, 18*(1), 146. https://doi.org/10.1186/s12916-020-01585-y

Chapter 6

Flexibility

I cling to my routines because I know they are safe and effective. Spontaneous things are a roll of the dice, and, frankly, nearly always lead to meltdowns that are not only agonizing but also cost me relationships. I can deviate from my routine, and will do if it's important or if the risks can be mitigated, but that also takes a lot of executive function and sensory resilience resources, so it has to be worth it.

–Peter B.

What people often think a lack of flexibility means:

Many clinicians think that all autistic people have rigid routines or rituals, and that they have meltdowns if they cannot follow their routines. Similarly, many clinicians believe that autistics are rigid in *all* interactions and areas of their lives. We frequently hear, "he can't be autistic, he doesn't have rigid routines," "she can't be autistic, she is highly flexible with others," or "he can't be autistic, he is capable of very flexible thinking on theoretical or intellectual matters." As you will see, however, there are actually many different types of inflexibility that can accompany autism.

Many of the behaviors and characteristics discussed in this chapter can be indicative of anxiety and/or OCD in a non-autistic person. And, of course, they can also reflect a co-occurring diagnosis of anxiety or OCD in an autistic person.

It is essential to consider signs of inflexibility in the larger context of an individual's presentation. That is, inflexibility

DOI: 10.4324/9781003242130-8

in the context of social difficulty may indicate the possibility of autism. If, however, there is no social difficulty – either by external behavior or internal experience – these features may be due solely to anxiety and/or OCD, rather than autism. We discuss differential diagnosis in more detail in the book, *Is This Autism? A Companion Guide for Diagnosing*.

What does this category really include?

While some autistic individuals are persistently rigid in many aspects of their lives, many can be highly flexible in some interactions and areas of their lives, but highly inflexible in others. Rather than looking for overall inflexibility, we find it helpful to look for *islands of rigidity*, which can take many different forms, such as:

Routines and rituals: This can manifest as a need to navigate through a daily routine with each task performed in the exact same order/manner, to demand that others follow the same routine for a given activity every time, and so on. We have heard countless examples of these kinds of routines.

Strong reactions to small changes: Sometimes this is clear and easy to spot. For instance, Donna worked with one 11-year-old who was still upset, and complained every single day, about the fact that her parents had painted the bathroom a different color *two years ago*. Donna also worked with an 8-year-old who burst into tears when her mother got a different haircut and took several months to adjust to the change. We have also seen children who melt down if their parents take a different route home from school. These examples are readily apparent and easy for parents to spot.

Other times, the issue is not so obvious, and it requires close attention from a parent or teacher to discern the pattern. For instance, some children have a really bad day *every* time there is a substitute teacher or bus driver, or plans change unexpectedly, or a teacher shifts to a new topic (e.g., switching from multiplication to division), or a food like macaroni cheese is made by a different manufacturer.

Of note, people who have very limited diets or who wear the same clothes every day may struggle with change because they are inflexible, but it is important to make sure the difficulty is not better explained by sensory challenges. If the latter are at the root of the inflexibility, then the issue would more appropriately be categorized under the *sensory* criterion.

> Every morning of his 5th grade year, Nico went into the classroom and immediately scanned the daily schedule, looking for any variation or unexpected changes. Only after doing this could he truly begin his day.

> Riley looked forward to her violin lesson every Tuesday. One week, her teacher needed to meet on Monday instead. Riley had a complete meltdown when her mother casually mentioned this on Sunday evening. She cried, "But violin lessons are on Tuesdays!"

> Adrian became incredibly frustrated when their father tried to demonstrate a different way to solve a math problem. Even though the father's way was easier, Adrian felt strongly that they could only do it the way the teacher showed them, not because they were afraid of getting it wrong on the test or displeasing the teacher, but because they truly felt that the first way they learned it was the **only** way to do it.

Difficulty coping with transitions: This is most noticeable when an autistic person is required to transition away from preferred activities, such as playing video games, and then to initiate non-preferred activities, such as homework. However, it can also happen with less stressful transitions, such as moving from subject to subject in school.

Sarah recalls that one of her sons always melted down on the way to his horse-riding lesson, even though once he got there, he was fully engaged and clearly loved the lesson. After coping with the meltdowns week after week but observing her son's joy while riding, Sarah finally realized that he was not scared of the horses or resistant to the lessons. Instead, he was simply struggling to cope with the transition from being at home to being at the stable.

Some autistics talk about *autistic inertia*, which refers to situations where it is difficult to get started on something or to stop doing something once started. We have recently started to see research on this, for example, by Karen Leneh Buckle and her colleagues. It is more difficult to manage *autistic inertia* when an individual is stressed, overloaded, or tired.

Parents sometimes don't realize that they have naturally adapted to this difficulty with transitions by giving lots of advance notice about upcoming changes or by allowing lots of extra time to make the transition.

Mason was a strong student who generally enjoyed school. However, every year it was a challenge for him to adjust to a new teacher and a new routine. He did his best, but he also frequently commented that, "[his] old teacher didn't do it that way." Additionally, Mason was consistently irritable every Monday morning and every Friday afternoon, as the shift between school days and non-school days was disorienting for him.

Black-and-white thinking: Autistic people can sometimes think about ideas, activities, or people in ways that feel like "all-or-none" thinking. This type of rigidity can result in increased interpersonal conflict because there are so many situations that require an understanding of the "gray" area.

Black-and-white thinking can occur about anything, even french fries! Matt loved french fries from a young age [who doesn't?]. However, when he was 5, Matt tasted mashed potatoes and was repelled by the texture. Since that day, Matt has refused to eat any potatoes, even french fries or potato chips, because, as he says, "I hate potatoes." His black-and-white thinking about potatoes was stronger than his love of french fries.

One example we see relates to a child's perception of their teachers. Some autistic kids will either love or hate a particular teacher. If a child feels comfortable with his teacher, he can be "on" (i.e., compliant, organized, and hardworking) in that class. If, however, he is not comfortable with a teacher, he may turn "off." In that case, regardless of the subject or how wonderful the teacher may be, the child may simply not engage in that class.

Jack has not had particular difficulty with change or transitions, and he has not exhibited rigid routines or rituals. However, he has always had very black-and-white thinking. He has never been able to let go of even a minor (perceived) transgression, and "a transgression from years ago feels as though it just happened." For example, during middle school, and then again in high school, Jack became upset with certain teachers. He stopped doing any work in their classes and would not interact with them in any way. He became so angry with one teacher that he never spoke to her again.

We also see black-and-white thinking about younger siblings at times. To their parents' great dismay, some autistic kids place a particular sibling in the "bad" category and seem unable to ever enjoy their company or see them in even a mildly positive light. This goes well beyond typical sibling rivalry.

Sadly, some autistic individuals engage in black-and-white thinking about themselves, too, and all too often their interpretations tend toward the negative. These individuals may think highly negative thoughts about themselves from a very young age. For example, we have seen preschoolers and early elementary school kids who think and state, "I'm the stupidest kid in the world," "I'm horrible," and "I don't deserve to live." These extreme thoughts are often in response to fairly typical experiences, such as coloring outside of the lines or making a spelling error. This type of black-and-white thinking puts these individuals at particularly high risk for developing a fixed mindset (e.g., "I can't do math" or "I'm a terrible writer") and ultimately for experiencing anxiety and/or depression.

My way or the highway: Some autistic individuals can be overtly inflexible in their interactions with others. With young children, this may be seen in play, where they may need to be in charge, choosing what game to play, what roles each child gets, the rules, and so on. Sometimes this causes conflict with other children, but not always. We have seen some autistic kids who are viewed as leaders in their younger years because they have a clear plan for play and take charge. However, this doesn't always last. By mid-elementary school, these children have often lost their status as leaders because of their difficulty with sharing control and being flexible.

This type of inflexibility can, of course, be seen as defiance when directed at parents or teachers. While some of these children are inflexible both at home and at school, many of them have a "Jekyll and Hyde" presentation. They may be rigid rule followers at school but quite defiant at home, or they may really struggle with the structure at school but do well at home, particularly if their parents are highly flexible with them. The parents of these inflexible kids often report feeling that they are always walking on eggshells or that the child seems to be running the household, especially if the child has extreme reactions to being told *no* or being denied a preferred or highly anticipated activity.

Getting "stuck" in their thinking: We hear about this from parents in many different contexts. "It's impossible to change his interpretation of a situation." "It's so hard for her to change her mind." "He always wants [something] to be a particular way."

"She is so rigid in her thought process and in how she needs to say what she needs to say." "He can't let things go." "He is very stuck in his viewpoint, to the point of insubordination." "She has a vision in her head, and she cannot be talked out of it."

Getting "stuck" like this can be externalized, resulting in defiant behavior or interpersonal conflict, or it can be internalized, resulting in "thought loops," (i.e., repetitive thoughts or ruminations) from which it can be very difficult to disengage. Either way, these are signs of rigidity that can affect academic, social, emotional, and/or behavioral functioning.

Unusually strong moral compass: This has become a bit complicated in the USA during the late 2010s and early 2020s because people are thinking more in extremes with regard to political and social justice issues, and so having strong moral convictions has become part of the culture. However, we observed this pattern (i.e., where an individual has incredibly strong feelings about social justice issues or about issues of fairness in general) long before the current status quo.

> When Jamika met Mamta at a conference, they quickly realized they were both autistic. They began exchanging stories, and were surprised at one of their common experiences. Each of them recalled that, during high school, if they were taking an exam and accidentally saw another student's response to a question, they would deliberately answer that question incorrectly, rather than taking the slightest chance of inadvertently cheating.

Rigid rule following: This one can be hard to spot because people that engage in rigid rule following are often considered to be model students or employees and may be less likely to present for an evaluation or treatment. Often, these individuals are referred for other reasons, such as anxiety, depression, or perfectionism. Indeed, adults often describe these kids as "the easiest kids in the world," "every teacher's dream," or "the neighbors' favorite kid to have over" because they can always be counted on to follow the rules and let the adults know when someone else isn't. However, when we are taking a child's history and we hear statements like, "she is always the teacher's favorite," "every year he is a model student," or "she has never required any discipline at all," we know that there is a chance that this child is a rigid rule follower.

Rigid rule following may be seen in the younger years as a child who refuses to color outside of the lines, or becomes upset with himself if he accidentally does so. It may be seen as an elementary school child who is not able to bend the rules when playing a board game, just for fun (e.g., "Let's change how we play so that if you roll doubles you lose a turn!"). As children get older, their rigid rule following can manifest as "policing" and alienate them from peers, who have a more typical and flexible understanding of the subtleties of bending and breaking rules and the reasons why that may be okay. We have seen more than one child get teased or bullied because they become upset or tell on other kids who curse, as well as one college student who felt that she could not be friends with anyone who ever cursed.

While many of these individuals rigidly follow rules and expect others to do the same, some of them are not concerned when they themselves break rules but become extremely upset when others do so. They may also be rigid about some rules, such as not stepping even one inch outside of a crosswalk, but quite flexible about others, such as not eating cookies right before dinner.

Another common example of rigid rule following is the feeling that one must be exactly on time for everything. For example, Sarah currently works with a client who gets very stressed if she thinks that her parents will be even one minute late to one of her appointments, and she harangues them if she thinks that they are not leaving home exactly on time.

Alex was a very bright and hardworking 12-year-old who was always a favorite of teachers and other adults because of his consistently excellent behavior. One day, Alex was in the car with his mom, dad, and sister. His mother had to quickly drop off a package, and there was no parking, so his father pulled into a handicapped space to let her out. The father and two children would remain in the car with the engine running, and the mother would be gone for less than a minute. Still, Alex, who was normally very calm, had a complete meltdown because his father was not supposed to be in a handicapped spot. He was entirely unable to understand that his father's action was consistent with the intent of the rule, if not the letter of the law.

Literal interpretations: Many clinicians know that autistics can be concrete or literal, but they are sometimes surprised to learn that this is considered an aspect of rigidity. Being literal is included in this category because it involves difficulty using context to *flexibly*, and thus accurately, interpret language. Understanding figurative or nonliteral language requires awareness that the words spoken have a different meaning than they usually do, requiring flexible interpretation. Donna was once walking home from the school bus stop with her son, who was about 10 at the time. As they began to walk, she said, "So, what's shakin'?" To her great chagrin, he looked around and (in all seriousness) replied, "Your arms."

We hear many examples like this from parents, though not all of them are so amusing. This type of inflexibility can cause significant communication problems. Donna recently worked with a very sweet and hardworking 8th grader who had frequent fights with her parents. If they gave her a few chores to do and then later remembered one more and tried to add it to the list, she would become uncharacteristically angry and accuse them of lying to her about how many chores she had.

Jasmine was a brilliant 26-year-old with an IQ well over 140. She was underemployed as an administrative support person at her father's company. One day, a coworker, Jim, asked her to make him a spreadsheet and gave her the specifics needed for the project. Jasmine made a beautiful spreadsheet, including everything that Jim had asked for. And then she resumed her regular work. It never once occurred to her that Jim's request implied an expectation that she would tell him that she had finished and send him the completed spreadsheet. She did exactly as requested; she made the spreadsheet.

Jasmine made errors like this every day. Despite her extremely high IQ and great work ethic, it was extremely hard, if not impossible, for Jasmine to function well at work without near constant supervision and clarification.

Of note, this is a good example of something that could be coded under multiple criteria, as Jasmine also demonstrated a lack of perspective-taking. However, one example should not be used to satisfy more than one criterion, and at times the clinician must simply make a judgment call about where an example best fits. We discuss this in the book *Is This Autism? A Companion Guide for Diagnosing*.

Donna has learned that she has to be very careful in testing sessions because of this inflexible interpretation of language. For instance, if she says, "this test takes about five minutes," some kids will look at the clock and at exactly five minutes will either stop working or become annoyed that she "lied" to them. She has also found it important to end the testing session exactly on time, or, if needed, to ask permission to go even a few minutes over time.

This aspect of rigidity can also affect humor, particularly sarcasm or dry humor. To be clear, autistic people can have a great sense of humor; in fact some of the wittiest people we know are autistic! However, some autistics do not pick up on other people's sarcasm. This is because we actually say the opposite of what we mean when we are being sarcastic ("Oh, you really are *so* much smarter than the rest of us"), which requires a spontaneous and flexible ability to interpret the words in a different way. It also requires an appreciation for changes in prosody, as described in Chapter 3.

Refusal to part with certain objects: We are not talking about messy rooms here. We are talking about adamant refusal to part with useless objects, such as paper plates, plastic forks, bottle caps, tissue boxes, worn-down pencils, old scraps of paper, and countless other examples we have seen. Parents often present this as being compulsive, being messy, or having collections.

It is important to differentiate this from having a particular interest in unusual objects or parts of objects, which can qualify as an unusual interest. It is also different from unusual *use* of objects, which can qualify as a repetitive or atypical behavior.

> Robert was a 21-year-old who treasured a bottle that had been given to him by a friend. His parents observed, "He really fixated on it, to the extent that it was very odd."

To illustrate the importance of looking beyond a behavior to the underlying reason for the behavior, let's look at children with different profiles who are extremely interested in cell phones.

- Sammy has a particular interest in repeatedly taking apart cell phones, which constitutes repetitive or atypical behavior.

- Ethan gets a new cell phone every year (lucky Ethan!), but he refuses to get rid of the old ones, accumulating them for years, thereby demonstrating inflexibility.

- Aiden is particularly interested in the size of people's phones, which is an atypical interest.

- Just for fun, let's add a sensory example: Amanda regularly holds her cell phone very close to her eyes for a few minutes at a time. She is demonstrating sensory craving.

From the experts: Reflections on areas of inflexibility

Yesterday the pizza place I've eaten at for years changed their sauce a little. I couldn't handle it and was stressed all night.
—Audrian F.

I don't have rigid routines when it comes to my schedule, but I do have rigid routines when it comes to certain activities. The steps I take while showering, down to how I dry myself off, is the same every time. When I eat my food, it has to be in a certain order. Small candies such as M&Ms and Skittles have to be eaten in even numbers and have to be eaten in the same color.

—Darci D.

I also have a hard time with rule flexibility. Whether the rule is spoken or unspoken, official or unofficial ... deviating from what's been actually established really gets my goat.

–Elise A.

One time, I was working in my home office while my wife was in the living room. She suddenly had the urge to rearrange the furniture, so she shuffled everything. When I got into the living room after she finished, I started crying because of the anxiety it caused me. I can't identify why it triggered me the way it did, but I couldn't handle it.

–Alexys H.

I have an oversized reaction to rule breaking. I remember as a kid I would be really careful about doing all the hand-signals when riding my bike, even if no one else was around. I would get annoyed when I saw other people ride bikes without doing the hand-signals. The worst version of this would be if someone gave me an instruction or rule, other people were breaking it, and then the person who originally made the rule indicated that the rule didn't matter.

–Drew R.

I think a big part of my masking is pretending I don't mind when things change or don't go my way. I learnt that people will consider me difficult and hard to live with when I ask for things to be done or to go my way.

–Charlotte R.

From the experts: Reasons for the preference/need for sameness

So many autistic teens and adults have explained the very logical reasons for their strong preference, or actual need, for predictability and sameness. Here are just some of the explanations:

I have really limited executive function resources. When I'm rested, I can make decisions, no problem, but I run out of that resource well before NT people. I get fatigued, then overwhelmed, and I just can't think of what to do, how to do it, and so on. I need to conserve that resource for the things that matter, like work, so I try not to use them on stuff I care about a lot less, like what I eat for lunch. I eat the same thing for lunch almost every day...

–Peter B.

I function better when things are predictable. I'll go to a McDonald's rather than a Subway because I know exactly what I need to say, in advance. At Subway they keep asking me questions, and I get flustered if I'm not expecting them. I'm all ready to say that I want a foot-long roll with chicken, and then they'll ask me what type of bread, or whether I want things toasted. If I know in advance what all the choices are, I can be ready to make them, but unexpected choices are difficult.

–Drew R.

I don't freak out when my routine changes because I'm too rigid; I freak out because now I'm going into something without being able to prepare. For some things, the amount of time I need to prepare myself for the interactions is small, so I'm fairly flexible about it. For example, if a friend asks me to get dinner right then I'm fine because I know generally what restaurants my friend likes and what I like to eat there. Some things, however, take more time for me to figure out what's expected of me, and so last-minute changes really freak me out. For instance, if my boss changes the daily schedule, I panic because now I don't have time to think through what is expected of me and how to execute it.

–Alix L.

When so much of the world is already so stressful and difficult to operate, I get comfort in the things I know and understand. Change, especially when I'm already under stress, and especially affecting the things I find comfort in, can be scary.

–Andi L.

I think my rigidity is also closely connected to my difficulties with switching from one task to another. I don't like to be interrupted at all!

–Leen V.

Sometimes patterns are just innately soothing. I used to go up and down staircases two steps at a time, and it feels wrong to finish on the last step instead of on the ground or landing. So, for every staircase I regularly went on, I knew whether to start on the first or second step. I'm also much more comfortable if I walk on a footpath with regular blocks, stepping in the middle of each block instead of across the dividing lines. Neither of these are big things. I won't get distressed if I don't do them .... If I spend time within patterns, I'm more on an even-keel.

–Drew R.

Inflexibility: What we've learned from the girls

Generally speaking, both on and off the autism spectrum, boys tend to externalize whereas girls tend to internalize. Thus, in general, boys' inflexibility tends to manifest in behavioral problems, which is probably why so many people believe that if you have autism you're going to have a lot of behavioral problems, and if you don't have behavioral problems you can't possibly be autistic. This is, of course, entirely untrue.

Autistic girls can certainly be inflexible in any of the ways that we have discussed. However, when they are coping with a situation that requires flexibility, they are less likely to outwardly fight against it and more likely to quietly try to cope. This results in tremendous anxiety, both in *anticipating* changes and transitions, as well as moving through them. Often, autistic girls do not have support in these stressful situations because (1) they have been so anxious for so long that they are not even aware that they are anxious – it is simply their normal state of being, and (2) even if they are aware that they are struggling, it may not occur to them or be comfortable for them to talk about this and self-advocate, even with their parents. Thus, the symptom of their inflexibility is a persistently high stress level and associated anxiety. There can also be anxiety related to change, even positively anticipated change, like a vacation.

Quite often, the adults in their lives know that these girls are anxious or having meltdowns, but they have not associated those emotional struggles with the girls' difficulty with flexibility. The adults (parents, teachers, counselors) don't understand the impact of the girl's difficulty coping with change, transitions, or other situations that require flexibility.

Additionally, autistic girls are often highly vulnerable to being obsessive and perfectionistic in their thinking and approach to tasks. We have seen this kind of rigidity manifest in countless ways, including not coloring outside the lines, having to take notes in a certain way, staying up all night doing homework "perfectly," refusing to go out if her hair is imperfect, getting upset if she gets less than a perfect score on schoolwork, and controlling every aspect of a social gathering – from the menu, to the seating, to the decorations.

Donna recently worked with a high-school student who was incredibly perfectionistic. If she was writing an essay and did not like one sentence, she would delete all of her work, even prior paragraphs, and start over again.

Frequently asked questions

- **Does a child have to have behavioral problems to be inflexible?** No. As discussed in the section on girls and rigidity, boys are more likely to have behavioral problems associated with rigidity, while girls are more likely to internalize, resulting in anxiety and perfectionism rather than defiance or meltdowns. Because many clinicians mistakenly equate rigidity with difficult behavior, *female rigidity* is much more likely to be overlooked.

- **Everyone can be inflexible sometimes. Where do we draw a line between typical inflexibility and that which would rise to the level of autism?** There is no easy answer for this, as it ultimately requires a subjective judgment call. However, we believe that inflexibility should be considerable for it to contribute to a diagnosis of autism. One or two examples of inflexibility are not sufficient; rather, there should be a clear *pattern*, with numerous examples. Moreover, the inflexibility needs to be problematic in some way. This can include behavior problems, anxiety, social challenges, or effects on academic functioning.

- **Why do we consider being concrete or literal in this category, rather than in the social communication domain?** Being overly literal can certainly cause a social disconnect for adolescents and adults, but it is included in this category because, at its core, being literal represents *inflexible* interpretation of language. The social disconnect is simply the *result* of the concrete interpretation.

- **Do people have to be inflexible in all environments for it to count?** No, they do not. While some individuals do show inflexibility in all environments, many of them have a "Jekyll and Hyde" presentation. Some do quite well with the structure and social expectations at school or work but fall apart as soon as they get home. Others struggle with the inflexibility of the school or work environment but do well at home, particularly if they have very flexible parents or partners.

- **Where does humor fit into this?** It is a myth that autistic people don't have a sense of humor. That said, they may sometimes miss sarcasm or irony in part because it requires flexible interpretation of language. That is, if I trip and fall, and you say, "Gee, you're so graceful," I intuitively know that those words have a different meaning, and I have to flexibly interpret them in a different way. Other reasons that humor can be problematic for some autistics are noted in the relevant chapters (e.g., nonverbal communication and co-occurring challenges).

- **Is inflexibility always bad?** Absolutely not! A preference for sameness, consistency, and routine can mean that regular activities are always completed, and completed well. In addition, following routines saves energy and gives people the freedom to devote more cognitive resources to other tasks. Furthermore, autistic people often excel at pattern- and rule-based activities like knitting, laying tiles, or playing poker.

References and related reading

American Psychiatric Association. (2022). *Diagnostic and statistical manual of mental disorders* (5th ed., text rev.). https://doi.org/10.1176/appi.books.9780890425787

Buckle, K. L., Leadbitter, K., Poliakoff, E. & Gowen, E. (2021). "No way out except from external intervention": First-hand accounts of autistic inertia. *Frontiers in Psychology*, *12*(Article: 631596). https://doi.org/10.3389/fpsyg.2021.631596

Dworzynski, K., Ronald, A., Bolton, P., & Happé, F. (2012). How different are girls and boys above and below the diagnostic threshold for autism spectrum disorders? *Journal of the American Academy of Child and Adolescent Psychiatry*, *51*(8), 788–797. https://doi.org/10.1016/j.jaac.2012.05.018

Henderson, D. (in press). *Is this autism? A companion guide for diagnosing*. New York: Routledge.

Hull, L., Mandy, W., & Petrides, K. V. (2017). Behavioral and cognitive sex/gender differences in autism spectrum condition and typically developing males and females. *Autism: The International Journal of Research and Practice*, *21*(6), 706–727. https://doi.org/10.1177/1362361316669087

Hull, L., Petrides, K. V., Allison, C., Smith, P., Baron-Cohen, S., Lai, M.-C., & Mandy, W. (2017). "Putting on my best normal": Social camouflaging in adults with autism spectrum conditions. *Journal of Autism and Developmental Disorders*, *47*(8), 2519–2534. https://doi.org/10.1007/s10803-017-3166-5

Kaat, A. J., Shui, A. M., Ghods, S. S., Farmer, C. A., Esler, A. N., Thurm, A., ... & Bishop, S. L. (2021). Sex differences in scores on standardized measures of autism symptoms: A multisite integrative data analysis. *Journal of Child Psychology and Psychiatry*, *62*(1), 97–106. https://doi.org/10.1111/jcpp.13242

Kirkovski, M., Enticott, P. G., & Fitzgerald, P. B. (2013). A review of the role of female gender in autism spectrum disorders. *Journal of Autism and Developmental Disorders*, *43*(11), 2584–2603. https://doi.org/10.1007/s10803-013-1811-1

Kopp, S., & Gillberg, C. (1992). Girls with social deficits and learning problems: Autism, atypical Asperger syndrome or a variant of these conditions. *European Child & Adolescent Psychiatry*, *1*(2), 89–99. https://doi.org/10.1007/BF02091791

Lai, M.-C., Lin, H.-Y., & Ameis, S. H. (2022). Towards equitable diagnoses for autism and attention-deficit/hyperactivity disorder across sexes and genders. *Current Opinion in Psychiatry*, *35*(2), 90–100. https://doi.org/10.1097/YCO.0000000000000770

Lai, M.-C., & Szatmari, P. (2020). Sex and gender impacts on the behavioural presentation and recognition of autism. *Current Opinion in Psychiatry*, *33*(2), 117–123. https://doi.org/10.1097/YCO.00000 00000000575

Mandy, W., Chilvers, R., Chowdhury, U., Salter, G., Seigal, A., & Skuse, D. (2012). Sex differences in autism spectrum disorder: Evidence from a large sample of children and adolescents. *Journal of Autism and Developmental Disorders*, *42*(7), 1304–1313. https://doi.org/10.1007/s10803-011-1356-0

Young, H., Oreve, M.-J., & Speranza, M. (2018). Clinical characteristics and problems diagnosing autism spectrum disorder in girls. *Archives de Pédiatrie*, *25*(6), 399–403. https://doi.org/10.1016/j.arcped.2018.06.008

Young, S., Hollingdale, J., Absoud, M., Bolton, P., Branney, P., Colley, W., & Woodhouse, E. (2020). Guidance for identification and treatment of individuals with attention deficit/hyperactivity disorder and autism spectrum disorder based upon expert consensus. *BMC Medicine*, *18*(1), 146. https://doi.org/10.1186/s12916-020-01585-y

Chapter 7

Intense or atypical interests

It's a lot like romantic infatuation, but without the sexual feelings. They're like having a huge crush, but on a topic rather than a person.

–Sara M.

What people often think a restricted interest means

Many people, including many healthcare professionals, seem to equate autism with overtly atypical interests, such as airport codes, traffic cones, or train schedules. Indeed, the DSM offers as examples a preoccupation with vacuum cleaners, a strong attachment to a pan, or spending hours writing out timetables.

As you may have guessed by now, this category includes so much more than overtly atypical interests.

What does this category really include?

According to the DSM-5, it includes "highly restricted, fixated interests that are abnormal in intensity *or* focus" (italics added). Let's clarify some important points associated with this wording.

- **Restricted:** In our opinion, this is a problematic term because there is no clear, objective way to know if something is truly *restricted*. Some clinicians interpret this quite strictly, believing that the interest "has to eclipse everything else in the person's life" (as explained to us by one psychiatrist who we fully respect but with whom we disagree). In our clinical experience, many

DOI: 10.4324/9781003242130-9

autistic individuals, particularly those with well-above-average intellectual functioning, do have more than one interest at a time.

Additionally, when children are young, their parents often place them in organized activities, such as soccer leagues, art classes, or Scouts, and the children may genuinely enjoy these activities. While some clinicians may believe that the enjoyment children derive from other activities rules out the possibility of restricted interests, we do not. According to the *Oxford English Dictionary*, the word "restricted" means "limited in extent, number, scope, or action." It does not mean "eclipsing everything else." That said, there are clinicians who disagree, and who feel that interests must be so restricted that the person cannot think about or enjoy anything else.

- **Fixated**: The term *fixated* can help clarify what qualifies as an interest that is *abnormal in intensity*. This can manifest as frequency (e.g., the person's thoughts frequently return to the same topic) and/or as intensity (e.g., the person has an intense emotional experience around the topic, activity, or object). As with so many of the diagnostic criteria, it's important to ask the person about their internal experiences rather than relying solely on external presentation. Many subtly autistic people have learned to explore their interests internally and privately, frequently after receiving (repeated) requests to talk about the topic less frequently.

- **Either/or**: To be considered significant for the purpose of diagnosis, the specialized interest must be *either* intense *or* atypical; it does not have to be both.

- **Abnormal**: We find the word *abnormal* pejorative, so we will instead use the term *atypical*, which has a similar meaning but does not imply that one experience is more *normal* than another.

Interests can be atypical: The obvious question here is: How atypical does the interest have to be? There is no set standard for this, and there seems to be a fair amount of variability from clinician to clinician (kind of like that other thing that's hard to define but "I know it when I see it.") To be atypical, the interest does not have to be completely bizarre; it simply has to be atypical *for that child in the context of his family and culture.*

Atypical interests can be about anything at all: In our informal survey of autistic adults (mostly female), we heard about an endless variety of interests, such as goat farming, indigenous land management, food storage, emergency preparedness, Korean cinema, restaurant menus, frozen meals, prime ministers, and 16th century common women's clothing. One individual talked about floor plans of houses, stating, *"I used to get thick magazines of them in the mail and I would spend all day looking at these and imagining myself living in them. I had a massive stack of them under my bed. And I would spend hours drawing my own."*

Alternatively, **interests can be typical but intense**. Defining *intense* is just as challenging as defining *restricted*, and to some extent it is subjective.

From the experts: Common intense interests

We informally asked a group of autistic adults about their interests, and the responses were highly consistent with our clinical experience. We offer percentages here, with the caveat that this was an informal survey and does not represent the autistic community at large; it is simply a sample of mostly female autistic adults. We should also note that these percentages add up to more than 100% because autistic individuals often have more than one special interest throughout their lives and can certainly have more than one special interest at a time.

The most common interests in our survey were:

- Animals, either in general or specific types (42%)

- Reading (32%)

- Human behavior, including body language, relationships, communication, and much more (26%)

- Human anatomy/medical sciences, including anatomy, surgery, obstetrics and gynecology, genetics, Civil War medicine, and many more (24%). As Allie S. recalled, *"Looking back, a 7-year-old talking constantly about childbirth to random people is embarrassing!"*

- Plants/gardening/nature (22%)

- Autism (20%). As Miko tells us, "*Like when I am now in a bad state, I read a book on autism to relax.*"

- Language/languages (16%). Miko reports, "*With languages I prefer to read about grammar and language structure more than I like to learn phrases to communicate. Phrases mean nothing to me if I don't know what each word means and why they have the declination they have and the sequence they do.*"

- Music (16%): for example, Mississippi Delta blues, Appalachian music, and African dancing and drumming (the latter from a woman with no personal connection to these geographical regions).

- Art/crafts (16%): for example, "endlessly" making cigar box guitars or painting peg dolls, cataloging and collecting art supplies.

- Research (14%). Margaret G. offers a great example: "*I know of an autist who will research any question to the ends of the earth. When I said I wanted a marble rolling pin for my graduation gift, he sent me an email with four different options from four different sellers, complete with the options available for each one and all the pros and cons. When his laptop died, he spent 6 months researching buying a new one and I didn't even come close to understanding all of the technical details he tried to describe.*"

- Numerous topics/activities were each noted by about 10% of respondents, such as maps/geography, fiber arts (e.g., knitting or spinning wool), and justice/morality. As Emily R. says, "*Knitting. And a lot of time was spent reading about knitting, or reading about people who knit, or reading about types of yarn. I learned to knit without looking because I was scared I'd lose my vision in old age and not be able to knit anymore – I think I was 10 at that time – and once I could do that, I started figuring out ways to prop books open so I could read and knit at the same time.*"

- Interests that were less common but came up more than once included specific celebrities, specific periods in history, homesteading, nutrition, and makeup/fashion. Nic A. tells us, *"I would make collages or outfits and try to design my own. I knew all the names of up-and-coming designers, I could tell if things were in season or last season, I could tell you where you bought your pants and shoes from just looking at them. I would spend hours just looking through shops at new fashion. Feeling all the clothes. Trying them on."*

Daydreaming as an intense interest

We have heard from many autistics about their daydreaming/fantasy life. This can be a completely immersive experience that is not only endlessly entertaining but can provide a much-needed respite from the outside world. While it is true that many non-autistic children have imaginary friends and even create imaginary worlds, some autistic children do this with an intensity and frequency that far outstrips their non-autistic peers. When an individual's daydreaming rises to the level of "intense" (as described elsewhere in this chapter), it should be considered toward a diagnosis. We asked autistic adults about their experience of daydreaming and its many benefits.

I used to daydream in and expand my own worlds every second I could. Usually, I could convince myself of the reality of these places, like there was a physical side of me stuck in the real world to keep up appearances, while my spirit or something was off in a complete other world. I recognize now that it was a way to escape a number of stressors.

–Marcelo H.

I would say that if I'm not doing anything else, I'm daydreaming with a very elaborate ongoing plot. I've had the current one going for about 8 months or so, but my longest ones have lasted years or more.

–Eleanor J.

I control what is said, where I am, what people look like, and who I am too – I can stop, start, skip, and rewind.

–S.E. Jones

I've been strongly obsessed with fantasy settings, wanting to either flesh them out in such intricate detail as to be able to fully imagine living there. I care a lot for things that 'nobody' cares about, as they don't impact the story or possibly gameplay. Specific cuisines, ingredients, non-narratively important mechanics of magic, how it feels to dream as a species that does it in a special way, how metallurgy develops besides high magic, and how it leads to later/modern sword designs. I want maximum detail.

–Rúna K.

I think a lot of autistic folks find it very difficult to understand injustice. There's too much here that you can't do anything really impactful about. But in a fantasy world, the heroes have power and opportunity, and they use it to grand effect. It makes sense to daydream about a world in which you can just stop people from being horrible. Fantasy offers worlds that make sense, where people who are good to each other are protected by other people who are good to each other. And the monsters, the demons, the bad guys? They get kicked out, or they learn to be better.

–Fabian B.

However, many autistics also tell us about the potential downsides of having such a rich inner world. Some refer to this as *maladaptive daydreaming*. Eli Somer and colleagues proposed diagnostic criteria for *maladaptive daydreaming*, in which an individual's daydreaming causes clinically significant distress or impairment, and we've known a number of autistic people who get so lost in their thoughts that they don't notice what is happening around them. This can have catastrophic consequences (e.g., crossing the street when there is oncoming traffic). We have heard many examples of challenges related to excessive or intense daydreaming.

Feeling split between two worlds and never being satisfied with either of them is the maladaptive part for me.

–Julia K.

When the real world is an unreal/shallow/husk compared with your inner world, it is hard to grasp the consequences of the real world. Why should I care about THIS world when there are thousands in my head? Why should I do anything when I could dream instead? Why should I care about a car hitting me when in my dreams I could survive far worse? Why should I care about social contacts when the ones in my head are far easier?

–Ale X.

I use it as a coping mechanism when I'm feeling emotionally flooded. I retreat inward and think about it, and it makes me happy, so I smile. Then the person who is talking to me gets mad because I'm not listening, but I can't, I literally can't.

–Bob W.

My parents and sisters constantly got mad at me for wanting silence in the car, but that was daydreaming time for me, and I needed silence for it.

–Jason L.

There have been moments when I am so completely lost in my daydream while walking outdoors that, when I "wake up," I am completely lost and don't know how I ended up in a neighborhood or forest I've never seen before.

–Isabella B.

Highly fixated or restricted interests can also include **particular attachments to objects**. Of course, it is not at all unusual for a young child to have a "lovey," or to sleep with a stuffed animal, but once children are school-aged, these attachments to objects begin to wane. Similar to interests, consider an attachment to an object as relevant if the attachment is either intense or atypical in nature or for the child's developmental level. Here are examples, all using different aspects of particular attachment to a stuffed animal.

- **Intense:** An elementary school student carries his stuffed animal everywhere, including school, birthday parties, sporting events, dance class, etc.

- **Atypical for developmental stage:** An adult is highly attached to a stuffed animal (i.e., not just for the nostalgic feeling) and brings it on vacation with him.

- **Atypical in focus:** A student is particularly attached to the ears of his stuffed animals.

Mrs. B reports that Marc "would bring things home, like a tire he found on the road. He was not quite a hoarder, but he collected things, like rubber bands...." Marc did not have specific intentions for these objects (such as arts and crafts or building with them), and he had great difficulty getting rid of them when asked to do so.

Jordan was a charming and attractive 17-year-old who appeared socially typical. She came for testing because she needed continued academic accommodations for her upcoming transition to college. When asked if she had any objects that she was particularly attached to, Jordan (quite unexpectedly) said, "Yes, my stuffed bunny." When asked if she brings him places with her, Jordan said, "Yes, I bring him everywhere, I have him right here in my backpack." She then pulled out her bunny to show me.

From the experts: How do our interests differ from "non-autistic interests"

The level of intensity: "*Being without a special interest can feel very similar to depression for me; my sense of self fades, and everything feels effortful – even passing interests. A special interest lends vitality and energy. It can make it hard to remember to sleep, because engaging with the special interest can be so exciting and energizing – it can look like hypomania from the outside, though not always. I think a lot of autistics 'charge their batteries' with special interests, in some ways even more so than with sleep.*"

–Emily R.

The depth and breadth it demands: Emily R. says, "*There's more emphasis on information rather than just engagement; like when my special interest was exercise, I didn't just exercise, but wanted to learn about exercise and read everything I could on different theories of what's most effective, etc.*" Similarly, Drew R. reflects, "*[it's about] the importance of details, and the importance of getting those details right – I can spend hours chasing down a detail that even other academics would happily just include in a paper even if they aren't 100% sure it is correct.*"

The inability to disengage: Holly G. reports, "*I cannot stop thinking about it no matter what other tasks I'm performing. … Agitated is an understatement if I'm disturbed or redirected away from it.*" Emily R. adds, "*If something is a special interest, it doesn't fade when you do other things. It's not out of your mind while you're in class, or watching TV.*"

The effect on the rest of one's life: As Holly G. says, "*It's a special interest and not a hobby if it affects ADLs [activities of daily living] – I don't eat or sleep, I forget to use the bathroom, I disengage from the outside world.*"

The all-or-nothing mentality: As Miko tells us, "*I feel as if it's pointless to know only a little bit about something. It's like*

my mind only works on or off with interests. ... I feel I can't
leave anything out and not know as much as possible, if it's
interesting to me. But if it's not interesting to me, I don't really
see the point in knowing anything at all about it."

Interests: What we've learned from the girls

Their interests are more likely to be intense rather than atypical.
While autistic females can certainly have atypical interests, they
are more likely than boys to have interests that are typical but
intense.

**They are more likely to have interests that are centered on people
or animals, rather than data or objects.** Some of the most common
intense interests for girls are animals (in particular, dogs, cats, and
horses).

Roxanne was an athletic teenager who had persistent difficulty
making friends or connecting with any of her teammates. Roxanne
had no interest in clothes, boys, or any aspect of pop culture, but she
did have an intense interest in sharks. When Donna asked her what
she loved about sharks, Roxanne replied, "Everyone thinks they're
mean, but they're not."

Another common intense interest for girls is reading. We have
seen girls who get in trouble for persistently reading during
class, bringing books to the dinner table or to birthday parties,
wanting to read on playdates, and reading in the shower (not
the bath, but the shower!). Of course, reading is a marvelous
activity for any child, but there can be too much of a good
thing, particularly if it interferes with basic social interactions,
developing relationships, doing homework or chores, sleeping,
or engaging in basic hygiene. As we've heard from more than
one autistic, *"The fire alarm has gone off while I was reading*
and I've not heard it!" and, *"My parents wanted to put me in*
addiction therapy for it!"

An intense interest can be both good and bad. Grace's teachers always commented that she persistently read during class. Over the years, some of Grace's teachers were not flexible and would reprimand her for not paying attention (even though she earned straight As). Other teachers were impressed by her constant reading. They realized that Grace was a bit bored by the curriculum, and they allowed her the flexibility to read in class after she completed assignments. Some of these teachers even allowed her to stay in the classroom during lunch and recess, reading on her own instead of interacting with her peers, which concerned her parents, as she became increasingly socially isolated. Fast forward 10 years: Grace is now the youngest student in her PhD program. She still spends all of her time reading and has had great difficulty making friends. On the one hand, Grace is often lonely and wonders if she will ever get married, have children, or have friends. On the other hand, she has found a way to read and write for a living, using her strengths to create a life that will enable her to support herself and contribute to the world in a meaningful way. Good? Bad? A bit of both, we suppose.

We also see girls who are intensely interested in pop culture. This can include famous people, such as Taylor Swift or members of a K-Pop band, or particular TV shows, such as *The Office*. Some autistic girls become superfans who amass a tremendous amount of knowledge about their interests. Writing fan fiction might be one way that they express this. While many other people may share these interests, for them they are generally far less intense.

Their intense interests are often quite typical, which can make them harder to notice as autistic. We've also met a number of autistic women who enjoy cooking and/or baking. This is a great example of an activity that non-autistic people enjoy; the difference for autistic women is the intensity and specific focus. For example, Sarah knows an autistic woman who spent 6 months perfecting her recipe for cream puffs, preparing a new batch for her coworkers to sample twice a week. Interests that are intense but typical in focus can be harder for clinicians to uncover, as parents do not think to mention passionate but typical interests, such as American Dolls,

Disney princesses, or movies such as *Frozen*. If clinicians only ask about *atypical* interests, these will be missed.

They may not talk about their interests as much as boys do. It is also important to note that, in general, girls tend to internalize while boys tend to externalize, so boys may talk excessively about their interests whereas girls may think excessively about theirs but not talk as much about them, which makes them harder for clinicians to identify.

While writing this section, Donna reviewed the previous 25 children she had diagnosed with autism. Not surprisingly, two-thirds were boys, and one-third were girls. As such, her clinical experience was consistent with the research. The boys had a wide variety of interests that might be considered atypical, such as flags, surgery, the macabre, rainbows, the *Titanic*, the *Silent Mary*, specific musical scores, *Star Wars*, punk music, water fountains, garbage trucks, stoves, fireplaces, and locks. No two boys (in this very small sample) had the same interests. In contrast, the girls whom Donna saw had intense interests in reading, animals, particular pop stars, and office supplies (which we have also seen several times). There was far less variety.

That said, **an intense interest can be about anything.** (Both Sarah and Donna's husbands joke that their intense interest is autism!) There are certainly many other possible intense interests for girls. Some others we have seen include anime, Manga, the *Cat Warrior* series, cosplay, My Little Pony, and microbes.

Frequently asked questions

- **Can electronics/video games count as intense interests?** We have asked numeous other autism specialists, "Do you count video games as an intense interest – if it is truly intense?" So far, the answer has always been *yes*. In fact, it is one of the most common intense interests that we have seen in recent years, particularly for adolescent boys. In addition to the game itself, there are also social communities that form around games (*fandoms*) and these can be a great way for people to connect around a shared interest.

To consider it a truly *intense* interest, the level of interest needs to rise above and beyond what is typical for people the same age. This can be hard to determine, and it became even harder during the COVID-19 pandemic, when so many students were stuck at home with few options for entertaining themselves. We would advise you to find out if the student has no other interests, or talks endlessly about their favorite game (and to an uninterested audience). Also consider whether their relationships with peers are centered on the game itself, without any other elements (such as having side conversations about other topics).

- **Does someone have to have the same interest for many years, or can the intense/atypical interest change over time?** The interest can certainly change. Many autistic kids go through intense phases: for instance, a boy may be "obsessed" with motor vehicles for a few years, then with *Minecraft* for a few years, then with computer coding. We sometimes call these kids "serial monogamists." Special interests may last days, weeks, years, or decades, and they may come and go.

- **Can there be more than one special interest at a time?** Absolutely! We have known many autistics who regularly juggle two or more intense or atypical interests.

- **Are intense or atypical interests always (or ever) a problem?** Intense or atypical interests are often characterized as "symptoms" that have no particular benefits, but it is very important to note that having an intense or atypical interest is *not* necessarily a problem and can actually be a tremendous asset to the individual and the community at large. Many adult autistics have built their careers and made major contributions to the world based on their interests. For instance, we have known more than one college professor who has studied one topic for years. They know more than anyone else about this topic, and they get to write and talk to people all day long about it. These interests only become problematic when the person is unable to talk about other things in order to maintain the interest of and connection with their conversation partners.

Additionally, a significant number of autistics describe a special interest in topics that can help them with challenges that are part of being autistic. These include topics like: forensic interrogation (to learn how to read others); language and linguistics; idioms; postures and gestures of people in movies; human behavior and relationships; specific psychiatric conditions (especially autism); and psychopharmacology.

One of our favorite examples of intense interests comes from the beloved comedian Dan Aykroyd, who grew up with intense interests in ghosts and crime fighting. If Dan weren't autistic, the world might not have had *Ghostbusters!*

References and related reading

American Psychiatric Association. (2022). *Diagnostic and statistical manual of mental disorders* (5th ed., text rev.). https://doi.org/10.1176/appi.books.9780890425787

Bargiela, S., Steward, R., & Mandy, W. (2016). The experiences of late-diagnosed women with autism spectrum conditions: An investigation of the female autism phenotype. *Journal of Autism and Developmental Disorders,* 46(10), 3281–3294. https://doi.org/10.1007/s10803-016-2872-8

Duvall, S., Armstrong, K., Shahabuddin, A., Grantz, C., Fein, D., & Lord, C. (2021). A road map for identifying autism spectrum disorder: Recognizing and evaluating characteristics that should raise red or "pink" flags to guide accurate differential diagnosis. *The Clinical Neuropsychologist,* 36(5), 1–36. https://doi.org/10.1080/13854046.2021.1921276

Dworzynski, K., Ronald, A., Bolton, P., & Happé, F. (2012). How different are girls and boys above and below the diagnostic threshold for autism spectrum disorders? *Journal of the American Academy of Child and Adolescent Psychiatry,* 51(8), 788–797. https://doi.org/10.1016/j.jaac.2012.05.018

Green, R. M., Travers, A. M., Howe, Y., & McDougle, C. J. (2019). Women and autism spectrum disorder: diagnosis and implications for treatment of adolescents and adults. *Current Psychiatry Reports,* 21(4), 22. https://doi.org/10.1007/s11920-019-1006-3

Hiller, R. M., Young, R. L., & Weber, N. (2014). Sex differences in autism spectrum disorder based on DSM-5 criteria: Evidence from clinician and teacher reporting. *Journal of Abnormal Child Psychology, 42*(8), 1381–1393. https://doi.org/10.1007/s10802-014-9881-x

Hiller, R. M., Young, R. L., & Weber, N. (2016). Sex differences in pre-diagnosis concerns for children later diagnosed with autism spectrum disorder. *Autism: The International Journal of Research and Practice, 20*(1), 75–84. https://doi.org/10.1177/1362361314568899

Hull, L., Mandy, W., & Petrides, K. V. (2017). Behavioral and cognitive sex/gender differences in autism spectrum condition and typically developing males and females. *Autism: The International Journal of Research and Practice, 21*(6), 706–727. https://doi.org/10.1177/13623 61316669087

Hull, L., Petrides, K. V., Allison, C., Smith, P., Baron-Cohen, S., Lai, M.-C., & Mandy, W. (2017). "Putting on my best normal": Social camouflaging in adults with autism spectrum conditions. *Journal of Autism and Developmental Disorders, 47*(8), 2519–2534. https://doi. org/10.1007/s10803-017-3166-5

Kaat, A. J., Shui, A. M., Ghods, S. S., Farmer, C. A., Esler, A. N., Thurm, A., … & Bishop, S. L. (2021). Sex differences in scores on standardized measures of autism symptoms: A multisite integrative data analysis. *Journal of Child Psychology and Psychiatry, 62*(1), 97–106. https:// doi.org/10.1111/jcpp.13242

Kirkovski, M., Enticott, P. G., & Fitzgerald, P. B. (2013). A review of the role of female gender in autism spectrum disorders. *Journal of Autism and Developmental Disorders, 43*(11), 2584–2603. https://doi.org/ 10.1007/s10803-013-1811-1

Kopp, S., & Gillberg, C. (1992). Girls with social deficits and learning problems: Autism, atypical Asperger syndrome or a variant of these conditions. *European Child & Adolescent Psychiatry, 1*(2), 89–99. https://doi.org/10.1007/BF02091791

Lai, M.-C., Lin, H.-Y., & Ameis, S. H. (2022). Towards equitable diagnoses for autism and attention-deficit/hyperactivity disorder across sexes and genders. *Current Opinion in Psychiatry, 35*(2), 90–100. https://doi.org/10.1097/YCO.0000000000000770

Lai, M.-C., Lombardo, M. V., Auyeung, B., Chakrabarti, B., & Baron-Cohen, S. (2015). Sex/gender differences and autism: Setting the scene for future research. *Journal of the American Academy of Child & Adolescent Psychiatry, 54*(1), 11–24. https://doi.org/10.1016/ j.jaac.2014.10.003

Lai, M.-C., & Szatmari, P. (2020). Sex and gender impacts on the behavioural presentation and recognition of autism. *Current Opinion in Psychiatry*, *33*(2), 117–123. https://doi.org/10.1097/YCO.00000 00000000575

Mandy, W., Chilvers, R., Chowdhury, U., Salter, G., Seigal, A., & Skuse, D. (2012). Sex differences in autism spectrum disorder: Evidence from a large sample of children and adolescents. *Journal of Autism and Developmental Disorders*, *42*(7), 1304–1313. https://doi.org/10.1007/ s10803-011-1356-0

Somer, E., Soffer-Dudek, N., & Ross, C. (2017). The comorbidity of daydreaming disorder (maladaptive daydreaming). *Journal of Nervous & Mental Disease*, *205*, 525–530. https://doi.org/10.1097/ NMD.0000000000000685

Young, H., Oreve, M.-J., & Speranza, M. (2018). Clinical characteristics and problems diagnosing autism spectrum disorder in girls. *Archives de Pédiatrie*, *25*(6), 399–403. https://doi.org/10.1016/j.arc ped.2018.06.008

Young, S., Hollingdale, J., Absoud, M., Bolton, P., Branney, P., Colley, W., ... & Woodhouse, E. (2020). Guidance for identification and treatment of individuals with attention deficit/hyperactivity disorder and autism spectrum disorder based upon expert consensus. *BMC Medicine*, *18*(1), 146. https://doi.org/10.1186/s12916-020-01585-y

Chapter 8

Sensory differences

I think there is this perception that sensory discomfort is experienced as solely pain. But, for me, I don't feel physical pain: I feel severe anxiety, overwhelmed, panicked, or at other times anger, irritability, rage even.

−Asiatu Lawoyin

You say reactive, I say responsive ...

The DSM-5-TR diagnostic criteria for autism use the terms hyper- and hypo-*reactivity*. But Carol Stock Kranowitz, author of *The Out-of-Sync Child*, prefers *sensory over-* or *under-responsivity* as well as *sensory craving*, as do the authors of *Sensory Integration: Theory and Practice*, Anita Bundy and colleagues. To make this more confusing, other people prefer the terms hyper- or hypo-*sensitivity*.

The DSM-5-TR also refers to an *unusual interest in sensory aspects of the environment*, and some people refer to this as *sensory seeking* or, more recently, *sensory craving*.

For the purpose of this book (except when quoting the DSM-5-TR), we have decided to use the terms *over-* and *under-responsivity*, as well as *sensory craving*.

DOI: 10.4324/9781003242130-10

What people often think atypical responsivity to sensory input means

When considering autistic sensory experiences, many people primarily think of sensitivity to noise, particularly children who are so sensitive to noise that they regularly cover their ears. People also think of sensitivity to texture, such as an intolerance of tags in T-shirts or seams in socks. Some people also think of sensory craving behaviors, such as staring at a fan or playing with water for an uncommonly long time. These examples are fairly common but, as you're probably expecting by now, there is more to this category than meets the eye.

What does this criterion really include?

In the DSM-5-TR, this category includes "hyper- or hypo-reactivity to sensory input or unusual interest in sensory aspects of the environment." We will review each of these, but first, let's discuss our sensory systems.

> While sensory issues are more common in autistics, they are certainly not specific to autism, and they should not be the sole determinant of an autism diagnosis.

Our sensory systems

In every moment of our lives, our bodies take in and process sensory input. This input comes from the external world (e.g., sights, sounds, and smells, to name a few) and from our internal world (e.g., heart rate, temperature, muscle tension, etc.). We constantly process this incoming information, contextualize it, give it meaning, and respond to it in our thoughts, actions, and emotions, often unconsciously.

Most people are aware of five of our sensory systems (vision, hearing, touch, smell, and taste), and these are explicitly mentioned in the DSM-5-TR diagnostic criterion for sensory issues. However, we actually have *eight* sensory systems. Let's review each of these before discussing how autistics may have altered sensory experiences.[1]

Hearing: Our auditory sense allows us to hear sounds in the environment, to discriminate the specific sounds that constitute language, and to discriminate language from non-language sounds. Furthermore, we have to contextualize these sounds; that is, sense where they are coming from, how close they are, and what they may tell us about our environment. For instance, hearing a dog bark is an entirely different experience if (a) you are playing with your new puppy, who is right in front of you; (b) you are walking alone in the woods, enjoying the quiet, and the bark comes unexpectedly from right behind you; or (c) you are in a doctor's waiting room with no dogs in sight but with a television playing in the background. The process of discriminating the volume, location, and possible movement of the sound gives you clues about the situation. It also helps you discern which sounds to attend to, which to ignore, and which are threats.

Touch: The skin covering our entire body has countless receptors that give us information about touching and being touched. Separate sensory pathways detect the sensations of pain, temperature, touch (both light touch and deep pressure), position, and vibration. This helps us to take in information in countless ways. For example, we might feel a piece of fruit to see if it's ripe, hug someone tightly to feel support, or put on our "comfort clothes" as soon as we get home from a long day at work.

Vision: Our visual sense codes the information we take in about the environment through our eyes. This includes data like color, brightness, shape, size, location, distance/depth, and motion (i.e., direction and speed of your own body and of objects in the environment). As with auditory processing, visual processing involves integrating these different types of information to form a contextual model of the world that allows you to recognize things like objects and faces, along with their location in space. This sense is tightly integrated with the systems that control movement, allowing people to move through space as they interact with objects and others in the environment.

Taste: We categorize taste as sweet, sour, bitter, salty, and savory, but any parent who regularly cooks dinner for the family knows all too well that each individual has their own complex and unique experience of taste. Taste allows us to distinguish edible from spoiled food and to experience pleasure while eating and drinking. It's important to note that food textures (e.g., smooth, crunchy, creamy, sticky) are also part of the gustatory experience, though technically those experiences are related to the sense of touch on the tongue. This is an excellent example of the countless ways in which our sensory systems act together, or integrate, to guide our experience of ourselves and the world around us.

Smell: We can recognize the smells of hundreds of thousands of different substances, and our reactions to those smells can range from positive to neutral to negative. More than any other sense, smell is linked to the creation of memories – a familiar smell can trigger recent memories or those from long ago. In this way, smell is also highly contextual, helping you to quickly assess a situation. For example, some smells might be pleasant, like that of a new book or a piece of toast, while others, such as rotten food or wet dogs, are often experienced as unpleasant. Of course, this is highly individualized. For example, Donna loves to inhale the scent of an infant, which her daughter finds perplexing! In addition to experiencing smells on a continuum from pleasant to unpleasant, we also experience different intensities. When two people are in a room with a scented candle, one of them may barely notice a vaguely pleasant aroma, while the other's attention is powerfully drawn to the intensity of the scent. Our sense of smell is tightly integrated with our sense of taste; chewing releases chemical compounds that are part of our experience of food.

Proprioception: Proprioception gives us information about our body's position and movement via sensations in our muscles, bones, and tendons that code for stretching versus contracting and tensing versus releasing. We use these sensations to move specific *parts* of our body to maintain posture and coordinate our movements. For instance, we intuitively know how much force to exert when handing an object to someone, spreading butter, erasing an error, or throwing a ball, how to move our legs as we walk faster or slower, and how high to raise and lower our legs to negotiate stairs.

Vestibular: The vestibular system, located in your inner ear, gives you information about the position and motion of your head and body. This system helps us keep our equilibrium, so we don't become dizzy or bump into things. It is also critical to our sense of balance and our ability to coordinate our body's movement through space. In addition, it allows us to stabilize our gaze while providing feedback to help us maintain head and body posture. Data from the vestibular system are tightly integrated with data from the other sensory systems, especially visual and proprioceptive, which helps us accurately experience motion. It also has a direct connection to the motor system, so we can make rapid adjustments to our movements based on the input we get from the inner ear. We use this information when we stand or sit up straight, move through space, turn our head, or ride in a car.

Interoception: How do you feel? Such a simple question, right? But to answer this question, we need to do a body check, either consciously or unconsciously, and take in information about our heartbeat, breathing, muscle tension in specific areas of our body, hunger, thirst, pain, and other sensations, which can be as specific and yet as vague as "butterflies in my stomach." These actual bodily sensations tell us how we are feeling in terms of homeostasis (e.g., my body needs food, movement, water, sleep, etc.) and in terms of emotions (I'm anxious, angry, sad, etc.). The awareness of these internal sensations is referred to as *interoception* (as opposed to *exteroception*, i.e., the awareness of sensations coming from *outside* of the body).

These sensory systems do not work in isolation from each other. We constantly take in, integrate, and act on information from multiple sensory systems. When our sensory systems work well, they protect us from danger or overwhelm, guide us toward pleasant experiences, and help us navigate the world in countless ways.

We do not currently have clarity about the extent to which differences in responsivity arise from differences in physiological sensitivity as opposed to differences in observable behavioral reactions to those sensations (i.e., sensitivity versus responsivity).

Our feeling is that, for purposes of diagnosis, it doesn't matter. What matters is that the individual perceives, experiences, *or* responds to sensory input in atypical ways.

So, what might this look like in an autistic person?

The DSM-5-TR breaks this category into three parts: over-responsivity, under-responsivity, and unusual interest in sensory aspects of the environment. Any of these three can occur in any of the eight senses, which makes for countless sensory profiles.

Over-responsivity: The DSM-5-TR notes that over-responsivity can be "manifested through extreme responses" and that "extreme reactions to or rituals involving taste, smell, texture, or appearance of food or excessive food restrictions are common" in autistic individuals. Over-responsivity is also referred to as sensory sensitivity and sensory defensiveness. Over-responsivity can manifest in externalizing behaviors (such as a meltdown), unusual responses (such as being startled by quiet sounds), or avoidance of the offending stimuli (with or without verbal clarification regarding the reason for the avoidance). However, there may also be *no observable behavioral manifestation.* In many cases, individuals have an internal reaction ranging from mild discomfort to distraction, irritation, overwhelm, or even rage.

An individual can experience over-responsivity in any and all senses. While not an exhaustive list by any means, examples include:

- Significant aversions to specific sounds, such as toilets flushing, other people chewing, or to sound in general;

- Discomfort with either natural or artificial light;

- Tactile defensiveness or significant discomfort with textures – seams on socks, tags on clothing, the feel of air or water on the skin;

- The feel of human touch or affection, particularly light touch (see the examples below);

- Aversions to specific smells, such as celery or soap, or a general sensitivity to all smells;

- Sensory aspects of hygiene, such as the feel of wet hair or wet skin, the taste of toothpaste, the sensation of a toothbrush or hairbrush, or the feel or sound of nail clippers;

- Excessive reactions to food or extreme food restrictions, resulting in a very limited diet;

- Overwhelm in crowds, due to overpowering combined visual, auditory, and olfactory input;

- Over-responsivity to internal sensations, most notably pain, manifesting as unusually low pain tolerance, or

- Fears related to heights, or fear/nausea/reactions related to movement, such as going down the stairs, swinging, or spinning.

From the experts: Reflections about over-responsivity

Certain types of smells, like bleach and fragrances, can quickly give me headaches.

–Taylor M.

I have extreme sensitivity to certain wavelengths of light, where I wear a pair of sunglasses which block 580 nm yellow light, even when it is cloudy, and when I see certain blue LED lights, they look so bright I have to look away.

–Eric O.

When I'm sleeping, the hair HAS to be off the back of my neck. If there is any hair on the back of my neck, I won't get any sleep.

–Grace O.

My main sensitivity is to touch. I literally go red and feel my skin burning for about 20 to 30 minutes if I am even playfully smacked or do a 'high five' or clap in applause or in time to music.

–Elizabeth B.

Smells can be the worst, the thing I'm most sensitive to. Certain smells can be so overwhelming, I can't really breathe without gagging.

–Zoe M.

My fingers feel heavy when I wear nail polish.

–Elizabeth B.

I don't like having multiple different textures in one bite, so salad is something I will never enjoy, despite liking most vegetables.

–Zachary M.

I can hear better than people. People will think I can't hear their conversations, but I can, and I also can't tune them out, so I couldn't stop listening even if I wanted to.

–Audrian F.

I get triggered when I am in a waiting room and a TV or radio is playing. I'm not sure where my reaction comes from, but when it goes on too long, I start crying and/or get angry.

–Leen V.

I used to get really motion sick as a kid. It's gotten better as I've gotten older, but I'll still have trouble in the car if there are a lot of twists and turns in the road, or if there are a lot of other sensory things happening. Like if I'm in a car with a lot of people talking, and there's also music playing or more sound around me, I'll get more sick than I would if there was less going on. And even though I'm mostly fine in cars now, a lot of the reason I chose to move to a city with a train system is so that I can avoid them for the most part.

–Zoe M.

From the experts: Firm versus light touch

We have heard from many autistics that light touch can be problematic, while deep touch is either neutral or enjoyable.

Light touch is THE WORST. Hard pass on light touch. I remember when I was a kid my mom was braiding my hair and her hand kept grazing the back of my neck and I kept pulling away and she kept yanking me back. It was a terrible tug of war with my head just because I couldn't stand her lightly touching me!

–Lauren O.

I don't like light touch sensations. It's almost alarming. Deep touch is more soothing to me, like a weighted blanket or long mutual hug. I can't really explain what about it is soothing, but it doesn't cause any alarms and is calming.

–Noelle B.

I immediately want it to stop. It's not painful. It's just overwhelming and anxiety-producing. And it's not exactly a thing intimate partners love when you tell them you don't want to be light touched.

–Lauren O.

Misophonia: A unique sensory challenge

Misophonia is an extreme emotional reaction to common sounds that most people don't even notice. Though any sound can be a trigger, the most frequent triggers are the noises related to eating or breathing. There are several notable characteristics of misophonia:

- **Extreme externalizing reactions**: Misophonia can create extreme emotional reactions. For most people with misophonia, hearing these sounds triggers feelings of disgust or intense irritability and, if unabated, can progress to anger or rage. Once triggered, an individual with misophonia can become so overwhelmed that they become aggressive or experience an intense need to escape from the source of the sound.

- **Misperceptions**: Typically, individuals who experience sensitivity to sensory input are aware that they react more strongly than others. In contrast, some misophonics may believe that other people are intentionally making noises to irritate them, or at least that other people are making an unreasonable amount of noise, and they may feel strong anger toward others who are simply breathing, chewing, or carrying out their daily activities in a normal fashion.

- **Needs**: Most individuals who have general auditory sensitivities do better in quiet environments with less stimulation overall. In contrast, a quiet environment can be particularly high risk for a misophonic, because any soft noise in the vicinity will be more noticeable and could trigger a reaction.

Under-responsivity: Under-responsivity occurs when an individual shows little to no response to a stimulus. The under-responsivity can be to external stimuli or to internal sensations. Examples include:

- Low reaction to pain, which is often described as an individual being unusually stoic or having a high tolerance for pain;

- Apparent indifference to temperature, either heat or cold;

- Low awareness of toileting needs, so a child might have frequent accidents;

- Low awareness of other internal signals, such as hunger or satiety, so that an individual may keep eating endlessly or never get hungry, may require external reminders to eat or go to the bathroom;

- Low sensitivity to tactile input, such as the feeling of food on one's face – individuals who have this experience may chronically appear unkempt, as they do not feel their messy hair or their twisted clothing;

- Low sensitivity to auditory input, such as not hearing a car coming;

- Poor postural control, due to low registration of vestibular/proprioceptive input;

- Insensitivity to visual input – for example, not being able to process motion, differentiate between colors, or know how far away something is;

- Low sensitivity to vestibular/proprioceptive input, so an individual may "trip on air";

- Being oblivious to the risk of heights or moving equipment;

- Not becoming dizzy, even with excessive spinning, or

- Having little awareness of the physiological sensations (interoception) associated with emotions (e.g., a rapid heart rate associated with anxiety or excitement), and thus being unaware of one's emotional state.

From the experts: Reflections about under-responsivity

I have no issues with any smells, tastes, textures, or sounds ... almost to the point of an oddity in certain situations – food that most people would find unpalatable due to one of those aspects generally does not bother me.

–Eric O.

I rarely get thirsty or hungry. I had no idea that was common. I forget to drink water or eat pretty often, especially in new environments where my routine is thrown off, such as a business trip or sleepover as a kid.

–Asiatu Lawoyin

I never know when I'm thirsty, so now I keep a water bottle with me and try to drink a lot. In the past I would forget about eating or drinking until it got to an extreme point. I have gotten to the point where I haven't noticed it until it's painful.

–Jack K.

I have problems knowing when I'm hungry. Some days I'll only eat one meal, and usually only because I realize I hadn't eaten anything else. I think my sense of hunger can also be triggered by checking the time because I find myself responding to the question "Are you hungry?" by checking the time. My dad joked once that I don't have a stomach, I have a watch.

–Angie L.

I broke my ankle 6 years ago – before I knew anything about autism. I didn't notice until the next morning. I thought I had just twisted my ankle really badly, so I went to bed. The next morning it was swollen up like a baseball, and I couldn't move it, so I went to the hospital. I got x-rayed, and the doctor told me it was a really bad break, and I was going to need surgery. I said, "OK." He kind of looked at me strangely and said, "This is a really bad break. I'm surprised you're not in more pain." Makes sense now.

–Cindy B.

I love shoes and can wear almost any shoe without discomfort. I can buy shoes without trying them on or wear shoes that are a size too small. I only notice they don't fit me well if I see blisters at the end of the day.

–Grace O.

I have trouble knowing when I'm hungry and remembering to eat throughout the day, and often rely on checking the time. When I do notice I'm hungry it's less because I feel it in my stomach and more because I can tell emotionally. I'll be more irritable and sad for no real reason.

–Zoe M.

Sensory craving: The DSM-5-TR includes "unusual interests in sensory aspects of the environment" and offers examples, including "excessive smelling or touching of objects, fascination with spinning lights or spinning objects." More examples include:

- Close visual inspection of objects, looking at objects from the corner of the eyes or through squinted eyes;

- Fascination with visual repetitive movement (such as fans or doors);

- Unusual sensory exploration, such as licking people or objects or excessively smelling unusual stimuli;

- Frequently chewing or sucking on sleeves or collars;

- Strong attraction to a particular texture, or

- Craving certain types of tactile input, such as deep pressure or weighted blankets.

From the experts: Reflections about sensory craving

I often feel a very strong urge to latch onto a friend or tuck my face against their clothes both for texture and scent reasons. I also like petting leaves or stuffed animals and rubbing against certain textures.

–Audrian F.

I was the kid who sniffed everything, especially aniseed, petrol (at the petrol station), liquid paper, black textas, and nail polish. I can smell when my kids are coming down with a cold. The scent of lavender is my happy place.

–Elizabeth B.

I have a ribbon that I love to run between my fingers and under my nails. I've had it in some form or another all my life, the original was the silky edge of my crib blanket!

–Amie H.

One of my favorite experiences growing up was the smell of my stuffed bunny's ears. I would smell them when I was falling asleep or when I was upset or lonely.

–Gabby H.

I like the smell of wet wool, or wool containing lanolin. Most of my friends and family hate it, even the friends who knit.

–Angie L.

Unusual sensory experiences: Although this is not part of the official diagnostic criteria, it's important to note that many autistic people experience their sensory world in very different ways than those who do not report sensory differences. For example, when there are many noises in an environment, like a restaurant, the sounds can blend together or be so distorted that some individuals have difficulty determining which sounds to attend to. Likewise, people can be extremely sensitive to one kind of noise (e.g., the whine of electronics), while oblivious to other sounds (e.g., someone saying their name). Autistic advocate and educational speaker Kim Clairy (personal correspondence, September 2021) tells a story of hiking with her husband on her honeymoon and coming upon a gap between some rocks that "you could drive a small car through" and freezing because she didn't think she could fit through the opening. Only after her husband showed her that he could walk through did she believe that she could do the same. Kim reports countless examples of being unable to reliably understand how big her body actually is.

Many autistic people also have *synesthesia*. Synesthesia is a neurologic phenomenon in which senses that are typically unconnected are stimulated simultaneously. While non-autistics may also experience synesthesia, one recent study by Simon Baron-Cohen and his colleagues found that the rate of synesthesia in autistic adults was almost three times greater than in non-autistics. Thus, it is essential to consider synesthesia as another example of atypical sensory experience that may be part of a larger presentation of autism.

We have heard many examples of synesthesia. For example, Charlotte R. reports that, "*Certain foods tasted of shapes. The strongest one was white grape juice, which tasted round.*" Similarly, Angie L. recalls, "*When I was in elementary school, I'd associate numbers, especially when used in simple addition or subtraction, with colors. For instance, 7 + 3 = 10 would be orange and green.*" According to Kim Clairy, her vision becomes unreliable when she is in a noisy environment, with some things blurring and blending together while individual features (like an eye or a mouth) appear in sharp focus.

We cannot overstate the overwhelming impact that sensory issues can have on an autistic's ability to function. Meng-Chuan Lai and colleagues remind us that sensory differences can be present very early in development. This can affect development in the earliest stages of life and may impact other domains of (what we understand as) autistic features. As Allie S. remarked, *"The sensory issues in public school really affected my ability to socialize. I stayed in with a teacher for lunch and recess because I couldn't deal with the noise. Once I was in a smaller school, I was able to socialize during lunch and free time."*

The impact of sensory issues on motor coordination: As already mentioned, our senses are integrated with our motor control system because accurately sensing the environment is a prerequisite for being able to move through it. Since the DSM-5-TR does not reference the motor aspects of sensory processing as part of the diagnostic criteria for autism, we leave that discussion for later.

The impact of sensory experiences on social interactions: As you can imagine, coping with all of these sensory challenges can be extremely draining and leaves little energy for social interactions, particularly when the social interactions themselves are effortful and exhausting. We find that our autistic clients, as well as our autistic friends and family members, have more successful social interactions when they are in a sensory-friendly environment.

Sensory experiences: What we've learned from the girls

Research on sensory differences in autistics of different genders is sparse, and the little that does exist is inconclusive. Some studies indicate similar sensory processing differences in males and females, while others report greater sensory differences in females. We have seen no studies suggesting that males have greater sensory differences than females.

In research settings, autistic females report the same or more significant sensory differences than autistic males. In clinical settings, it may be particularly important to query non-males about their sensory experiences because, as a general rule, **males tend to externalize more, while females tend to internalize more** (and we look forward to research on sensory differences in people of all genders). Thus, it is possible that males (both autistic and not) will have observable behavioral manifestations of sensory differences that are more likely to be reported by parents or teachers. In contrast, girls may be more likely to have sensory differences with no observable behavioral correlates. We have had numerous females tell us things like, "the sound of light bulbs makes me insane, but I've never told anyone." Thus, the most reliable way to truly understand a girl's sensory challenges is to directly query her about them.

Finally, it is important to highlight the relevance of sensory differences in eating disorders for autistic girls. Research suggests that there is a high prevalence of autism in girls with eating disorders and that there is a high prevalence of eating disorders in autistic girls. Sensory differences are relevant to this topic for a few reasons. First, autistic girls are at higher risk than typical girls for being picky eaters, and the resulting restricted food choices, due to taste, smell, or texture issues, can lead to restricted calorie intake. Second, some autistic girls have trouble feeling or interpreting physiological hunger signals, so they rarely feel hungry and thus eat very little. This can easily be misinterpreted as intentional restriction of calories in order to lose weight. Of course, the opposite can also be true; some autistic girls do not register the feeling of being full and thus overeat. Careful assessment is necessary to tease out contributing factors so that treatment can be appropriately targeted.

Kim Clairy had a severe eating disorder, and her autism made it even more challenging to get appropriately targeted help. For instance, when Kim was in a treatment center, she was asked to eat predetermined amounts of specific foods, which was challenging because of her sensory sensitivities to the smell, taste, and/or texture of some of those foods. Staff at Kim's treatment center believed that her difficulty eating these foods resulted from concern about calories, which was not in fact the case. Additionally, when stressed, Kim needed to pace back and forth, a common repetitive movement among autistic females. However, the staff at her eating disorders program interpreted this behavior as an attempt to burn calories.

Frequently asked questions

- Do non-autistic people also have atypical sensory experiences? Absolutely! Sensory sensitivities in particular are common in many people. It is challenging to get a clear estimate of how many children without disabilities have significant sensory processing issues, in part because studies use different criteria. However, it is clear that a significant percentage of non-disabled children do indeed have sensory processing challenges. For instance, Roianne Ahn and her colleagues found that between 5.3% and 13.7% of non-referred, presumably typically developing children in kindergarten had sensory processing disorder, and Ayelet Ben-Sasson and colleagues found that 16% of parents reported significant sensory over-responsivity in their elementary school-aged children. That said, the prevalence rate is much higher in autistic children – as high as 95% according to Tomcheck & Dunn. As we noted at the beginning of this chapter, while sensory issues are more common in autistics, they are certainly not specific to autism, and they should not be the sole determinant of an autism diagnosis.

- **Can an individual be over-responsive to some things and under-responsive to others?** Absolutely, and this is typical.

- **Can an individual's sensory experiences change?** Yes, and this, too, is common. Sensory experiences can change in general as a person matures, and they can also change from day to day, depending on the situation and the individual's state of mind. For instance, a person can be exquisitely sensitive to noise while they are taking a test, to the point where they can have a strong reaction to the sound of the fluorescent lights, and the same individual may enjoy playing their favorite video game with the volume turned up high.

- **What if the sensory experience only occurred when the client was younger, and they have outgrown it?** It still counts. Remember, these criteria need to be met either currently *or* by history.

- **Are autistics the only people who experience altered interoception?** No. Anyone can experience altered interoceptive awareness, though some groups of people are more vulnerable to this. In addition to autistics, this includes some individuals with ADHD, as well as people who have experienced trauma and people who are persistently emotionally dysregulated.

- How is sensory craving behavior different from *stimming*? Stimming is an informal term that means different things to different people. This can include sensory craving, repetitive behavior, and for some people spending time with their intense interest. Stimming serves a purpose. If a client mentions stimming, we recommend that you simply ask them what the experience and behavior mean for them and what purpose stimming serves.

Note

1 We are indebted to Carol Stock Kranowitz, MA, for her work communicating these differences to the general public in her book *The Out-of-Sync Child*. We are especially grateful to her for the comments she made on a draft of this book, and particularly on this chapter.

References and related reading

Ahn, R. R., Miller, L. J., Milberger, S., & McIntosh, D. N. (2004). Prevalence of parents' perceptions of sensory processing disorders among kindergarten children. *American Journal of Occupational Therapy*, 58(3), 287–293. https://doi.org/10.5014/ajot.58.3.287

American Psychiatric Association. (2022). *Diagnostic and statistical manual of mental disorders* (5th ed., text rev.). https://doi.org/10.1176/appi.books.9780890425787

Baron-Cohen, S., Johnson, D., Asher, J., Wheelwright, S., Fisher, S. E., Gregersen, P. K., & Allison, C. (2013). Is synaesthesia more common in autism? *Molecular Autism*, 4(1), 40. https://doi.org/10.1186/2040-2392-4-40

Ben-Sasson, A., Carter, A. S., & Briggs-Gowan, M. J. (2009). Sensory over-responsivity in elementary school: Prevalence and social–emotional correlates. *Journal of Abnormal Child Psychology*, 37(5), 705–716. https://doi.org/10.1007/s10802-008-9295-8

Ben-Sasson, A., Carter, A. S., & Briggs-Gowan, M. J. (2010). The development of sensory over-responsivity from infancy to elementary school. *Journal of Abnormal Child Psychology*, 38(8), 1193–1202. https://doi.org/10.1007/s10802-010-9435-9

Ben-Sasson, A., Cermak, S. A., Orsmond, G. I., Tager-Flusberg, H., Carter, A. S., Kadlec, M. B., & Dunn, W. (2007). Extreme sensory modulation behaviors in toddlers with autism spectrum disorders.

American Journal of Occupational Therapy, 61(5), 584–592. https://doi.org/10.5014/ajot.61.5.584

Ben-Sasson, A., Hen, L., Fluss, R., Cermak, S. A., Engel-Yeger, B., & Gal, E. (2009). A meta-analysis of sensory modulation symptoms in individuals with autism spectrum disorders. *Journal of Autism and Developmental Disorders*, 39(1), 1–11. https://doi.org/10.1007/s10803-008-0593-3

Bertone, A., Mottron, L., Jelenic, P., & Faubert, J. (2005). Enhanced and diminished visuo-spatial information processing in autism depends on stimulus complexity. *Brain*, 128(10), 2430–2441. https://doi.org/10.1093/brain/awh561

Board on the Health of Select Populations, Board on Children, Youth, and Families, Institute of Medicine, & Division of Behavioral and Social Sciences and Education. (2015). Prevalence of learning disabilities. In T. F. Boat, J. T. Wu, & J. T. Wu (Eds.), *Mental disorders and disabilities among low-income children* (Ch. 16). National Academies Press (US). www.ncbi.nlm.nih.gov/books/NBK332882/

Bundy, A. C., Lane, S., Mulligan, S., Reynolds, S., & Fisher, S. J. (2020). *Sensory integration: Theory and practice*. F. A. Davis.

Danielson, M. L., Bitsko, R. H., Ghandour, R. M., Holbrook, J. R., Kogan, M. D., & Blumberg, S. J. (2018). Prevalence of parent-reported ADHD diagnosis and associated treatment among U.S. children and adolescents, 2016. *Journal of Clinical Child and Adolescent Psychology*, 47(2), 199–212. https://doi.org/10.1080/15374416.2017.1417860

Dworzynski, K., Ronald, A., Bolton, P., & Happé, F. (2012). How different are girls and boys above and below the diagnostic threshold for autism spectrum disorders? *Journal of the American Academy of Child and Adolescent Psychiatry*, 51(8), 788–797. https://doi.org/10.1016/j.jaac.2012.05.018

Falkmer, M., Stuart, G. W., Danielsson, H., Bram, S., Lönebrink, M., & Falkmer, T. (2011). Visual acuity in adults with Asperger's syndrome: No evidence for "eagle-eyed" vision. *Biological Psychiatry*, 70(9), 812–816. https://doi.org/10.1016/j.biopsych.2011.07.025

Green, S. A., Hernandez, L., Lawrence, K. E., Liu, J., Tsang, T., Yeargin, J., … & Bookheimer, S. Y. (2019). Distinct patterns of neural habituation and generalization in children and adolescents with autism with low and high sensory overresponsivity. *The American Journal of Psychiatry*, 176(12), 1010–1020. https://doi.org/10.1176/appi.ajp.2019.18121333

Hull, L., Mandy, W., & Petrides, K. V. (2017). Behavioral and cognitive sex/gender differences in autism spectrum condition and typically developing males and females. *Autism: The International Journal of Research and Practice*, 21(6), 706–727. https://doi.org/10.1177/13623 61316669087

Hull, L., Petrides, K. V., Allison, C., Smith, P., Baron-Cohen, S., Lai, M.-C., & Mandy, W. (2017). "Putting on my best normal": Social camouflaging in adults with autism spectrum conditions. *Journal of Autism and Developmental Disorders*, 47(8), 2519–2534. https://doi.org/10.1007/s10803-017-3166-5

Jussila, K., Junttila, M., Kielinen, M., Ebeling, H., Joskitt, L., Moilanen, I., & Mattila, M.-L. (2020). Sensory abnormality and quantitative autism traits in children with and without autism spectrum disorder in an epidemiological population. *Journal of Autism and Developmental Disorders*, 50(1), 180–188. https://doi.org/10.1007/s10803-019-04237-0

Kaat, A. J., Shui, A. M., Ghods, S. S., Farmer, C. A., Esler, A. N., Thurm, A., ... & Bishop, S. L. (2021). Sex differences in scores on standardized measures of autism symptoms: A multisite integrative data analysis. *Journal of Child Psychology and Psychiatry*, 62(1), 97–106. https://doi.org/10.1111/jcpp.13242

Kopp, S., & Gillberg, C. (1992). Girls with social deficits and learning problems: Autism, atypical Asperger syndrome or a variant of these conditions. *European Child & Adolescent Psychiatry*, 1(2), 89–99. https://doi.org/10.1007/BF02091791

Kranowitz, C. S. (2020). *The out-of-synch child: Recognizing and coping with sensory processing differences.* TarcherPerigee, an imprint of Penguin Random House.

Lai, M.-C., Lin, H.-Y., & Ameis, S. H. (2022). Towards equitable diagnoses for autism and attention-deficit/hyperactivity disorder across sexes and genders. *Current Opinion in Psychiatry*, 35(2), 90–100. https://doi.org/10.1097/YCO.0000000000000770

Lai, M.-C., & Szatmari, P. (2020). Sex and gender impacts on the behavioural presentation and recognition of autism. *Current Opinion in Psychiatry*, 33(2), 117–123. https://doi.org/10.1097/YCO.00000 00000000575

Lane, S. J., Reynolds, S., & Thacker, L. (2010). Sensory over-responsivity and ADHD: Differentiating using electrodermal responses, cortisol, and anxiety. *Frontiers in Integrative Neuroscience*, 4. https://doi.org/10.3389/fnint.2010.00008

Maenner, M. J. (2020). Prevalence of autism spectrum disorder among children aged 8 years: Autism and Developmental Disabilities Monitoring Network, 11 sites, United States, 2016. *MMWR*

Surveillance Summaries, 69. https://doi.org/10.15585/mmwr.ss 6904a1

Mandy, W., Chilvers, R., Chowdhury, U., Salter, G., Seigal, A., & Skuse, D. (2012). Sex differences in autism spectrum disorder: Evidence from a large sample of children and adolescents. *Journal of Autism and Developmental Disorders*, 42(7), 1304–1313. https://doi.org/10.1007/s10803-011-1356-0

Moseley, R. L., Hitchiner, R., & Kirkby, J. A. (2018). Self-reported sex differences in high-functioning adults with autism: A meta-analysis. *Molecular Autism*, 9(1), 33. https://doi.org/10.1186/s13229-018-0216-6

Schoen, S. A., Miller, L. J., & Green, K. E. (2008). Pilot study of the sensory over-responsivity scales: Assessment and inventory. *American Journal of Occupational Therapy*, 62(4), 393–406. https://doi.org/10.5014/ajot.62.4.393

Tomchek, S. D., & Dunn, W. (2007). Sensory processing in children with and without autism: A comparative study using the short sensory profile. *American Journal of Occupational Therapy*, 61(2), 190–200. https://doi.org/10.5014/ajot.61.2.190

Young, H., Oreve, M.-J., & Speranza, M. (2018). Clinical characteristics and problems diagnosing autism spectrum disorder in girls. *Archives de Pédiatrie*, 25(6), 399–403. https://doi.org/10.1016/j.arcped.2018.06.008

Young, S., Hollingdale, J., Absoud, M., Bolton, P., Branney, P., Colley, W., … & Woodhouse, E. (2020). Guidance for identification and treatment of individuals with attention deficit/hyperactivity disorder and autism spectrum disorder based upon expert consensus. *BMC Medicine*, 18(1), 146. https://doi.org/10.1186/s12916-020-01585-y

Part Two

What else might be part of this presentation?

This section of the book serves two purposes. The first is to help you understand autistic people by describing related experiences they may have. The second is to alert you to patterns that should cue you to step back and consider whether someone may be autistic.

Chapter 9 describes co-occurring conditions that may be part of an autistic person's profile, and which can impact their day-to-day functioning and experience. We categorize these as challenges in processing emotions, cognition, medical/health conditions, and other experiences.

Chapter 10 discusses some of the many potential strengths of autistic people. So far, the focus of this book has been on the challenges autistic people must navigate. The chapter on autistic strengths will help you identify possible strengths in the autistic people you know. Clinicians can use this understanding with their autistic clients – to build on and celebrate as you work together.

As you read the chapters in this section, keep in mind that differential diagnosis will be discussed in Donna Henderson's *Is This Autism? A Companion Guide for Diagnosing* (in press, Routledge). Here we focus only on how these experiences may appear when you see them in autistic people.

DOI: 10.4324/9781003242130-11

Chapter 9

Common co-occurring challenges

In this chapter, we describe co-occurring challenges that some autistic people may also experience. These conditions occur more frequently in autistic people and can have an enormous impact on their functioning and/or their well-being. Because our focus is on people with a less obvious presentation of autism, we will describe conditions that are more common in that population. We will not report the prevalence rates of many of these co-occurring conditions because estimates vary widely and usually include autistic people with high support needs. Furthermore, prevalence rates are not as thoroughly researched for autistic people with a less obvious presentation.

The DSM-5-TR autism criteria describe *associated features* that include language impairment, difficulty with adaptive functioning, motor deficits, self-injury, disruptive behaviors, anxiety, depression, and catatonic-like motor behavior. But, like Susanne Duvall and her colleagues, we have also found it helpful to consider other behaviors and traits that are not specific to autism but are signs that the clinician may want to consider it. Dr. Duvall and her colleagues call these "pink flags." We agree that one or two pink flags are not necessarily significant, but a *pattern* of pink flags certainly warrants further investigation.

We cannot stress this enough: The experiences discussed in this chapter are not specific to autism. However, if there is a *pattern* of these experiences, in the context of social difficulty

DOI: 10.4324/9781003242130-12

(either externally manifested or internally experienced), we encourage you to consider the possibility that, in addition to these challenges, your client may be autistic.

This chapter has two aims. First, we highlight traits and behaviors that may cue you to consider whether autism is part of the picture. Second, we alert you to the fact that some of these conditions may present differently in autistic people than they do in non-autistic people. Differential diagnosis is discussed in *Is This Autism? A Companion Guide for Diagnosing*; here we focus on *what else* may occur in autistic clients and *how* these conditions may appear in these individuals.

We categorize these challenges into emotional, cognitive, medical/health, and "not easily classified into one of these groups." While some of these conditions are listed in the DSM-5-TR, many are not. Space does not allow us to provide a thorough review of each condition. As mentioned above, there is little research exploring co-occurring conditions specifically in autistics with low support needs, so our decisions about what to include in this chapter, and what to leave out, are based largely on our experience.

Possible Emotional Conditions[1]

Many people who are later diagnosed with autism first present for assessment or treatment because they are depressed, anxious, shut down, or having intense meltdowns. Because it is impossible to disentangle the extent to which emotional challenges are a result of stressors like being misunderstood, or related to a person's wiring (e.g., vulnerability to sensory overwhelm), we will sidestep this question and focus on the *impact* of these challenges on autistic people.

In this section we cover:

* Anxiety

* Obsessive-compulsive disorder (OCD)

* Depression

* Autistic burnout

- Emotional intensity and lability
  - Neuro-crash
  - Extreme empathy (emotional disequilibrium)
  - Rejection sensitive dysphoria (RSD)
  - Bipolar disorder
  - Repeated self-injury
  - Suicide
- Trauma
- Alexithymia
- Pathological demand avoidance/pervasive drive for autonomy (PDA)

Emotional challenges may present differently in autistic people than they do in non-autistic people. As with non-autistic people, if you notice a change – be it a decline in adaptive or academic functioning, intensity of an interest (either more intense or less intense), more repetitive behaviors, withdrawal, or increased irritability, aggression, or repeated self-injury – consider whether the person may be struggling with an emotional challenge. Also, keep in mind that formal screening tools for diagnoses in the DSM may not be valid with some autistic clients. Researchers are aware of this problem and, as we are writing, numerous labs are investigating whether some currently used assessment tools are appropriate for autistics or if new or revised tools are needed.

Anxiety

Most of the research on anxiety in autistic individuals has been done with children. However, anxiety is also quite common in autistic adults and the findings for children certainly seem to apply to the autistic adults we know. Lawrence Scahill and his colleagues at Emory University found that the best observable indicators of anxiety in autistic children were irritability, social withdrawal and avoidance, hyperactivity, offensive speech, increased insistence on sameness, increased intensity of restricted interests, and behaviors that are repetitive, self-injurious, compulsive, or ritualistic.

Anxiety itself is neither good nor bad; some anxiety can help focus your attention and orient you to action so you can more effectively navigate a dangerous or uncertain situation. When anxiety is overwhelming, it can spark a fear response that causes a person to fight, run, or freeze. These responses, too, can be helpful, effective, or necessary when circumstances demand them, but they can cause problems when the response is out-of-proportion to the danger inherent in the situation. Furthermore, anxiety can lead people to *avoid* situations that trigger or worsen their symptoms. As our colleague Dr. Jonathan Dalton (personal communication, 2020) reminds us, "Anxiety itself is not harmful, but avoidance ruins lives." It can also lead people to try to control things that are uncontrollable, affecting job performance, school, and/or personal relationships.

Certain anxiety disorders are much more common in autistic people. In 2010, Cruz and colleagues presented work at the International Meeting for Autism Research (IMFAR) in which they surveyed autistic children aged 7–14, with IQ > 70, who had at least one co-occurring anxiety disorder. They found that generalized anxiety disorder, specific phobias, social anxiety disorder (SAD), and separation anxiety disorder were the most common; selective/situational mutism was also present.

Generalized anxiety disorder (GAD) is quite common in autistic individuals. Boon Yen Lau and colleagues analyzed anxiety triggers in autistic children at ages 6 to 18 and found that they were anxious about many of the same things as non-autistic children (e.g., performance, social situations, weather, supernatural phenomena, health), though they also worried about autism-specific triggers like change/novelty/uncertainty, social confusion, and sensory overwhelm. Furthermore, they had a high rate of *specific phobias*. The authors noted, as have we, that these specific phobias can be quite unusual (e.g., eyes). We have also noticed in our own clients that phobias can also be typical but intense (e.g., a child refusing to go outdoors all summer long because they might encounter a bee).

We have also observed that a number of our anxious autistic clients do not respond to cognitive behavior therapy (CBT) as quickly as our non-autistic clients. This is so common that we consider autism when a client reports that CBT was not helpful.

People with *separation anxiety disorder* can become *extremely* upset when a person to whom they are strongly attached is not present, fearing that either they, or the other person, will be harmed while they are apart. Adults as well as children can experience separation anxiety. Autistic individuals may experience separation anxiety due to worry about harm befalling their loved one, or because their departure represents a change in routine, or both.

Social anxiety disorder (SAD) is a "marked fear or anxiety about one or more social situations" in which the individual worries that they may be scrutinized by others. People with SAD fear that others will negatively evaluate them. In turn, they may become hypervigilant or interpret the neutral reactions of others as hostile. (It is easy to understand why autistic people might have anxiety about social situations, given their frequent history of social situations going awry.)

The DSM-5-TR describes *selective mutism (SM)* as a "consistent failure to speak in specific social situations in which there is an expectation for speaking, despite [being able to speak] in other situations." Some autistics prefer the term *situational mutism*, as they find the implication that they are *selecting* when to be mute inaccurate. We have also encountered clinicians who use the phrase *situational mutism* differently – to indicate episodes of mutism that are shorter in duration and thus do not meet the one-month duration criteria for SM.

The thoughtful article by Peter Muris and Thomas Ollendick, *Selective Mutism and Its Relations to Social Anxiety Disorder and Autism Spectrum Disorder*, makes a compelling argument that it is nearly impossible to disentangle SAD from SM. They also note that while the DSM-5-TR does not permit a simultaneous diagnosis of SM and autism, autism explains a large percentage (63–80%) of children with SM. They conclude that SM, SAD, and autism "can be considered to be a unified trinity of social disorders." The differences in social communication styles, the preference for sameness, and the sensory hyper-responsivity of autistic people can make social interactions even more difficult, triggering social anxiety and "promoting the persistent non-speaking behavior displayed by children with SM." Thus, when working with a client who has SM or a history of SM, the possibility of autism should be considered.

From the experts: Reflections on anxiety

When I see people I don't know very well, I have no idea what to say. Then I start freaking out because I'm worried that they'll judge me. Once that starts, I can't make myself talk, no matter how nice the other person is.

–Namik T.

I learned a couple years ago that my child therapist thought I had social anxiety, and that's why I didn't like to spend time in large groups of people. I had to explain that I didn't have serious social anxiety as a child, though I do now, and it was all sensory. I wish she had asked instead of assuming.

–Allie S.

Obsessive-compulsive disorder (OCD)

People with OCD have, according to the DSM-5-TR, "recurrent and persistent thoughts, urges, or images that are ... intrusive or unwanted," cause anxiety and/or distress, and which they may try to suppress or neutralize with a thought or action (a compulsion) that is seemingly unrelated to the obsession. These compulsions are usually repetitive behaviors or rituals that the individual feels driven to perform. Because both OCD and autism involve repetitive behaviors, intense or persistent thoughts, sensory hyper-responsivity, and a feeling that things are "not right," the two conditions can reinforce each other when both are present. Furthermore, because it can be difficult to distinguish between a stim (which does not cause the person distress, but may distress those around them) and a compulsion (which bothers or even distresses the person and interferes with their lives), it can be difficult to determine how to appropriately understand and thus address the behavior. Likewise, addressing an intense interest as if it is an obsession is not helpful and can, in fact, be harmful.

Take, for example, the act of repeatedly opening and closing a door. For a person with OCD (without autism), this act might be a ritual performed to protect themselves and/or others from a threat. It provides temporary relief from anxiety. This is different from the motivation of an autistic person (without OCD) who might open and close the door because it is interesting or pleasant. The experience is pleasurable or self-soothing, as opposed to the experience of *needing* to perform the act in order to ward off intense anxiety. Further, the autistic person with OCD may find it difficult to distinguish between behaviors driven by sensory cravings versus those driven by the compulsive need to perform the ritual. This can make treatment quite challenging.

There can be a complex and challenging relationship between autistic experiences and OCD. For example, something that starts out as a sensory reaction can trigger an OCD behavior. One client noted that her son found the texture of fleece extremely aversive, and, whenever he touched it, he was so repelled by the feeling that he needed to wash his hands repeatedly, which in turn triggered his OCD. His compulsive behavior was not initially related to an obsessive thought; it was related to a sensory experience.

Depression

The symptoms of depression may include feelings of intense sadness, hopelessness, or emptiness, in addition to changes in sleep, appetite, energy levels, concentration, daily behavior, adaptive skills, or self-esteem. Mood swings, apathy, guilt, hopelessness, and anxiety can lead to agitation, excessive crying, self-isolation, or irritability. In addition, autistic people who become depressed may have less energy to mask, with previously acquired skills appearing to regress; increases in repetitive behaviors (and especially negative thought loops – a.k.a. rumination), new or increased areas of inflexibility, anxiety, aggression, and self-injury, and/or changes in how they engage with their intense interests. They may intensify their focus on a current interest, lose passion for it, or shift their interest to a new topic (perhaps with darker or more morbid content).

Rates of depression are much higher in autistic than in non-autistic people, and this may be particularly true in autistics with average to above-average intellectual functioning – some estimates indicate that as many as 65% of these adults are clinically depressed. Chloe Hudson and her colleagues found that depression is worse in autistic people who have higher verbal abilities and also in those with lower support needs. The factors that contribute to depression in autistic people come from many of the same sources as those affecting non-autistic people. These include unsupportive or limited social connections, poor achievement in school or at work, and a lack of agency and independence. Bullying of school-aged children (both autistic and non-autistic) leads to higher rates of depression, and autistic school-aged children are much more likely to be bullied than those without autism.

The developmental course of depression may differ depending on the autistic person's gender. The rates of depression in autistic males are higher than in non-autistic males, and they remain stable from childhood through adulthood. The rates of depression in autistic females, in contrast, are similar to their non-autistic peers in childhood, but are higher than their non-autistic peers in adolescence and adulthood. Felicity Sedgewick and her colleagues found that there was an elevated risk of depression for autistic adults regardless of gender, and that it was the same rate as found in non-autistic nonbinary and trans individuals.

Autistic burnout

Burnout is a deep fatigue that results from long-term exposure to challenging situations from which there is no adequate time for recovery. Autistic individuals are particularly vulnerable to burnout, which can last months to years, and is often first experienced during adolescence. According to Dora Raymaker and her colleagues, autistic people say that *trying to pass as non-autistic* is the most common reason for autistic burnout. Burnout can look like depression; however, unlike depression, people suffering from burnout can still feel pleasure, and they do not have feelings of worthlessness. Burnout can lead to depression, and both depression and burnout can lead to increased risk for suicide.

Autistics suffering from burnout may become unable to speak or care for themselves and they report memory challenges, especially short-term memory. The burnout that results from this kind of long-term depletion does not respond to medication or to therapeutic interventions that depressed people find helpful (e.g., considering alternative interpretations of events). What is required for recovery is relief from the demands that are taxing their systems.

From the experts: Reflections on burnout

I withdraw from others ... trying to stay makes me feel so drained. I withdraw because alone time is my safe place. I feel tired, brain fog, don't want to talk to people as much or don't feel okay without talking to someone, meltdowns, shutdowns, extreme dissociation, derealization. I usually stop feeling real, my head constantly hurts, I feel sick all the time, and don't have the energy to stand in the shower or sit up at my desk. I basically feel like I'm internally rotting when burnt out.

–Spencer C.

I used to have a phenomenal memory. I never used an agenda or a shopping list, but since my burnout in 2012, I lost this. It's getting a bit better, but I'm afraid it will never be the same again.

–Leen V.

Emotional intensity and lability

The DSM states that "disruptive challenging behavior" is a feature associated with autism, even though the emotional intensity and lability that drive such behavior are not part of the diagnostic criteria. One way to think of this emotional intensity is as resulting from an extremely sensitive *threat detection system*, creating a powerful response to situations that non-autistic people may not find as threatening.

In young children, emotional overwhelm is often labeled as a *temper tantrum*, but that language implies that the behavior is deployed willfully by the child in order to get something they want. Such manipulative behavior is not the same as a *meltdown*, which is an uncontrollable physiological and instinctual response to an overwhelming situation. Of course, children do have temper tantrums, but treating a meltdown like a temper tantrum is ineffective and possibly traumatizing.

Your body deploys natural defense mechanisms when you are faced with a real *or perceived* threat. *Fight* and *flight* are your sympathetic system's response to threat. The parasympathetic system's response kicks in when your body believes there is a possibility of imminent death; this more primitive defense mechanism is known as *freeze* (think of an animal "playing dead"). In the subsections that follow, we describe some of the conditions that trigger these intense emotional responses.

Neuro-crash: The short-term overwhelm of a system pushed beyond its limit in the moment can lead to a fight, flight, or freeze response (also called a meltdown/shutdown). The term *neuro-crash*, coined by autistic adult Raun Kaufman, aptly captures the essence of this response. He identifies seven factors that can lead to a neuro-crash: (1) being around agitated people; (2) being rushed, or pushed to do something that is too difficult; (3) invasions of personal space; (4) sensory overload; (5) lack of predictability; (6) unclear expectations; and (7) physiological reactions. While many clinicians code neuro-crash as anxiety, we've had autistic clients who strongly feel that they are not experiencing anxiety.

From the experts: Reflections on neuro-crash

A few years ago, my work team had a karaoke event ... I had to leave well before it was over. I was shaking and about to start crying just from overwhelm. In the car, I just leaned back in the seat and closed my eyes and tried not to shake or cry, to let everything just disappear.

–Charlotte R.

I can handle a party for all of about 30, maybe 45 minutes, and seem to be doing fine. What people don't recognize is that afterwards, I'm going to collapse for a day and a half and hide.

–Pat G.

I am very sensitive to loud noises. Going to concerts or being near a train when it rolls into the station can send me over the edge. I feel an intense need to hide or get away from the noise. When I can't, my mind goes dark and I can't move. Later, I can't remember exactly what happened.

–Tom W.

Extreme empathy (emotional disequilibrium): By now it is clear – to researchers as well as autistic people and those who love them – that many autistics have tremendous *affective empathy*. In fact, we've observed autistic people who are so highly empathic that they shut down when someone near them (or even a fictional character) experiences a big emotion. This can happen whether or not the other individual overtly displays their emotions. When the other person is not calm (e.g., a crying baby), the combined sensory and empathic overwhelm can be incredibly dysregulating to an autistic person. This dysregulation might look like a lack of empathy, but that interpretation puts the focus on the external behavior (e.g., yelling at a crying baby) instead of the internal experience.

From the experts: Reflections on extreme empathy

Nicole R. says that sometimes she has to leave the room sobbing in reaction to movie scenes, and it can take her hours, days, or even weeks to recover. "*Now I mostly just zone out when awful things happen on screen, because I don't like people to see my internal reaction. I can't take the stress while waiting for the scene to resolve. My husband says I watch the movies as if we are the characters.*"

I soak up the mood of the room but I can't normally name the exact emotion – only positive/negative – or put it on a person. Group therapies are hell. People in the office who just argued with their spouses are hell. Any transmission from a war zone or natural disaster area is hell. I can't watch people playing contact sports such as rugby, boxing, or even roller derby because I get upset instantly.

–Alis C.

Rejection sensitive dysphoria (RSD): We include RSD here not because it's a formal diagnosis, but because it is embraced by many ADHDers, some of whom are also autistic. The intense emotional pain of RSD is triggered when a person thinks they have disappointed others or themselves, or when they feel rejected, teased, or criticized. The response is rapid and quite dramatic. Dr. William Dodson has observed that "about a third of adolescents and adults list rejection sensitive dysphoria (RSD) as the most impairing aspect of their ADHD." Non-autistic people with RSD are prone to interpreting small signals (e.g., a sideways glance or small shifts in tone of voice) as a devastating rebuke. But autistic people with RSD may also misinterpret these cues, or be confused about the underlying intent behind them. This confusion can compound their dysregulation. Because the response is so immediate and visceral, it often doesn't respond well to behavioral or cognitive interventions; the most effective treatment may be medication.

Bipolar disorder: Although autism is sometimes misdiagnosed as bipolar disorder (BD), autistic people can also have BD. As with non-autistics, autistics with BD experience cyclic patterns of hypomania, mania, and/or depression that is distinct from their baseline. Jean Frazier and her colleagues observed that the typical manic/hypomanic risk-taking behaviors like overspending, gambling, or excessive shopping aren't observed as frequently in autistic people with BD. Instead, they are more likely to be verbally aggressive, socially intrusive, or restless. Like their non-autistic counterparts, they may have feelings of grandiosity, a decreased need for sleep, and pressured speech. Autistic people also had increased difficulty thinking clearly and they engaged more deeply with their intense interests.

Repeated self-injury: Most of the research on self-injury in autism focuses on self-injurious behaviors (SIBs) like head-hitting and biting, while the literature on self-injury in non-autistics focuses on non-suicidal self-injuries (NSSIs), such as cutting. The distinction between these two types of self-injury is not entirely clear to us. What is clear is that autistic people engage in self-injury at a rate (50–65%) that is more than twice that of non-autistic people (17–26%). As mentioned in Chapter 5, SIBs may function to provide proprioceptive input, and may sometimes, but not always, be an attempt to regulate intense emotions. Determining the function of the self-injury can make it easier to create a helpful plan for intervention.

Suicide: Suicide is a devastating problem, and both ideation and attempts appear to be particularly prevalent in autistic people. In 2018, Sarah Cassidy's team found that a shocking 72% of autistic adults scored highly for suicide risk. Tatja Hirvikoski and her colleagues reviewed the records of over 27,000 people and found that eight times more autistic people died by suicide (31%) than did non-autistic people (4%)! While immediate stressors like bullying and abuse are clear triggers for considering suicide and developing a plan to carry it out, there are other risk factors that can also make suicidal ideation more likely in an autistic person. These include traits like difficulty seeing alternative ways to approach a problem, perfectionism, all-or-none thinking, rumination, negative memory biases, and difficulty thinking about the future. Autistic individuals are more likely to complete suicide when there is a late diagnosis of autism, plus lack of access to psychiatric support and treatment, unemployment, lack of education, and/or a sense that they do not belong.

Meng-Chuan Lai and his colleagues also report that autistic people who die of suicide are more likely to be aggressive, unafraid of death, and to have an increased tolerance for pain. They have often previously self-harmed, previously attempted suicide, and have a co-occurring health or mental health condition. Sarah Cassidy's team found that additional triggers included financial stress, recent unemployment, bullying, abuse, bereavement, relationship breakdown, social isolation, recent changes to a living situation, and exposure to others' suicidal behavior. One of these factors alone was not predictive; those who died had an average of *six* of these conditions. Finally, those who died of suicide were often noted to have been impulsive, as reflected by the fact that most of their deaths were not planned or premeditated. Instead, these autistic people likely died because of their reaction to the overwhelming feelings of the moment.

Trauma

It is quite difficult to determine the proportion of autistic people who have experienced trauma for numerous reasons. These include: trauma assessments that have mostly been developed and normed on non-autistic populations, symptoms of trauma may be different in autistic and non-autistic individuals, and the fact that autistics report a wider range of traumatizing events.

Autistics are more likely to have *adverse childhood experiences* (ACEs). As Sara Griffiths and her colleagues have noted, "research reports shockingly high rates of trauma among autistic people." This includes income insufficiency, parental separation or divorce, neighborhood violence, maltreatment, victimization, removal from birth family, bullying, school discipline, police contact, psychiatric hospitalization, and living with individuals with mental health problems and/or substance abuse.

Autistic people are also much more vulnerable to *victimization*, including hate crimes, sexual and financial victimization, and other types of deceit. And though we have not seen research on this topic, we know a number of autistics (and their parents) who have experienced *healthcare trauma* as a result of being chronically misunderstood, misdiagnosed, and invalidated.

Autistic people may also experience events as traumatic that would not technically qualify as traumatic in the DSM-5-TR. In 2020, Freya Rumball, Francesca Happé, and Nick Grey asked a group of autistic adults who reported exposure to traumatic events about their experiences and found that many of the life events they experienced as traumatic were not recognized as traumas in the DSM (e.g., bullying, navigating mental health challenges, and social difficulties).

Furthermore, the autistic community reports that it can be traumatizing to do things that are not distressing for non-autistics, like making eye contact, hearing someone chew, or going to school. Coping with the typical daily sensory experiences that accompany brushing one's teeth, eating, or wearing clothes can also be sources of chronic trauma for some autistic people (just picture yourself being forced to eat live bugs or wear scratchy, prickly clothes every day). The fact that current assessment tools don't query for these kinds of experiences raises concerns that autistic people may not receive treatment for the trauma they have experienced (and that they feel pressured to remain in traumatic situations).

Autistic people respond to traumatic events in much the same way as non-autistics – they are more easily startled, struggle to concentrate, have more difficulty sleeping, and are more emotionally reactive. There may also be an increase in self-injury, as well as an increase in the expression of autistic traits like unusual repetitive behaviors, rigidity, and increased rumination, not to mention regression in adaptive life skills or ability to communicate. Other reactions, including debilitating depression, may be quite severe.

Assessment can be quite challenging in part because current assessment tools rely on self-reported distress. Because autistics can have trouble conveying their distress to medical professionals – because of issues that include difficulty with interoception and communicating their emotions (alexithymia, see below), as well as flat or restricted affect – standard self-report measures may be inadequate to assess the possibility of trauma in autistic individuals. Significant people in the person's life are sometimes unaware of the signs of distress, which limits the accuracy of teacher- or parent-report measures and collateral interviews. In recent years, researchers like Daniel Hoover and Elizabeth Romero have attempted to address this shortcoming by developing screening tools (e.g., the Interactive Trauma Scale) for assessing trauma in autistic children.

Alexithymia

The term alexithymia (having no words [a lexi] for state of mind [thymos]) refers to a condition in which people have great difficulty describing or naming their emotions. People with alexithymia appear to have trouble:

- Noticing their own bodily sensations (a.k.a., difficulty with interoception);

- Relating those sensations to the situation in which they are occurring; and/or

- Accurately labeling the emotions that correspond to the bodily sensations they are experiencing in that situation.

To better understand the challenge, consider the process of determining what an emotion is. If someone senses their stomach clenching and their heart pounding when they are first in line for a new roller coaster, they might label the feeling as *excitement*. If they have the same physical sensations during a confrontation with a coworker, they are more likely to label the feeling as *anxiety*. Accurately identifying emotions requires an understanding of both the internal bodily state *and* the context. Without access to both types of information, alexithymic people have difficulty communicating their emotions.

A therapist working with one of Donna's clients noted that their shared client, who had never experienced trauma, was entirely unaware of his emotions. "When I show him an emotional video, tears will stream down his face, but he can't describe the emotional state. He insists that he isn't feeling anything." As you might imagine, it is very difficult to regulate your emotions if you don't even realize which emotions you are having! For this reason, people with alexithymia can find it extremely challenging to apply cognitive strategies for managing their emotional responses to situations.

During an interview with Donna, Vidhi was unable to express how she experiences emotions in her body, which was a striking change from her usual incredibly fluent and mature oral expression. For instance, when asked what anger feels like to her, Vidhi responded, "That's a very hard question to answer. I don't know how to explain that with words. I feel it in this part of my body" (indicating her face). When asked how anxiety feels in her body, Vidhi (who has a 99.6th percentile vocabulary) reported, "these are specific physical feelings that I know but I can't describe or explain. It's in this part of my body (indicating her abdomen)."

Alexithymia can also lead to inaccurate diagnosis because therapists and other healthcare professionals may not understand the nature or intensity of the physical and/or psychological pain their clients are experiencing. When the autistic person has flat affect in addition to alexithymia, it further complicates the diagnostic picture, as those individuals cannot use *either* words *or* other nonverbal cues to convey their pain. It is critically important for clinicians to be aware of this when treating their autistic clients.

From an expert: A reflection on alexithymia

I know I have emotions. I can see the effects of them. When I get sad, I cry. When I get mad, my muscles tense up. I can't tell if I'm enjoying something. I see the physical traits, but I can't put words to them, and I don't know what emotions I'm having when I'm having them. Sad is pressure behind my eyes. When people talk about emotions, I don't know what they mean; it's like trying to describe a color. That makes it hard for me to advocate for myself.

–Jack K.

Pathological demand avoidance/pervasive drive for autonomy (PDA)

PDA has long been acknowledged as a subtype of autism in the UK. Although clinicians in the USA are becoming more aware, it is still not listed in the DSM-5-TR or the ICD-11. While PDA is clinically referred to as *pathological demand avoidance*, we prefer Tomlin Wilding's re-interpretation, *pervasive drive for autonomy*, which more accurately reflects the core issue: an anxiety-driven need for self-determination and independence. PDAers experience external demands as impinging on their freedom.

This need for autonomy leads people with PDA to avoid demands and expectations *for the sole purpose of remaining in control*. When faced with a demand, even a tiny one (e.g., putting one glass in the dishwasher, doing a single math problem, or taking a shower), they can have extreme reactions. The external presentation of the emotion can be misinterpreted, and they are sometimes so intense that these individuals are misdiagnosed with oppositional defiant disorder, bipolar disorder, or intermittent explosive disorder.

One of PDA's most frustrating features is that this intense negative reaction can be triggered by a demand that the person with PDA *wants to meet* (e.g., to be productive, to be nice to their parents, colleagues, or friends, to learn, to do their homework, to have a job, etc.). But *they cannot force themselves to do these things if they feel that someone else wants or expects them to do it* because their fear of the loss of autonomy is so intense. As such, they are at high risk for school or work avoidance and may have particular difficulty launching into adulthood.

As Elizabeth Newson et al. reported in 2003, PDAers have superficially functional social skills that can lead people to wonder whether or not they are really on the autism spectrum (although in our experience, they are). The characteristics that are typical of PDAers but not of other autistics may include needing more novelty than most autistics, engaging in more pretend play and role playing (sometimes to an extreme), or having particularly strong superficial social skills that lack depth.

Like other autistics, some PDAers only show evidence of difficulty in one setting. They might camouflage well at work or in school only to fall apart at home. Or they might do well at home, where there are lower demands, and struggle at school or work. Another hallmark of PDA is that they can do well for short periods of time and then suddenly stop doing well (family members report that it is like living with Dr. Jekyll and Mr. Hyde.) This inconsistent presentation can be particularly confusing: "They did it yesterday! Why can't they do it today?" It is easy to interpret this inconsistency as indicating that the behavior is entirely volitional, but it isn't.

As a result, these individuals are highly misunderstood. In addition to the trauma of living with PDA, the chronic misinterpretation, invalidation, and lack of support add new layers of anxiety and depression. This is especially true for adult PDAers, who can alienate partners and friends – the very relationships necessary for buffering the impact of chronic stress, anxiety, and depression.

PDA is also incredibly hard on families. It can dominate the household, wreak havoc with marriages, and affect siblings. Parents of children with PDA have often tried everything (therapy, medication, behavior plans, private schools, etc.) to no avail, leaving them feeling hopeless, helpless, incredibly frustrated, and often wrongly judged by others for what seems to be overly permissive parenting.

Possible Cognitive Differences

Autistic people process information in fundamentally different ways than non-autistic people, and they can also have co-occurring traits that impact their cognition.

In this section we will cover:

- Attention

- Executive functioning

- High need for explicit context (as well as weak central coherence)

- Spoken language (understanding and speaking)

- Academics

- Slow processing speed

- Prosopagnosia

- Giftedness

There is no *one autistic cognitive profile*. While it is true that there are some differences that frequently co-occur in autistic people (e.g., difficulty with attention regulation, executive functioning, and need for explicit context), it is inaccurate to assume that all autistic people will have the same profile. That said, it is common for autistics to have an *uneven profile*, with significant strengths in some areas and notable challenges in others. Of course, non-autistics can also have uneven profiles, and an uneven cognitive profile should not, in and of itself, be taken as indicative of autism.

Attention

Individuals with attention-deficit/hyperactivity disorder (ADHD) have difficulty regulating attention, with or without hyperactivity and impulsivity. Many less obviously autistic people are first diagnosed with ADHD, only to receive an autism diagnosis many years later (if at all). Benjamin Yerys and his colleagues have consistently found that autistic individuals with ADHD rate themselves as having a poorer quality of life than autistic people who do not have ADHD. The reasons include a less robust response to external interventions like parent training or coaching, atypical responses to medications (more severe side-effects, with less symptom relief), and difficulty communicating effectively.

Executive functioning

Executive functions (EFs) are neurologically based skills that govern how we manage ourselves and our resources to achieve a goal. These skills include inhibition, shifting (flexibility), emotional control, initiation, working memory, planning, organization, generativity, and self-monitoring. Cara Pugliese and her colleagues noted in 2021 that "recent meta-analyses support the identification of EF as a primary deficit in autism with many domains of EF affected." Chun Lun Eric Lai and his colleagues' careful study in 2017 of EF in autistic children and adolescents with average to above-average IQs identified verbal and spatial working memory, flexibility, and ability to generate multiple options as problematic, even in the absence of ADHD.

High need for explicit context

Before discussing this important difference, it will help to first understand why it matters.

Understanding the world requires interpreting information with the larger context in mind. There's a lot of uncertainty and ambiguity in what is seen, heard, read, and felt that cannot be resolved without taking context into consideration. For example:

- What does it mean if my heart is pounding?

- Is it OK to lie?

- What's a good present to buy?

- When is "later"?

- What do you do when a traffic light turns yellow?

- How close should I stand to another person?

To cope with ambiguity, non-autistic brains make subconscious educated guesses, using context as a guide. Subcortical systems process information instantly and generally without conscious awareness, guiding attention to the relevant details so those that don't matter can be ignored. Without context, every detail must be taken in, relevant or not, and integrated to create a meaningful whole.

It has been suggested that autistic individuals do not automatically use context as their guide, and that they use a slower and more effortful detail-oriented process by default. In 2005, Dinah Murray and her colleagues proposed that autistic people have a *monotropic mind* that leads them to notice details and recognize objects because of a narrow and intense focus of attention that enhances perceptual clarity within the area of focus. In 2006, Francesca Happé and Uta Frith argued that this detail-focused cognitive style operated with little attention to the bigger picture. The experience would be like doing a jigsaw puzzle when none of the pieces have any straight edges and there is no picture to guide you. Putting the pieces together is certainly possible, but it would be difficult and time consuming. This refinement of Dr. Frith's original theory of *weak central coherence* has been challenged by a number of researchers. Laurent Mottron and his colleagues, for example, proposed that autistic people are perfectly able to attend to the bigger picture when they know they need to do so; it's just that their *default* is to focus on the details.

Peter Vermeulen reviewed the literature on this processing bias towards "absolute thinking in a relative world" as it applies to perception, social interactions, communication, and knowledge, and made a strong argument for the need to explicitly describe context when interacting with autistic individuals. By making the context explicit, he posited that non-autistics would be able to more effectively interact with autistics because they would make it easier for autistic people to interpret and integrate details into a unified whole. In his book, *Autism as Context Blindness*, he gives an example of asking a young man what kinds of support he received in his home. The young man answered, "The floor."

Dr. Vermeulen realized that he should have provided more context by asking about the support he received in his home from people or organizations.

In a personal communication, Dr. Vermeulen observed that *providing context is critically important when any person – not just an autistic person – is overwhelmed*, noting that he saw "a very strong link between absolute thinking and stress."

Connecting culture: Speakers in *low-context cultures* (e.g., the United States, Australia, and the United Kingdom; Germany, Scandinavia, and Sweden) *provide more context* by default, which may make it easier for autistic people who live in those countries to understand and be understood by others. Speakers in *high-context cultures* (e.g., Japan, China, Korea, Arab countries, France, Spain, and many South American and African countries) *expect listeners to have figured out the context themselves*. Due to these (potentially erroneous) assumptions, autistic listeners in these cultures may be more likely to misunderstand/misinterpret what they are being told.

Spoken language

In 2009, Helen Tager-Flusberg and her colleagues noticed that autistic children with language disorders have strikingly asynchronous development across language domains. Autistic people, even those with average to above-average intellectual functioning, can have challenges expressing themselves and understanding what others are saying. The issues can be deceptive because the expressive language skills of many autistics are often much better than their comprehension. There are also distinct patterns of language acquisition. For example, they might have an extremely advanced vocabulary, but have trouble constructing grammatically complex sentences. Informally, we have noticed that the language skills of our autistic clients are best when talking about their intense interests.

There are specific areas of asynchronous development that are more frequently observed in autistic individuals. Dr. Tager-Flusberg and her colleagues described the following possible language differences in autistics.

Vocabulary:

- Limited/unusual/extensive vocabulary.

- Difficulty with or sensitivity to words that have more than one meaning (e.g., pound).

- Difficulty updating a word's meaning or pronunciation based on new data (e.g., do not pronounce the "l" in "salmon").

- Very formal or precise words and phrases.

- Difficulty with figurative language (e.g., metaphors, similes, allusions).

Grammar and morphology:

- Limited *syntactic repertoire* (e.g., don't vary their use of different sentence structures as much as non-autistic speakers).

- Less sensitive to the importance of word order in meaning.

- Misinterpret and misuse prepositions (to, in, on, at, over, under, etc.).

- Difficulty with conjunctions (and, but) and pronouns (esp. I/ you).

- Difficulty with third person singular (he/she/it).

Organization:

Comprehension:

- Difficulty with inferencing (drawing a conclusion based on data – e.g., the ground is wet so it must have rained).
- More likely to misinterpret what was happening in a story.

Production:

- When telling a story, difficulty communicating the sequence of events and the processes that connect them.
- Topical discontinuities.
- Too much or too little detail.

Conversational style:

- Less responsive (may not respond to questions and comments).

- Difficulty understanding indirect requests (e.g., "This trash can needs emptying!").

These are possible language differences; individual profiles will of course show varying patterns of strength and weakness. It's also critical to remember that some autistic individuals have perfectly intact or even stellar language skills, and that excellent language and communication skills do not rule out autism.

Academics

Academic challenges often result from a convergence of other conditions like learning disorders, ADHD, executive dysfunction, difficulty with fine motor control, and/or a high need for explicit context. It is impossible to summarize all possible areas of academic impact, so instead we will focus on some that we more commonly observe in our autistic clients: hyperlexia, difficulty with reading comprehension, challenges with written expression, and difficulty with the language-based components of math.

Hyperlexia is characterized by an advanced ability to sound out words (decoding skills). Students with hyperlexia often learn to read very early without being explicitly taught, are strongly drawn to the written word, and are often excellent spellers. This profile is strongly associated with autism, as reported by Alexia Ostrolenk and her colleagues.

Rohan was a quiet child. He didn't speak in full sentences until he was 6. But he wanted to share what he was thinking with his family, and at 2 years old he taught himself to read. His parents had magnetic letters on the refrigerator, so he started spelling words with them to communicate. When his dad came home from the hospital after his little brother was born, 4-year-old Rohan had arranged the letters to spell "Mama and baby" on the refrigerator.

Reading comprehension difficulties can be traced to difficulties with language processing, fluctuating attention, linking prior knowledge and personal experiences to the information in the passage, understanding character motivations, sequencing events, making connections between events in the passage, creating mental images, and determining the gist. Furthermore, autistic people sometimes focus on the details in the story, missing the bigger picture. Of course, other autistic individuals are highly superior readers.

Written expression is perhaps the most complex of all academic skills, as it requires fine motor coordination, precise wording, attending to grammar, organization and planning, taking the reader's needs and preferences into account, coping with ambiguity, etc. While non-autistic individuals may experience any of these, in our experience, autistic individuals can be particularly vulnerable to any or all of these factors (while others can be phenomenal writers).

Mathematical skills can be a strength for some autistics, but aspects of math can be hard for some autistic students. For instance, they may have difficulty with word problems, related to their difficulties with language processing and/or difficulty identifying the most germane details. Understanding concepts like *less* versus *more*, or that *of* means *multiply*, involves learning the vocabulary of math and knowing when to apply it. Likewise, showing your work involves relating the mathematical concept to a real-world situation, or writing each step out so that another person can follow your thought process. Other challenges that may make math difficult for autistic people include poor working memory (making it difficult to hold numbers in memory when working on multistep math problems), poor fine motor or visual-motor skills (making it difficult to line up numbers when doing complex calculations), inattention (leading them to miss differences between symbols like + and *x*), knowing when to apply different mathematical rules, and flexible problem-solving skills (i.e., knowing that there are multiple ways to solve a problem).

Slow processing speed

One of the indices measured on some IQ tests is processing speed – how quickly and efficiently you can complete a task.

Sometimes these scores are quite low in autistic individuals (and others!), but saying that they process information slowly doesn't necessarily help to identify the *reason* for being slow. And if you don't know the reason, it's difficult to figure out how to address it. Additionally, some people can earn high scores on these very brief tests, but their working tempo in real life is much slower (in personal correspondence during 2019, our colleague Dr. Bill Stixrud refers to these individuals as *cognitive sprinters*).

Some factors that can contribute to the appearance of slow processing speed include: difficulty retrieving words, difficulty understanding what other people say, having trouble organizing thoughts, and being emotionally overwhelmed by anxiety or depression. Working style can also contribute. If a person needs breaks, needs to check and re-check their work because of poor working memory or anxiety, or is working at a less-than-ideal time of day for them, they will work more slowly. We really noticed the impact of working at our best time of day as we collaborated on this book. Donna works more efficiently in the morning, and Sarah works more efficiently at night.

Another possible reason for apparent slow processing speed is the *bottom-up* processing style that requires an individual to sort through relevant *and irrelevant* details. In these cases, the speed itself isn't necessarily slow, but the individual is processing more information, so it takes longer.

Prosopagnosia

Also known as face blindness, people with prosopagnosia have trouble recognizing and identifying a face that they have seen before. They can have this trouble with people they know casually, but also with people they know well. The problem is not in associating a name with a face (as many people, both autistic and not, have difficulty with name retrieval). Rather, it relates to a more basic perceptual difficulty perceiving and integrating facial features into a unitary whole, and connecting what they see with prior experience and context.

People with prosopagnosia are forced to rely on a person's individual features like shoes, hair, skin color, body shape, and the sound of their voice to identify them. As you might imagine, this can make it very difficult to keep track of people, and socializing can be incredibly difficult. Because people with prosopagnosia have trouble identifying characters easily, they can also find it difficult to follow the plot of TV shows and movies. While prosopagnosia is relatively rare in non-autistics (2–3% of the general population), Ilaria Minio-Paluello and her research team found that nearly one-third of autistic people are *face blind*.

From an expert: A reflection on prosopagnosia

Being face blind is TOUGH. Everyone thinks you don't care. I thought I was an awful person for years, because so many people knew me and I didn't know them. It's hard to shift from casual contact to a real relationship when you aren't sure, when you see them, whether you know them or not. But that doesn't make you uncaring. It makes you lonely.

–Charlotte R.

Giftedness

We discuss differentiation of gifted people from autistic people in *Is This Autism? A Companion Guide for Diagnosing*. Here, we want to spotlight gifted children who are also autistic. In an unpublished survey of 1,263 gifted children conducted in 2020, Drs. Jessica Koehler and Samantha Buell (personal communication, 2021) asked parents whether their gifted children had any co-occurring diagnoses. They found that 7.77% of their sample had been identified as autistic, and the authors were fairly certain this was an underestimate of the actual prevalence. This is far higher than the prevalence rate in the general population (just over 2% as of this writing). It's also worth noting that many gifted people are adept at problem solving, which may translate to strong impression management skills. If they are also autistic, they may well be using their intellectual and problem-solving talents to hide their autistic traits.

Medical/health

Autistic people have numerous differences related to health and physiology. One point we want to emphasize: **addressing emotional and/or cognitive challenges often requires attending to medical issues as well.** In 2015, Lisa Croen and her colleagues reviewed the healthcare records for medical conditions in 1,507 insured autistic adults and compared incidence rates for the same conditions in an age- and sex-matched sample of 15,070 non-autistic adults. The results were shocking. Autistic people have a higher incidence of health problems across every body system studied. We cannot know to what extent these differences are due to difficulty accessing healthcare, providers not taking the complaints of autistics seriously, higher stress levels, higher ACEs, medication side-effects, diet, lifestyle, and/or challenges with self-care. However, the data are incontrovertible: *autistic people are much more likely to be ill than non-autistics and health challenges can cause or exacerbate cognitive and behavioral problems.* Treating an underlying medical condition can make it easier for an autistic person to manage other aspects of their profile.

In this section we discuss:

- Common concerns, including sleep, eating, gastrointestinal issues, dental issues, atypical reactions to medications, obesity, menstruation, and menopause.

- Neurological challenges, including motor skills (fine motor, gross motor, hypotonia), tic disorders and Tourette (sometimes called Tourette's) syndrome, seizures, and migraines.

- Other health challenges, including autoimmune conditions, connective tissue disorders, dysautonomia/POTS, and genetic disorders.

Common concerns

Sleep: Difficulty sleeping is seen so often in autistic people that we are surprised when our autistic clients report no issues with sleep, and this is reflected in the research. Claudia Carmassi and her colleagues found that autistic people sleep for shorter periods of time and that their sleep isn't as efficient – they take longer to doze off and spend less time in REM sleep. Furthermore, autistics tend to be night-owls – going to sleep two or more hours after the conventional bedtime – with associated difficulty waking up in the morning. A meta-analytic review by Amparo Díaz-Román, Junhua Zhang, and their colleagues reported that autistic children resisted bedtime more often than their non-autistic peers and they had more anxiety about going to sleep. Sleep-disordered breathing (sleep apnea) and parasomnias (sleep terrors, sleepwalking, nightmares, and sleep paralysis) are also common.

Eating: difficulty with eating starts early for many autistics, especially if they have trouble with the fine motor coordination necessary to eat neatly, not to mention worry about triggering gastrointestinal symptoms. Over-responsivity to taste, smell, and texture at a young age leads to a limited set of acceptable foods that are often light brown or white in color – Sarah fondly refers to this eating style as the *beige diet*. Other autistic individuals have the opposite of the beige diet (and we informally refer to this as the *green diet*). These people become quite rigid about nutrition guidelines, overgeneralizing principles of healthy eating to the point of not getting enough calories or nutrients. Additionally, under-responsivity to taste or smell carries its own challenges, sometimes leading to disinterest in food and eating. Stimulant medications can exacerbate the problem, as these medications can temporarily suppress the normal cues for hunger.

Avoidant/restrictive food intake disorder (ARFID) is diagnosed when a person has difficulty meeting their nutritional needs because of a lack of interest in eating, sensory aversion to foods, or concern about triggering symptoms like choking, vomiting, or gastrointestinal distress. Some people with ARFID are significantly underweight, and may resort to getting necessary calories through oral nutritional supplements. They are often told that they are "too skinny," which can make them feel confused or ashamed about their diet, compounding the challenges they have with meeting their nutritional needs. Tanner Koomar and his colleagues found that 21% of autistic people had ARFID. No wonder so many parents of autistic children worry about their children's diets!

> *Paul Micallef, an autistic trainer, has a script he uses to explain what it is like for autistic people with sensory issues to eat foods they don't like (personal correspondence, 2022).*
>
> Imagine if someone served you a dish, and it had carrots in it. How do you feel about eating that dish?
>
> Oh sorry, not carrots, I meant maggots. I serve you a dish, and it has maggots in it. How do you feel now? Do you still want to eat that?
>
> What if there is nothing else to eat? Would you go hungry?
>
> What if I picked them out? Would you still eat it?
>
> What if I mashed them in?
>
> Are any of these getting better? Am I getting any closer to something you want to eat right now?

There can also be sensory craving for certain foods, which can look like a binge-eating disorder (BED). BED is characterized in the DSM by eating more food "in a discrete period of time" than needed. BED is also characterized by a "lack of control over eating during the episode" with episodes at least weekly over a 3-month period. The episodic nature of a BED is quite different from the constant difficulty limiting food intake, which can be due to poor impulse control, stress eating, or low interoceptive awareness of satiation.

Another challenge that some autistic people face is difficulty knowing when they are hungry or when they have eaten enough. This can be due to difficulty with interoception, and can lead them to not notice when they should start eating, or to continue eating long after they have taken in enough calories.

The overlapping symptoms of autism and eating disorders can be difficult to disentangle. The distinction is complicated by the fact that 22.9% of people with BED, anorexia nervosa (AN), or bulimia nervosa (BN) also have autism, according to Vanessa Huke and her colleagues.

Take autism into account when treating eating disorders

It is extremely important for clinicians to understand how autism can complicate treatment for eating disorders. Failing to do so can be unhelpful at best and fatal at worst. Kim Clairy, an autistic occupational therapist who nearly died from an eating disorder, has described at least three issues with her treatment.

(1) Difficulty with proprioception made it difficult for Kim to estimate her body size (which was not an "undue influence of body weight or shape on self-evaluation").
(2) Vomiting met an intense sensory need for rhythmic movement (though it was misinterpreted as purging associated with anorexia nervosa by her healthcare professionals).
(3) Kim's intense need for frequent movement was not because she wanted to exercise in order to burn calories. Instead, it was because motion helps her to focus and regulate her nervous system so she can carry out daily tasks.

As with other aspects of diagnosis, it is essential to understand the underlying reason(s) for restricted eating and related activities.

From an expert: Reflection on a special interest and eating disorders

Soccer was my special interest. I played in college and I would practice before and after scheduled practice. I even dribbled the ball to classes. My coach told the team that during the season we needed to stay away from 'unhealthy foods' as they would hinder our playing. I took it to heart and eliminated most foods. The soccer obsession and limited food led to overtraining and weight loss, which was part of the eating disorder.

–Kim Clairy, OTR/L

Gastrointestinal (GI) issues: Many autistic people suffer from chronic abdominal pain, and have a much higher rate of gastrointestinal disorders (see the review by Lisa Croen and her colleagues), including constipation, diarrhea, and gastroesophageal reflux disease (GERD). They also have higher rates of esophageal disease and problems with both their upper and lower GI tracts. Autistics are vulnerable to trouble with bowel and bladder control due to low interoceptive awareness; it's common to see encopresis (fecal incontinence or soiling) or enuresis (loss of bladder control) long past the usual age range for these. GI issues can be a primary symptom of an underlying medical condition, or a symptom/ side-effect of other conditions and/or treatments, including but not limited to anxiety/stress and medication side-effects. It makes sense that autistic people, and the people who love them, look to dietary solutions for these chronic and highly uncomfortable problems.

Dental issues: Dental issues are also common in autistics. Many autistic children avoid brushing their teeth because of sensory issues (the feel of the brush on their gums or their teeth, foaming toothpaste that tastes awful to them, the pain of flossing) and/or difficulty with fine motor control. Tolerating dental visits can be even harder. The sensory overwhelm, lack of control, and demand to sit still is challenging for many kids, and it can be even harder for autistic kids (and some adults as well). It can be very difficult to cope with the sound of the drill, the angle of the light, and the scraping sensations involved in removing plaque. This can set up a pattern of poor dental hygiene that can result in serious dental issues. Muhammed Abdullah Jaber found that autistic people had significantly more decayed, missing, or filled teeth than non-autistics, and they needed more restorative dental treatment. The majority of the autistic individuals in his study had poor oral hygiene and 97.0% of them had gingivitis.

Atypical reactions to medications: In their excellent chapter on medications in *The Oxford Handbook of Autism and Co-Occurring Psychiatric Conditions*, Bryan King and his colleagues reviewed studies of the responses of autistic people to a variety of medications. The autistic participants had lower response rates to methylphenidate, guanfacine, and SSRIs, and all had much higher rates of side-effects. SSRIs were not tolerated well at all; 78% of the autistic participants became unpleasantly activated, which may be experienced as agitation, hyperactivity, and sometimes even aggression. And while 49% of autistic participants with ADHD responded well to methylphenidate, that response rate was far lower than that of non-autistics (73.4%), and 18% of the autistic participants were unable to tolerate it due to a significant increase in irritability, lethargy, and social withdrawal. Only 3% of non-autistic people with ADHD suffered similar side-effects. Guanfacine led to more reliable improvement in ADHD symptoms, but 13.3% of the autistic participants dropped out because of intolerable effects like fatigue and drowsiness, likely due to substantially lowered heart rate and blood pressure. Informally, Sarah and Donna have noticed that their autistic clients seem to respond atypically to many medications – both target symptoms and side-effects can be experienced differently in autistics than in non-autistics.

Obesity: There is no doubt that autistic people are more often overweight than their non-autistic counterparts. It's unclear, however, to what extent these higher obesity rates are due to diet, difficulty with interoception (i.e., not feeling satiated), stress-related eating, inflammation, medication side-effects, and/or lower rates of exercise. Furthermore, there are no studies that specifically look at weight in people who have a less obvious presentation of autism. One promising study, by Tslil Simantov and her colleagues, found that autistic females were more likely to have a higher body mass index (BMI) and/or prediabetes symptoms than their non-autistic counterparts. The more autistic traits an undiagnosed female had, the more likely she was to have a higher BMI and/or prediabetes symptoms.

Menstruation: Tslil Simantov and her colleagues also measured reproductive system diagnoses, irregular puberty onset (either early or delayed), and menstrual irregularities. These diagnoses were significantly more frequent in autistic females, compared to their non-autistic counterparts.

The changes of puberty can be challenging for non-autistic girls but can be particularly hard on autistic females. This transition requires girls to cope with changes in their body, new clothing (e.g., bras), cramps and other physical symptoms of menstruating, as well as emotional symptoms associated with the hormonal cycle.

Menopause: The hormonal changes of menopause can be difficult for some autistic females. One study by Rachel Mosely and her colleagues found that sensory issues, difficulty communicating needs, and problems socializing with others became much worse during menopause, to the point that some participants were no longer able to mask their struggles. The same challenges that autistic teens experience at the onset of menstruation can also apply during menopause. Dr. Mosely and colleagues' study also noted an increase in meltdowns, anxiety, depression, and suicidal feelings.

Neurological challenges

Motor skills: Developmental coordination disorder (DCD), also known as dyspraxia, is so common in autistic people that Susanne Duvall and her colleagues listed it as a "pink flag" for autism. Physical therapist Anjana Bhat surveyed 11,814 parents of autistic children between the ages of 5 and 17 with no intellectual delays and found that 86.9% of them were at risk for a diagnosable motor impairment!

Both fine and gross motor control can be affected, as well as muscle tone. *Fine motor control*, sometimes called manual dexterity, is used in tasks like handwriting, buttoning clothing, tying shoe laces, and using silverware, but also for the oral-motor control involved in speaking, chewing, and swallowing. Reduced grip strength is common. *Gross motor control* is used for walking, running, jumping, lifting, etc. Some people with gross motor challenges have trouble synchronizing the movements of their arms, hands, legs, and feet, leading to difficulty with gait. People with *hypotonia* are "floppy," with poor core muscle strength, which leads to a need for some support while sitting, standing, or walking. People with hypotonia will sometimes toe walk after the age of 2, and can have poor balance, postural instability, and a clumsy gait. They touch the wall to stabilize themselves as they go downstairs or walk down the hall, and kids with hypotonia frequently lean on other kids during circle time. Another sign of hypotonia is W-sitting, in which the person sits on their bottom with their ankles and feet to either side of their hips, and their knees in front, creating a W shape if you look at their legs from above. This position allows a person to sit upright, even if they have weak core muscles.

Susanne Duvall and her co-authors note that motor challenges like these can have life-long consequences. Motor impairments can make it harder for children to play with others; adults and children with motor challenges can't participate as easily in games and sports. Difficulty with coordination can restrict vocational options, and make it harder to complete activities of daily living such as cooking, cleaning, self-care, and hygiene.

Tic disorders and Tourette syndrome: Tics are sudden, brief, repeated movements that are more likely to involve muscles in the eyes, face, head, and shoulders. Some tics involve vocalizations or sounds, like clicking the tongue. When both verbal and motor tics are present for more than a year, Tourette syndrome may be diagnosed. Tics are different from autistic motor stereotypies, which are typically more complex (involving the hands, arms, or entire body), more rhythmic, longer lasting (e.g., hand-flapping or finger-flicking), and have a purpose.

Another of Susanne Duvall and colleagues' "pink flags" for autism, tic disorders, and Tourette syndrome are much more common in autistic people than in the general population, where only 0.3–0.9% of people have them. Efrosini Kalyva's research team reported that 9–12% of autistic people have tic disorders (TDs), with Tourette syndrome present in 20% of autistics with average to above-average intelligence.

Seizures: Seizure disorders and epilepsy are much more common in autistic people. Lisa Croen's research team found that autistic people were 16 times more likely to have a seizure disorder than non-autistics! Susanne Duvall and her colleagues noted even higher prevalence rates, stating that "approximately 25–30% of individuals with [autism] experience seizures; patients with both [autism] and [intellectual disability] show the greatest risk for epilepsy." Interestingly, nearly 60% of autistic individuals have abnormal EEGs in the absence of clinical seizures, according to a study conducted by Howard Kim and his colleagues. This has functional implications; Jamie Capal and her research team noted that individuals who developed seizures were less able to care for themselves, more hyperactive, and rated themselves as having lower physical quality of life.

Migraines: While migraines are not more common in autistic people, neurologist Audrey Brumback (personal communication, 2021) suspects that they are grossly underdiagnosed because people who get them don't often know that debilitating headaches, nausea, fatigue, and malaise are not typical. Autistic people with low interoceptive awareness and alexithymia may have a more difficult time noticing that a migraine is imminent (when experiencing symptoms typical of prodrome and aura), and may experience something that looks to an outsider like fatigue, overwhelm, or just a regular headache.

Other health challenges

As mentioned earlier, autistic adults are much more likely than non-autistics to have *major chronic medical conditions affecting nearly every system* – immune, cardiovascular, metabolic, endocrine, neurological, gastrointestinal, hearing, vision, musculoskeletal, and pulmonary. Lisa Croen and her colleagues found that autistic women were more likely to have these conditions than their male counterparts, but all autistics were in worse health than otherwise similar non-autistics. We cannot describe all these conditions in the depth they deserve, so we will focus on three areas that can be particularly overlooked and underappreciated in autistic individuals. These include autoimmune conditions, dysautonomia/POTS (postural orthostatic tachycardia syndrome), and connective tissue disorders. And because these issues are often heritable, we end this section with a brief discussion of genetic disorders.

Autoimmune conditions: Guifeng Xu and her colleagues found that food, respiratory, and skin allergies are more common in autistic people, and a review by Amanda Enstrom and her colleagues found increased rates of type I diabetes, rheumatoid arthritis (RA), hypothyroidism, psoriasis, and systemic lupus erythematosus in the first-degree relatives of autistic individuals. Findings like these have led researchers to hypothesize that inflammatory responses may be associated with autism. This finding is corroborated by Theoharis Theoharides and his team at Tufts University School of Medicine. Over the past two decades, they have published numerous studies documenting the connection between stress and mast cell activation (MCAS), especially in autistic people. They hypothesize that it is this process that leads to the differences in synaptic pruning and neuronal connectivity in autism, resulting in a more sensitive stress response.

Dysautonomia/postural orthostatic tachycardia syndrome (POTS): The autonomic nervous system (ANS) regulates all of the physiological functions of our bodies that we do not consciously think about or control, such as heart rate, blood pressure, GI function, temperature regulation, circulation, and respiration (among others). Dysregulation of the ANS (dysautonomia) can be mild to debilitating, and usually involves multiple organ systems. Symptoms can include trouble with balance, dizziness, chronic tiredness and weakness, heart palpitations, swings in heart rate and blood pressure, exercise intolerance (heart rate doesn't adjust to changes in activity level), migraines or frequent headaches, difficulty regulating body and skin temperature, hypoglycemia, nausea, GI problems, dehydration, incontinence, sleep problems, noise/light sensitivity, blurred vision, forgetfulness and difficulty focusing, and mood swings.

A common sign of dysautonomia is orthostatic intolerance, which means it is difficult to stand still for long periods of time (10 minutes) without feeling faint or dizzy. Postural orthostatic tachycardia syndrome (POTS), a dysautonomia of the circulatory system, is not uncommon in the autistic people we see. When people with POTS stand up too quickly, they can experience a rapid increase in heartbeat, become lightheaded, and may even pass out (and POTS can bring other symptoms as well).

Connective tissue disorders: Connective tissue holds the structures of our body together. Defects in the genes that govern the formation of connective tissue can have an impact on many body systems, including the musculoskeletal system, the cardiovascular system, lungs, eyes, and skin. One of the more common connective tissue disorders is hypermobile Ehlers–Danlos Syndrome (hE–DS).

In 2020, Emily Casanova and her colleagues published a paper documenting the overlap in symptoms between people with Ehlers–Danlos syndromes/hypermobility spectrum disorders and autism. They found overlap in many areas that should, by now, be familiar. These include: DCD/dyspraxia, ADHD, learning disabilities, proprioception, anxiety, depression, bipolar disorder, suicidal behavior, eating disorders, seizure disorders, sleep disorders, over- and under-sensitivities – due to small fiber neuropathy that can lead to hyperalgesia (increased sensitivity to feeling pain and an extreme response to pain) and allodynia (extreme sensitivity to touch) – tachycardia, hypotension, gastrointestinal disorders (particularly those relating to motility), bladder dysfunction, poor temperature regulation, dysautonomias, instability/deformation of the brain stem/spinal cord, and mast cell activation syndrome.

In 2021, Andrew Owens and his colleagues in the UK examined the co-occurrence of autism, dysautonomia, and hE–DS by assessing the neuro-cardiovascular autonomic function in autistic and non-autistic populations. They found that many autistic individuals had difficulty modulating cardiovascular and temperature regulation systems, a finding that was even more pronounced in autistics with hE–DS.

More recently, Jennie Csecs and her colleagues investigated hypermobility, dysautonomia, and pain in neurodivergent adults with ADHD, Tourette's, and autism. Half of the neurodivergent adults had hypermobile joints. Importantly, the more hypermobile joints a neurodivergent participant had, the more likely they were to experience dysautonomia and musculoskeletal pain.

Genetic disorders: There have been countless studies dedicated to identifying how genetic variation is expressed in autism. Guillaume Huguet and his colleagues were able to identify a genetic cause for nearly 25% of the autistic people they studied. They noted that the genes they identified largely governed homeostasis in the nervous system. Likewise, Amanda Enstrom and her colleagues identified candidate genes governing the function of the immune system in autistic people. More recent work by Somer Bishop and her colleagues (2017) found that children with de novo (not inherited) mutations walked later than their peers with inherited genetic markers, but were otherwise less obviously autistic – they met fewer of the social communication criteria, and had better language skills. Clearly, genetic makeup contributes to each individual's presentation (autistic or not), though of course there are also neurobiological and environmental factors that can have an impact.

Other experiences

Having described emotional, cognitive, and medical conditions that are common in autistic people, there are four more areas of experience that don't fall into one of the above categories.

- Adaptive functioning

- Driving avoidance

- School avoidance

- Gender and attraction

Adaptive functioning

One of the more disconcerting realities of autism, increasingly apparent as autistic individuals move through adolescence and into adulthood, is that cognitive skills (and especially IQ) do not necessarily predict outcomes. Instead, outcomes are better predicted by an individual's ability to meet the demands of everyday living (a.k.a., *adaptive functioning*). These skills are the ones needed to navigate life independently – skills like personal care, managing a home, keeping a schedule, getting around in the community, and preparing meals.

In 2017, Julia Bascom and Gregory Wallace pointed out that an individual's quality of life relies heavily on these adaptive functioning skills. This has long been understood in autistic people with IQ < 70, but it is becoming increasingly clear that it is also true for autistic people with average or above-average IQs. Dr. Wallace was on a research team, headed by Cara Pugleise and her colleagues at the Children's National Medical Center, that was working to better understand this disconnect between IQ and adaptive functioning. Dr. Pugleise's team tracked adaptive skills through adolescence and found that the gains of autistic youth did not keep pace with those of their non-autistic peers through adolescence. A later study out of the same research center, this time headed by Catherine Kraper, tracked the gap between IQ and adaptive functioning and found that larger gaps between IQ and adaptive functioning predicted higher rates of depression and anxiety.

Ms. Bascom and Dr. Wallace wrote, "Poor adaptive skills without adequate supports may explain the dismal higher-education and employment rates among autistic adults. This is particularly true for those without intellectual disabilities, who may be presumed capable of attending college or pursuing competitive employment without a need for significant supports. In fact, however, these individuals often have significant impairments in basic day-to-day functions." This reflects our clinical experience and the lived experience of countless autistic individuals. Moreover, in these cases, these individuals must also cope with the blame and shame of "not living up to their potential."

Difficulty with adaptive functioning skills may become more evident or more pronounced with the transition to adulthood. Julie Lounds Taylor & Marsha Mailick Seltzer found that a significant number of autistic young adults experienced a substantial decline in independence and engagement in daily living skills over time; women were particularly vulnerable. And the worse the adaptive functioning, the lower the rates of employment.

The point here is not that all autistic people will have poor adaptive functioning; they won't. The point is that if you are working with a client whose adaptive functioning is surprisingly poor, consider whether there are other possible pink flags for autism.

Driving avoidance

In 2018, Nathan Wilson and his colleagues surveyed studies from around the world and found that between 66% and 91% of autistic people do not drive (as opposed to 32% of non-autistic people), and they get their driver's licenses two years later on average. Even when they do learn to drive, Brian Daly and his colleagues found that autistic drivers had more traffic violations than their non-autistic counterparts. Dr. Wilson's team reported that autistic people were concerned about their difficulties with multitasking, motor coordination, attention, planning, mental flexibility, and visual perception.

Dr. Wilson's team found that autistic drivers often took longer to master driving skills, and greatly benefited from training programs that used driving simulators. This led them to argue that new autistic drivers may eventually be successful with driving safely in many environments, though it may take them longer to qualify for their license.

From an expert: Reflection on driving

There is no way I could handle driving in Washington DC. Everything just moves too fast. I'd much rather take a bus than risk an accident just so I could get somewhere faster in a car.
                                                                    –Tom W.

Connecting culture: For a BIPOC autistic person and their family, especially for males, the fears around driving do not solely rest in the mechanics of driving or the anxiety the autistic person might have if pulled over by the authorities. For these adults and their families, driving avoidance and fears are entrenched in the historical racial biases and prejudices faced by people of color (especially males of color). For example, the racial profiling that is a reality for many Black males becomes a paralyzing fear for parents and partners of autistic Black males as they are keenly aware of the emotion dysregulation that could be triggered if their loved one were to be pulled over for a reason that didn't make sense to him.

Furthermore, behaviors that are viewed as obstinate in a non-Black autistic person may be viewed as aggressive and threatening in an autistic BIPOC male. This bias, combined with ignorance about the less effective nonverbal and verbal communication skills of autistic people, can lead to significantly negative outcomes.

School avoidance

We do not use the term *school refusal* because saying that a student is refusing school implies that they have made a conscious decision to avoid school. The term *school avoidance* allows for a broader range of motivations, including fear or overwhelm. It also acknowledges that the person may well want to go to school but may be too scared to do so.

Ellen Katherine Munkhaugen and her colleagues at Oslo University Hospital surveyed teachers in public schools in 2016, and found that school avoidance was significantly higher in autistic school-aged students (42.6%) compared to non-autistic students (7.1%). It is, in fact, so common among autistic students that, prior to the COVID-19 pandemic, when we saw clients who were avoiding school, we considered it to be a significant pink flag for autism.

Gender and attraction

We hesitated to include gender variation and attraction in a chapter on co-occurring conditions, because these are not conditions or disorders. However, it is also true that autistic people more often have non-cisgender identities, as well as variation in attraction to different genders.

Gender: The construct of *gender* is evolving along with our understanding of the many ways people can experience gender. By the time you read this, our understanding will almost certainly have evolved. This is our best attempt to capture what we know as of this writing in 2022.

- *Gender diversity* refers to the range of possible gender identities. Cultures around the world have long recognized that there are many genders; the gender binary that is dominant in current American society is only one possible social construct.

- *Gender assigned at birth*: Classification based on a combination of anatomy, hormones, and chromosomes as male, female, intersex, or another sex.

- *Gender identity*: A person's innate sense of their own gender – male, female, neither of these, both of these, or another gender(s).

  - *Transgender*: When the sex a person is assigned at birth and their internal sense of gender identity are not the same.

  - *Cisgender*: When sex assigned at birth and internal sense of gender identity are the same.

  - *Genderqueer*: a person who identifies as neither gender, both genders, or a combination.

    - *Non-binary*: Gender identity that is not solely male or female, that blends elements of being male or female, or is something other than male or female.

    - *Agender*: A person who does not identify as a particular gender or identifies outside of the gender spectrum altogether.

- *Gender expression/presentation*: The way people present their gender through behavior, clothing, hairstyle, makeup, interests, body shape, or choice of activities.

- *Gender fluidity*: When a person's gender expression and/or gender identity change over time, or consistently fluctuates across the gender spectrum.

There is another kind of gender that's not currently described in the research but is a part of some autistic people's experiences. *Autigender* is so influenced by being autistic that the very definition of gender (which is, after all, a social construct) cannot be unlinked from the person's way of thinking and being. David Jackson-Perry explains this by referring to the autistic trait of processing the world from the bottom up, without attending to the top-down constraints of social expectations about gender. "In this way, possibilities of gender expression are dictated not by what has been learnt to be possible but by what is experienced as real." This way of processing gender allows autistic people to "hold off from categorising themselves," so they can identify their gender "more loosely, until sufficient data [are] available, if at all." Autigender can and does coexist with other gender identities.

So, what does the research say about the autistic experience of gender? In 2014, John Strang and his colleagues found that autistic children were seven times more likely to be non-cisgendered than their non-autistic counterparts. In 2022, a team at the same clinic led by Blythe Corbett administered a more detailed questionnaire and learned that autistic children were specifically more likely to be transgender or genderqueer. We are not yet aware of any research on the long-term experiences of these individuals.

The parents of autistic children reported significantly more gender–body incongruence, with those who were assigned female at birth having significantly more gender–body incongruence than those assigned male at birth. This incongruence can cause a lot of distress, especially during puberty for those assigned female at birth. If your client is genderqueer or transgender, and has other pink flags, we strongly encourage you to consider the possibility of autism.

One of the more concerning findings from Dr. Strang's team is that 32% of gender-minority autistic people say their gender identity was questioned because of their autism diagnosis. This has an impact on the well-being of transgender and genderqueer autistic youth, who have higher rates of depression and anxiety. Varun Warrier and his team also found that transgender and genderqueer people have higher rates of other forms of neurodivergence, including ADHD, bipolar disorder, learning disorders, OCD, and schizophrenia.

From the experts: Reflections on gender

I don't think I'll ever label myself. I just don't get gender. My gender is a clearing in the woods, with a bunch of light shining on it, and there's a big tree stump. That's my gender.

–Josie E.

Gender, as well as the social norms based on it, has never made sense to me, especially after realizing that it's a social construct. As an autistic child, my disconnection from the human experience included gender. Growing up with my brother who is 17 months older than me, experiencing rules along with limitations that he did not, only deepened my disdain for the construct of gender, especially the binary. As an adult, I currently identify as an agender, autigender person.

—Asiatu

Attraction: Gender identity is different from attraction, which can be assessed across many distinct dimensions – including, for example, sexual, romantic, emotional, aesthetic, and platonic. As with gender, attraction is not binary and can be felt to differing degrees with people of different genders. Some autistic people identify as aromantic/asexual (sometimes referred to as *aro/ase*).

In part because of the autistic ability to evaluate gender and attraction without taking prior social constraints into account, our understanding is constantly evolving. When a client approaches you about their experiences in these domains, your acceptance, openness, and curiosity can establish trust as you help guide them through a process of better understanding themselves.

Note

1 The *Oxford Handbook of Autism and Co-Occurring Psychiatric Conditions* (2020) edited by Susan White, Brenna Maddox, and Carl Mazefsky has proven to be an invaluable resource for the sections of this chapter covering diagnoses recognized in the DSM-5-TR and the ICD-11. We refer you to that book for more detailed information regarding prevalence, presentation, and treatment options.

References and related reading

Antshel, K. M., Polacek, C., McMahon, M., Dygert, K., Spenceley, L., Dygert, L., Miller, L., & Faisal, F. (2011). Comorbid ADHD and anxiety affect social skills group intervention treatment efficacy in children with autism spectrum disorders. *Journal of Developmental & Behavioral Pediatrics*, 32(6), 439–446. https://doi.org/10.1097/DBP.0b013e318222355d

Au-Yeung, S. K., Bradley, L., Robertson, A. E., Shaw, R., Baron-Cohen, S., & Cassidy, S. (2019). Experience of mental health diagnosis and perceived misdiagnosis in autistic, possibly autistic and non-autistic adults. *Autism*, 23(6), 1508–1518.

Baron-Cohen, S., Johnson, D., Asher, J., Wheelwright, S., Fisher, S. E., Gregersen, P. K., & Allison, C. (2013). Is synaesthesia more common in autism? *Molecular Autism*, 4(1), 40. https://doi.org/10.1186/2040-2392-4-40

Bascom, J., & Wallace, G. (2017, November 28). Why intelligence scores do not predict success for autistic adults. *Spectrum | Autism Research News*. www.spectrumnews.org/opinion/viewpoint/intelligence-scores-not-predict-success-autistic-adults/

Bhat, A. N. (2020). Is motor impairment in autism spectrum disorder distinct from developmental coordination disorder? A report from the SPARK study. *Physical Therapy*, 100(4), 633–644. https://doi.org/10.1093/ptj/pzz190

Bishop, S. L., Farmer, C., Bal, V., Robinson, E. B., Willsey, A. J., Werling, D. M., ... & Thurm, A. (2017). Identification of developmental and behavioral markers associated with genetic abnormalities in autism spectrum disorder. *American Journal of Psychiatry*, 174(6), 576–585. https://doi.org/10.1176/appi.ajp.2017.16101115

Bishop, S. L., Thurm, A., Robinson, E., & Sanders, S. J. (2021). Prevalence of returnable genetic results based on recognizable phenotypes among children with autism spectrum disorder. *medRxiv*. https://doi.org/10.1101/2021.05.28.21257736

Capal, J. K., Macklin, E. A., Lu, F., & Barnes, G. (2020). Factors associated with seizure onset in children with autism spectrum disorder. *Pediatrics*, 145(Suppl. 1), S117–S125. https://doi.org/10.1542/peds.2019-1895O

Carmassi, C., Palagini, L., Caruso, D., Masci, I., Nobili, L., Vita, A., & Dell'Osso, L. (2019). Systematic review of sleep disturbances and circadian sleep desynchronization in autism spectrum disorder: toward an integrative model of a self-reinforcing loop. *Frontiers in Psychiatry*, 10. www.frontiersin.org/article/10.3389/fpsyt.2019.00366

Casanova, E. L., Baeza-Velasco, C., Buchanan, C. B., & Casanova, M. F. (2020). The relationship between autism and Ehlers–Danlos syndromes/hypermobility spectrum disorders. *Journal of Personalized Medicine*, 10(4), 260. https://doi.org/10.3390/jpm10040260

Cassidy, S. (2020). Suicidality and self-harm in autism spectrum conditions. In S. W. White, B. B. Maddox, & C. Mazefsky (Eds.), *The Oxford handbook of autism and co-occurring psychiatric conditions*. Oxford University Press.

Cassidy, S., Bradley, L., Shaw, R., & Baron-Cohen, S. (2018). Risk markers for suicidality in autistic adults. *Molecular Autism*, 9(1), 42. https://doi.org/10.1186/s13229-018-0226-4

Corbett, B. A., Muscatello, R. A., Klemencic, M. E., West, M., Kim, A., & Strang, J. F. (2022). Greater gender diversity among autistic children by self-report and parent-report. *Autism: The International Journal of Research and Practice.* https://doi.org/10.1177/13623613221085337

Croen, L. A., Zerbo, O., Qian, Y., Massolo, M. L., Rich, S., Sidney, S., & Kripke, C. (2015). The health status of adults on the autism spectrum. *Autism: The International Journal of Research and Practice, 19*(7), 814–823. https://doi.org/10.1177/1362361315577517

Cruz, F., Pulido, A., Ampolos, L., LaMarca, K., Keehn, R., & Lincoln, A. (2010). Characteristics of anxiety in children with co-occurring autism spectrum and anxiety disorders. Poster session presented at the International Meeting for Autism Research, Philadelphia, PA.

Csecs, J. L. L., Iodice, V., Rae, C. L., Brooke, A., Simmons, R., Quadt, L., ... & Eccles, J. A. (2022). Joint hypermobility links neurodivergence to dysautonomia and pain. *Frontiers in Psychiatry, 12.* www.frontiersin.org/article/10.3389/fpsyt.2021.786916

Daly, B. P., Nicholls, E. G., Patrick, K. E., Brinckman, D. D., & Schultheis, M. T. (2014). Driving behaviors in adults with autism spectrum disorders. *Journal of Autism and Developmental Disorders, 44*(12), 3119–3128. https://doi.org/10.1007/s10803-014-2166-y

Danielsson, S., Gillberg, I. C., Billstedt, E., Gillberg, C., & Olsson, I. (2005). Epilepsy in young adults with autism: A prospective population-based follow-up study of 120 individuals diagnosed in childhood. *Epilepsia, 46*(6), 918–923. https://doi.org/10.1111/j.1528-1167.2005.57504.x

Díaz-Román, A., Zhang, J., Delorme, R., Beggiato, A., & Cortese, S. (2018). Sleep in youth with autism spectrum disorders: Systematic review and meta-analysis of subjective and objective studies. *Evidence-Based Mental Health, 21*(4), 146–154. https://doi.org/10.1136/ebmental-2018-300037

Dinkler, L., Yasumitsu-Lovell, K., Eitoku, M., Fujieda, M., Suganuma, N., Hatakenaka, Y., ... & Gillberg, C. (2021). Early neurodevelopmental problems and risk for avoidant/restrictive food intake disorder (ARFID) in the general child population: A Japanese birth cohort study. *medRxiv.* https://doi.org/10.1101/2021.11.08.21265646

Dodson, J. (2020, July 29). New insights into rejection sensitive dysphoria. *ADDitude.* www.additudemag.com/rejection-sensitive-dysphoria-adhd-emotional-dysregulation/

Duvall, S., Armstrong, K., Shahabuddin, A., Grantz, C., Fein, D., & Lord, C. (2021). A road map for identifying autism spectrum disorder: Recognizing and evaluating characteristics that should raise red or "pink" flags to guide accurate differential diagnosis. *The Clinical Neuropsychologist*, *36*(5), 1–36. https://doi.org/10.1080/13854046.2021.1921276

Eigsti, I.-M., de Marchena, A. B., Schuh, J. M., & Kelley, E. (2011). Language acquisition in autism spectrum disorders: A developmental review. *Research in Autism Spectrum Disorders*, *5*(2), 681–691. https://doi.org/10.1016/j.rasd.2010.09.001

Ekinci, O., İpek Baş, S. A., Ekinci, N., Doğan, Ö. I., Yaşöz, C., & Adak, İ. (2021). Sluggish cognitive tempo is associated with autistic traits and anxiety disorder symptoms in children with attention-deficit/hyperactivity disorder. *Revista Brasileira de Psiquiatria*, *43*(2), 153–159. https://doi.org/10.1590/1516-4446-2020-0965

Ellis Weismer, S., Lord, C., & Esler, A. (2010). Early language patterns of toddlers on the autism spectrum compared to toddlers with developmental delay. *Journal of Autism and Developmental Disorders*, *40*(10), 1259–1273. https://doi.org/10.1007/s10803-010-0983-1

Enstrom, A. M., Van de Water, J. A., & Ashwood, P. (2009). Autoimmunity in autism. *Current Opinion in Investigational Drugs*, *10*(5), 463–473.

Fosdick, C. M., Wink, L. K., McClellan, L., Dominick, K. C., Pedapati, E. V., & Erickson, C. A. (2017). Pharmacologic treatment options for children and adolescents with autism spectrum disorder. *The Pharmaceutical Journal*. https://pharmaceutical-journal.com/article/research/pharmacologic-treatment-options-for-children-and-adolescents-with-autism-spectrum-disorder

Frazier, J. A., Doyle, R., Chiu, S., & Coyle, J. T. (2002). Treating a child with Asperger's disorder and comorbid bipolar disorder. *American Journal of Psychiatry*, *159*(1), 13–21. https://doi.org/10.1176/appi.aip.159.1.13

Gioia, G. A., Isquith, P. K., Guy, S. C., & Kenworthy, L. (2000). Test review: Behavior Rating Inventory of Executive Function. *Child Neuropsychology*, *6*(3), 235–238. https://doi.org/10.1076/chin.6.3.235.3152

Griffiths, S., Allison, C., Kenny, R., Holt, R., Smith, P., & Baron-Cohen, S. (2002). The Vulnerability Experiences Quotient (VEQ): A study of vulnerability, mental health and life satisfaction in autistic adults. *Autism Research*, *12*(10), 1516–1528. https://doi.org/10.1002/aur.2162

Happé, F., & Frith, U. (2006). The weak coherence account: Detail-focused cognitive style in autism spectrum disorders. *Journal of Autism and Developmental Disorders*, *36*(1), 5–25. https://doi.org/10.1007/s10803-005-0039-0

Henderson, D. (in press). *Is this autism? A companion guide for diagnosing.* New York: Routledge.

Hill, A. P., Zuckerman, K. E., & Fombonne, E. (2015). Obesity and autism. *Pediatrics, 136*(6), 1051–1061. https://doi.org/10.1542/peds.2015-1437

Hirvikoski, T., Mittendorfer-Rutz, E., Boman, M., Larsson, H., Lichtenstein, P., & Bölte, S. (2016). Premature mortality in autism spectrum disorder. *The British Journal of Psychiatry: The Journal of Mental Science, 208*(3), 232–238. https://doi.org/10.1192/bjp.bp.114.160192

Hoover, D. W., & Romero, E. M. G. (2019). The Interactive Trauma Scale: A web-based measure for children with autism. *Journal of Autism and Developmental Disorders, 49*(4), 1686–1692. https://doi.org/10.1007/s10803-018-03864-3

Hossain, M. M., Khan, N., Sultana, A., Ma, P., McKyer, E. L. J., Ahmed, H. U., & Purohit, N. (2020). Prevalence of comorbid psychiatric disorders among people with autism spectrum disorder: An umbrella review of systematic reviews and meta-analyses. *Psychiatry Research, 287*, 112922. https://doi.org/10.1016/j.psychres.2020.112922

Hudson, C. C., Hall, L., & Harkness, K. L. (2019). Prevalence of depressive disorders in individuals with autism spectrum disorder: A meta-analysis. *Journal of Abnormal Child Psychology, 47*(1), 165–175. https://doi.org/10.1007/s10802-018-0402-1

Huguet, G., Ey, E., & Bourgeron, T. (2013). The genetic landscapes of autism spectrum disorders. *Annual Review of Genomics and Human Genetics, 14*(1), 191–213. https://doi.org/10.1146/annurev-genom-091212-153431

Huke, V., Turk, J., Saeidi, S., Kent, A., & Morgan, J. F. (2013). Autism spectrum disorders in eating disorder populations: A systematic review. *European Eating Disorders Review, 21*(5), 345–351. https://doi.org/10.1002/erv.2244

Jaber, M. A. (2011). Dental caries experience, oral health status and treatment needs of dental patients with autism. *Journal of Applied Oral Science, 19*(3), 212–217. https://doi.org/10.1590/S1678-775720 11000300006

Jackson-Perry, D. (2020). The autistic art of failure? Unknowing imperfect systems of sexuality and gender. *Scandinavian Journal of Disability Research, 22*(1), 221–229. https://doi.org/10.16993/sjdr.634

Jónsdóttir, S. L., Saemundsen, E., Antonsdóttir, I. S., Sigurdardóttir, S., & Ólason, D. (2011). Children diagnosed with autism spectrum disorder before or after the age of 6 years. *Research in Autism Spectrum Disorders*, 5(1), 175–184. https://doi.org/10.1016/j.rasd.2010.03.007

Kalyva, E., Kyriazi, M., Vargiami, E., & Zafeiriou, D. I. (2016). A review of co-occurrence of autism spectrum disorder and Tourette syndrome. *Research in Autism Spectrum Disorders*, 24, 39–51. https://doi.org/10.1016/j.rasd.2016.01.007

Kaufman, R. (n.d.). Your child is having a neuro-crash: What it is, how to spot it, and ways to prevent it. *Exceptional Needs Today*. https://issuu.com/exceptionalneedstoday/docs/ent_n3_final/s/12110492

Kim, H. L., Donnelly, J. H., Tournay, A. E., Book, T. M., & Filipek, P. (2006). Absence of seizures despite high prevalence of epileptiform EEG abnormalities in children with autism monitored in a tertiary care center. *Epilepsia*, 47(2), 394–398. https://doi.org/10.1111/j.1528-1167.2006.00434.x

King, B., Rynkiewicz, A., Janas-Kozik, M., & Tyszkiewicz-Nafor, M. (2020). Medications to treat co-occurring psychiatric conditions in autism spectrum disorder. In S. W. White, B. B. Maddox, & C. Mazefsky (Eds.), *The Oxford handbook of autism and co-occurring psychiatric conditions* (370–386. Oxford University Press.

Klein, E. R., Ruiz, C. E., Morales, K., & Stanley, P. (2019). Variations in parent and teacher ratings of internalizing, externalizing, adaptive skills, and behavioral symptoms in children with selective mutism. International *Journal of Environmental Research and Public Health*, 16(21), 4070. https://doi.org/10.3390/ijerph16214070

Koomar, T., Thomas, T. R., Pottschmidt, N. R., Lutter, M., & Michaelson, J. J. (2021). Estimating the prevalence and genetic risk mechanisms of ARFID in a large autism cohort. *Frontiers in Psychiatry*, 12. www.frontiersin.org/article/10.3389/fpsyt.2021.668297

Kraper, C. K., Kenworthy, L., Popal, H., Martin, A., & Wallace, G. L. (2011). The gap between adaptive behavior and intelligence in autism persists into young adulthood and is linked to psychiatric comorbidities. *Journal of Autism and Developmental Disorders*, 47(10), 3007–3017. https://doi.org/10.1007/s10803-017-3213-2

Lai, C. L. E., Lau, Z., Lui, S. S. Y., Lok, E., Tam, V., Chan, Q., ... & Cheung, E. F. C. (2017). Meta-analysis of neuropsychological measures of executive functioning in children and adolescents with high-functioning autism spectrum disorder. *Autism Research*, 10(5), 911–939. https://doi.org/10.1002/aur.1723

Lai, M.-C., Kassee, C., Besney, R., Bonato, S., Hull, L., Mandy, M., ... & Ameis, S. H. (2019). Prevalence of co-occurring mental health diagnoses in the autism population: A systematic review and meta-analysis. *Lancet Psychiatry*, 6(10), 819–829. https://doi.org/10.1016/S2215-0366(19)30289-5

Lau, B. Y., Leong, R., Uljarevic, M., Lerh, J. W., Rodgers, J., Hollocks, M. J., ... & Magiati, I. (2020). Anxiety in young people with autism spectrum disorder: Common and autism-related anxiety experiences and their associations with individual characteristics. *Autism*, 24(5), 1111–1126. https://doi.org/10.1177/1362361319886246

Leyfer, O. T., Folstein, S. E., Bacalman, S., Davis, N. O., Dinh, E., Morgan, J., Tager-Flusberg, H., & Lainhart, J. E. (2006). Comorbid psychiatric disorders in children with autism: Interview development and rates of disorders. *Journal of Autism and Developmental Disorders*, 36(7), 849–861. https://doi.org/10.1007/s10803-006-0123-0

Mahler, K., McLaughlin, E., & Anson, D. (2020). Interoception across varying degrees of mental wellness. *American Journal of Occupational Therapy*, 74(S1), https://doi.org/10.5014/ajot.2020.74S1-PO9513

Mantzalas, J., Richdale, A. L., Adikari, A., Lowe, J., & Dissanayake, C. (2022). What is autistic burnout? A thematic analysis of posts on two online platforms. *Autism in Adulthood*, 4(1), 52–65. https://doi.org/10.1089/aut.2021.0021

Matthews, N. L., Smith, C. J., Pollard, E., Ober-Reynolds, S., Kirwan, J., & Malligo, A. (2015). Adaptive functioning in autism spectrum disorder during the transition to adulthood. *Journal of Autism and Developmental Disorders*, 45(8), 2349–2360. https://doi.org/10.1007/s10803-015-2400-2

Minio-Paluello, I., Porciello, G., Pascual-Leone, A., & Baron-Cohen, S. (2020). Face individual identity recognition: A potential endophenotype in autism. *Molecular Autism*, 11(1), 81. https://doi.org/10.1186/s13229-020-00371-0

Moseley, R. L., Druce, T., & Turner-Cobb, J. M. (2020). 'When my autism broke': A qualitative study spotlighting autistic voices on menopause. *Autism*, 24(6), 1423–1437. https://doi.org/10.1177/1362361319901184

Mottron, L., Dawson, M., Soulières, I., Hubert, B., & Burack, J. (2006). Enhanced perceptual functioning in autism: An update, and eight principles of autistic perception. *Journal of Autism and Developmental Disorders*, 36(1), 27–43. https://doi.org/10.1007/s10803-005-0040-7

Munkhaugen, E. K., Gjevik, E., Pripp, A. H., Sponheim, E., & Diseth, T. H. (2017). School refusal behaviour: Are children and adolescents with autism spectrum disorder at a higher risk? *Research in Autism Spectrum Disorders*, 41–42, 31–38. https://doi.org/10.1016/j.rasd.2017.07.001

Muris, P., & Ollendick, T. H. (2021). Selective mutism and its relations to social anxiety disorder and autism spectrum disorder. *Clinical Child and Family Psychology Review*, 24(2), 294–325. https://doi.org/10.1007/s10567-020-00342-0

Murray, D., Lesser, M., & Lawson, W. (2005). Attention, monotropism and the diagnostic criteria for autism. *Autism*, 9(2), 139–156. https://doi.org/10.1177/1362361305051398

Naigles, L. R., Cheng, M., Xu Rattanasone, N., Tek, S., Khetrapal, N., Fein, D., & Demuth, K. (2016). "You're telling me!" The prevalence and predictors of pronoun reversals in children with autism spectrum disorders and typical development. *Research in Autism Spectrum Disorders*, 27, 11–20. https://doi.org/10.1016/j.rasd.2016.03.008

Newson, E., Le Maréchal, K., & David, C. (2003). Pathological demand avoidance syndrome: A necessary distinction within the pervasive developmental disorders. *Archives of Disease in Childhood*, 88, 595–600. http://dx.doi.org/10.1136/adc.88.7.595

Ostrolenk, A., Forgeot d'Arc, B., Jelenic, P., Samson, F., & Mottron, L. (2017). Hyperlexia: Systematic review, neurocognitive modeling, and outcome. *Neuroscience & Biobehavioral Reviews*, 79, 134–149. https://doi.org/10.1016/j.neubiorev.2017.04.029

Overweg, J., Hartman, C. A., & Hendriks, P. (2018). Children with autism spectrum disorder show pronoun reversals in interpretation. *Journal of Abnormal Psychology*, 127(2), 228–238. https://doi.org/10.1037/abn0000338

Owens, A. P., Mathias, C. J., & Iodice, V. (2021). Autonomic dysfunction in autism spectrum disorder. *Frontiers in Integrative Neuroscience*, 15. www.frontiersin.org/article/10.3389/fnint.2021.787037

Poquérusse, J., Pastore, L., Dellantonio, S., & Esposito, G. (2018). Alexithymia and autism spectrum disorder: A complex relationship. *Frontiers in Psychology*, 9, 1196. https://doi.org/10.3389/fpsyg.2018.01196

Pugliese, C. E., Anthony, L., Strang, J. F., Dudley, K., Wallace, G. L., & Kenworthy, L. (2015). Increasing adaptive behavior skill deficits from childhood to adolescence in autism spectrum disorder: Role of executive function. *Journal of Autism and Developmental Disorders*, 45(6), 1579–1587. https://doi.org/10.1007/s10803-014-2309-1

Pugliese, C. E., Wallace, G. L., Anthony, L. G., & Kenworthy, L. (2020). Understanding executive function challenges in autism spectrum disorder. In S. W. White, B. B. Maddox, & C. Mazefsky (Eds.), *The Oxford handbook of autism and co-occurring psychiatric conditions* (305–325). Oxford University Press.

Raymaker, D. M., Teo, A. R., Steckler, N. A., Lentz, B., Scharer, M., Santos, A. D., ... & Nicolaidis, C. (2020). "Having all of your internal resources exhausted beyond measure and being left with no clean-up crew": Defining autistic burnout. *Autism in Adulthood.* https://doi.org/10.1089/aut.2019.0079

Rumball, F., Happé, F., & Grey, N. (2020). Experience of trauma and PTSD symptoms in autistic adults: Risk of PTSD development following DSM-5 and non-DSM-5 traumatic life events. *Autism Research*, *13*(12), 2122–2132. https://doi.org/10.1002/aur.2306

Scahill, L., Lecavalier, L., Schultz, R. T., Evans, A. N., Maddox, B., Pritchett, J., ... & Edwards, M. C. (2019). Development of the Parent-Related Anxiety Scale for youth with autism spectrum disorder. *Journal of the American Academy of Child and Adolescent Psychiatry*, *58*(9), 887–896. https://doi.org/10.1016/j.jaac.2018.10.016

Scarborough, H. S., Rescorla, L., Tager-Flusberg, H., Fowler, A. E., & Sudhalter, V. (1991). The relation of utterance length to grammatical complexity in normal and language-disordered groups. *Applied Psycholinguistics*, *12*(1), 23–46. https://doi.org/10.1017/S014271640000936X

Schöttle, D., Briken, P., Tüscher, O., & Turner, D. (2017). Sexuality in autism: Hypersexual and paraphilic behavior in women and men with high-functioning autism spectrum disorder. *Dialogues in Clinical Neuroscience*, *19*(4), 381–393. https://doi.org/10.31887/DCNS.2017.19.4/dschoettle

Sedgewick, F., Leppanen, J., & Tchanturia, K. (2020). Gender differences in mental health prevalence in autism. *Advances in Autism*, *7*(3), 208–224. https://doi.org/10.1108/aia-01-2020-0007

Serdarevic, F., Ghassabian, A., van Batenburg-Eddes, T., White, T., Blanken, L. M. E., Jaddoe, V. W. V., Verhulst, F. C., & Tiemeier, H. (2017). Infant muscle tone and childhood autistic traits: A longitudinal study in the general population. *Autism Research*, *10*(5), 757–768. https://doi.org/10.1002/aur.1739

Simantov, T., Pohl, A., Tsompanidis, A., Weir, E., Lombardo, M. V., Ruigrok, A., ... & Uzefovsky, F. (2022). Medical symptoms and conditions in autistic women. *Autism*, *26*(2), 373–388. https://doi.org/10.1177/13623613211022091

Smith, L. E., Maenner, M. J., & Seltzer, M. M. (2012). Developmental trajectories in adolescents and adults with autism: The case of daily living skills. *Journal of the American Academy of Child and Adolescent Psychiatry*, *51*(6), 622–631. https://doi.org/10.1016/j.jaac.2012.03.001

Solmi, F., Bentivegna, F., Bould, H., Mandy, W., Kothari, R., Rai, D., Skuse, D., & Lewis, G. (2021). Trajectories of autistic social traits in childhood and adolescence and disordered eating behaviours at age 14 years: A UK general population cohort study. *Journal of Child Psychology and Psychiatry*, 62(1), 75–85. https://doi.org/10.1111/jcpp.13255

Steffenburg, H., Steffenburg, S., Gillberg, C., & Billstedt, E. (2018). Children with autism spectrum disorders and selective mutism. *Neuropsychiatric Disease and Treatment*, 14, 1163–1169. https://doi.org/10.2147/NDT.S154966

Strang, J. F., Kenworthy, L., Dominska, A., Sokoloff, J., Kenealy, L. E., Berl, M., ... & Wallace, G. L. (2014). Increased gender variance in autism spectrum disorders and attention deficit hyperactivity disorder. *Archives of Sexual Behavior*, 43(8), 1525–1533. https://doi.org/10.1007/s10508-014-0285-3

Strang, J. F., Powers, M. D., Knauss, M., Sibarium, E., Leibowitz, S. F., Kenworthy, L., ... & Anthony, L. G. (2018). "They thought it was an obsession": Trajectories and perspectives of autistic transgender and gender-diverse adolescents. *Journal of Autism and Developmental Disorders*, 48(12), 4039–4055. https://doi.org/10.1007/s10803-018-3723-6

Tager-Flusberg, H., Rogers, S., Cooper, J., Landa, R., Lord, C., Paul, R., ... & Yoder, P. (2009). Defining spoken language benchmarks and selecting measures of expressive language development for young children with autism spectrum disorders. *Journal of Speech, Language, and Hearing Research*, 52(3), 643–652. https://doi.org/10.1044/1092-4388(2009/08-0136)

Taylor, G. J., Bagby, R. M., Parker, J. D. A., & Grotstein, J. (1997). *Disorders of affect regulation: Alexithymia in medical and psychiatric illness* (1st ed.). Cambridge University Press. https://doi.org/10.1017/CBO9780511526831

Taylor, J. L., & Seltzer, M. M. (2010). Changes in the autism behavioral phenotype during the transition to adulthood. *Journal of Autism and Developmental Disorders*, 40(12), 1431–1446. https://doi.org/10.1007/s10803-010-1005-z

Taylor, J. L., Smith, L. E., & Mailick, M. R. (2014). Engagement in vocational activities promotes behavioral development for adults with autism spectrum disorders. *Journal of Autism and Developmental Disorders*, 44(6), 1447–1460. https://doi.org/10.1007/s10803-013-2010-9

Tek, S., Mesite, L., Fein, D., & Naigles, L. (2014). Longitudinal analyses of expressive language development reveal two distinct language profiles among young children with autism spectrum disorders. *Journal of Autism and Developmental Disorders*, 44(1), 75–89. https://doi.org/10.1007/s10803-013-1853-4

Theoharides, T. C., Kavalioti, M., & Tsilioni, I. (2019). Mast cells, stress, fear and autism spectrum disorder. *International Journal of Molecular Sciences*, 20(15), 3611. http://dx.doi.org/10.3390/ijms20153611

Thompson, H. (2019). *The PDA paradox: The highs and lows of my life on a little-known part of the autism spectrum.* Jessica Kingsley Publishers. https://uk.jkp.com/products/the-pda-paradox

Tye, C., Runicles, A. K., Whitehouse, A. J. O., & Alvares, G. A. (2019). Characterizing the interplay between autism spectrum disorder and comorbid medical conditions: An integrative review. *Frontiers in Psychiatry*, 9. www.frontiersin.org/article/10.3389/fpsyt.2018.00751

Vermeulen, P. (2012). *Autism as context blindness.* AAPC Publishing.

Vermeulen, P. (2021). *Autisme en het voorspellende brein: Absoluut denken in een relatieve wereld.* Pelckmans Publishers.

Vivanti, G., & Hamilton, A. (2014). Imitation in autism spectrum disorders. In *Handbook of autism and pervasive developmental disorders: Diagnosis, development, and brain mechanisms* (4th ed., Vol. 1, pp. 278–301). John Wiley.

Warrier, V., Greenberg, D. M., Weir, E., Buckingham, C., Smith, P., Lai, M.-C., Allison, C., & Baron-Cohen, S. (2020). Elevated rates of autism, other neurodevelopmental and psychiatric diagnoses, and autistic traits in transgender and gender-diverse individuals. *Nature Communications*, 11(1), 3959. https://doi.org/10.1038/s41467-020-17794-1

Wechsler, D. (2014). *Wechsler Intelligence Scale for Children* (5th ed.). Bloomington, MN: NCS Pearson.

Weimer, A. K., Schatz, A. M., Lincoln, A., Ballantyne, A. O., & Trauner, D. A. (2001). "Motor" impairment in Asperger syndrome: Evidence for a deficit in proprioception. *Journal of Developmental & Behavioral Pediatrics*, 22(2), 92–101.

White, S. W., Maddox, B. B. & Mazefsky, C. (Eds.). (2020). *The Oxford handbook of autism and co-occurring psychiatric conditions.* Oxford University Press.

Wilding, T. (2020, April 4). Changing the name PDA. *Tomlin Wilding: Neuropsychology Specialist.* https://tomlinwilding.com/changing-the-name-pda/

Williamson, P., Carnahan, C. R., & Jacobs, J. A. (2012). Reading comprehension profiles of high-functioning students on the autism spectrum: A grounded theory. *Exceptional Children*, 78(4), 449–469. https://doi.org/10.1177/001440291207800404

Wilson, N. J., Lee, H. C., Vaz, S., Vindin, P., & Cordier, R. (2018). Scoping review of the driving behaviour of and driver training programs for people on the autism spectrum. *Behavioural Neurology*, *2018*, 6842306. https://doi.org/10.1155/2018/6842306

Xu, G., Snetselaar, L. G., Jing, J., Liu, B., Strathearn, L., & Bao, W. (2018). Association of food allergy and other allergic conditions with autism spectrum disorder in children. *JAMA Network Open*, *1*(2), e180279. https://doi.org/10.1001/jamanetworkopen.2018.0279

Yerys, B. E., Bertollo, J. R., Pandey, J., Guy, L., & Schultz, R. T. (2019). Attention-deficit/hyperactivity disorder symptoms are associated with lower adaptive behavior skills in children with autism. *Journal of the American Academy of Child & Adolescent Psychiatry*, *58*(5), 525–533. https://doi.org/10.1016/j.jaac.2018.08.017

Chapter 10

Autistic strengths

When someone enters therapy or requests an assessment, it is often because they are having trouble effectively navigating their world. They, or their parents, want to understand whether there is something that is making it particularly difficult for them to function, meet their goals, or feel safe and content. This leads clinicians to focus on the challenges, but it's important to remember that all people are complex, and that each of us has our own pattern of strengths as well as weaknesses. This understanding is an important part of the neurodiversity paradigm.

It's also true that a **weakness in one situation may be a strength in a different situation.** Someone who has trouble listening when there is a lot of background noise may look "impaired" when talking with friends in a restaurant. But that same person may be a terrific audio engineer; their ability to analyze and segment different sounds will allow them to seamlessly edit voice samples or create compelling soundtracks. As Temple Grandin so eloquently stated in her book with Richard Panek, *The Autistic Brain: Thinking Across the Spectrum*, "If people can consciously recognize the strengths and weaknesses in their ways of thinking, they can then seek out the right kinds of minds for the right reasons. And if they do that, then they're going to recognize that sometimes the right mind can belong only to an autistic brain." (Temple Grandin is one of the few people who has studied autistic strengths in depth. For this reason, she is frequently quoted in this chapter.)

DOI: 10.4324/9781003242130-13

Some people believe that autistic people have superpowers. This is reinforced by popular culture depictions of autistic people with *savant syndrome* (for example, Raymond Babbitt's incredible memory, as depicted in the movie *Rain Man*). Individuals with savant syndrome have profound abilities that are unexpected, given their abilities in other areas. While savant syndrome occurs more often in autistic people (10–28% of the time) than in the general population (where it occurs only 1% of the time), it is certainly not part of every autistic person's profile. It is critically important to allow autistic people the privilege of having no superpowers, just as we allow non-autistic people that privilege. That said, everyone has a profile with relative strengths and challenges. Highlighting individual strengths is important, because when a person knows what they are good at, it can help them focus on developing and nurturing their strengths. This is much more heartening and hopeful than focusing all their energy on "fixing" themselves.

In this spirit, we encourage you to consider the talents, skills, and qualities that may be present in the autistic individuals in your life. And while no autistic person will have all the strengths we describe, our hope is that reading this chapter will prompt you to consider some possibilities. This chapter covers seven areas in which we have noted substantial strengths in our autistic clients. These include: (1) sensory differences; (2) cognition; (3) intense interests; (4) consistency; (5) social communication; (6) humor; and (7) grit. Some of these areas were discussed earlier as part of the diagnostic criteria; here you will learn about how they can be strengths in the right environment. As you will see, these traits allow autistic people to contribute to society and the world in unique and valuable ways.

Sensory differences

As noted earlier, enough autistic people have sensory differences to warrant their inclusion in the diagnostic criteria for autism. While these sensory experiences can interfere with a person's life, there are also contexts in which they can be helpful. For example, many autistic people report that their heightened sensory awareness keeps them alert to danger in their surroundings even while they focus on another task. They might smell something burning or notice a chemical odor indicating a leak long before other people do. Or they might hear rodents in the walls or detect a sagging floor when looking for a new place to live.

Visual: Autistic people can be **highly attuned to visual information**. There are countless reports of autistic people noticing visual details that others miss, and even seeing things that others cannot. This is not necessarily due to better visual acuity; rather, it seems to be the result of different wiring that can allow them to notice details and recognize objects more easily. This ability to notice details can contribute to unique problem-solving abilities.

Auditory: Some autistic people are **attuned to different aspects of sound**. In addition to hearing sounds that are imperceptible to others, roughly 5% of autistic people can accurately identify the pitch of a tone without comparing it to a known standard (like a pitch pipe or a tuning fork). This ability to determine absolute pitch is seen in only 0.05% of the general population and can be invaluable to musicians, composers, and sound engineers, among others.

Other auditory abilities involve accurately discriminating between frequencies (pitches), or tracking many sounds simultaneously or monitoring for a particular sound in a noisy environment. This skill can help in a wide range of tasks, from diagnosing mechanical issues in a motor to listening for a visitor to arrive. These abilities can extend to the realm of spoken language, with some autistic people showing a remarkable sensitivity to changes in a person's emotional state, as reflected in the rhythm, melody, and volume of their speech, or noticing speech sounds (phonemes) in a new language they are learning.

> Marguerite was very sensitive to sounds and easily overwhelmed during concerts or movies. As an adult, she became a sound engineer. Her ability to hear the subtle transitions in speech and music allowed her to create soundtracks from multiple sources that sounded like they were recorded in one uninterrupted session.

Smell, taste, touch, proprioception, and vestibular sensations: Other sensory differences can also prove invaluable. Being able to smell food that is about to go bad, or taste something that is off in your dinner, can make you less likely to eat something that will give you food poisoning. It can also give you an excellent nose for wine or enable you to create amazing recipes. A woodworker relies on sensitivity to textures (touch) to create a perfect finish, and a baker has to know when the dough they are kneading has developed just the right consistency. Athletes develop an exquisite understanding of how their bodies are positioned and how they need to move (proprioception), and roofers need to be able to keep their balance in high places (vestibular sensations). Alternatively, people with high pain tolerance can wear clothing that others may not be able to tolerate (fashion!) or do things that would cause pain to others (e.g., pull a hot pan out of the oven with flimsy pot holders).

From the experts: Reflections about sensory strengths

> I would say that I'm both quite detail attentive and very visual – this is my main strength I believe. I can remember visual details [which] made my mapping/GIS courses a lot less difficult.
>
> –Zachary M.

> I'm super observant. I'm always scanning around my environment and processing information. Because of that, I pick up on many things that others don't even notice.
>
> –Noelle B.

> It doesn't bother me when clothes are too tight or shoes are too small. I can wear anything I want to!
>
> –Grace O.

Cognitive processes

Autistic people can have many cognitive strengths. Their different wiring means that they may process information in ways that others don't, potentially resulting in unusual problem-solving abilities, creativity, and insights.

Memory: Some autistic people also have an **astonishing ability to absorb and retain detailed information** in areas of interest. They might have an uncanny memory for dates, train schedules, software product codes, sports statistics, history, geography, and other areas.

> When Jon was 4 years old, his parents discovered that he was able to remember a person's birthday (day, month, and year) after hearing it only once. For years, they would host parties at their house and ask their son to recite the birthdays of their friends he had previously met, but whom he hadn't seen in many months. As an adult, Jon remembers dates that are important for his job, which allows him to manage complex projects without ever missing a deadline.

Associative thinking: Some autistic people are remarkable at **making associations** that others would not think of. These range from unexpected connections between ideas to generating creative breakthroughs in science and art. As Allie S. tells us, "*I am a crafter/ artist, and the way I think about and sometimes spontaneously create art involves creative and unexpected associations. I also think it makes me a good teacher.*"

Attention: In 2005, Dinah Murray and her colleagues proposed that a **narrow and intense focus of attention** is a core feature of autistic nervous systems. Though *monotropism* explains challenges such as difficulty shifting attention, it also explains some autistic strengths, including an ability to focus deeply on an intense interest, and attention to detail, among others. The remarkable **ability to notice details** that other people miss is not necessarily due to better visual perception. Rather, the narrow and intense focus of attention enhances perceptual clarity in the regions where the focus is directed. People with this intense ability to focus can be extremely thorough and accurate – for instance, when looking for mistakes in computer code, inventory, or data in a spreadsheet. This narrow focus of attention does not just apply to visual information; it can apply to any realm – sensory, physical, cognitive, etc.

Because their attentional resources can be so narrowly focused, the autistic people who have this ability may be **much less distractible** when working on something they are interested in. This can allow them to focus deeply (or hyperfocus) for extended periods of time while working on a project of interest.

[Authors' note: We had many reviewers for this book. A subset of our autistic reviewers noticed countless errors – small details as well as big-picture issues – that had been overlooked by our copy editor, our non-autistic reviewers, and us!]

From the experts: Reflections on attention and hyperfocus

The [strengths] that are most practical for my freelance translation business are attention to detail and the ability to focus well and for long periods.

–Leen V.

Recently, I ended up pulling an all-nighter to design a cross-stitch Stardew Valley themed clock idea I had. I don't think I've ever devoted that much focus or energy to any of my school assignments.

–Angie L.

I've found myself in multiple situations where I am unaffected by the 'shiny object chasing' that seems to dog my neurotypical colleagues.

–Eric O.

System(at)izing: In 2009, Simon Baron-Cohen and his colleagues at the University of Cambridge's Autism Research Centre presented evidence that some autistic people have an incredibly strong drive to analyze information and construct systems to make sense of that information. They argued that this is a direct consequence of excellent attention to detail. They called this skill *systemising* (spelled with an s, following the UK spelling convention); in the United States, we call it *systematizing*.

The result is that these autistic people are extremely good at organizing, categorizing, and discovering *patterns* in numerous domains. This is possible, in part, because they take in information without preconceived notions about how that information fits into the bigger picture and, instead, initially focus on unrelated or fragmented low-level details. This ability to spot patterns and repetition can make it easier for them to do things like recognize figures embedded in a complex scene, find errors in computer code, masterfully play strategy games such as chess, or create art.

Temple Grandin describes these thinkers as *bottom-up thinkers* because they are driven to **analyze details, exploring their organization until the structure becomes clear.** This way of thinking does *not* involve collecting data to support ideas based on prior experiences, like most non-autistic thinkers do. Because the autistic mind is not constrained by collecting data to support a pre-existing hypothesis, *bottom-up thinkers* can often more easily come up with novel and innovative solutions. (We will describe a phenomenon called context blindness later in the book; *bottom-up thinkers* do not use context to constrain their data collection and analysis. The context determines whether this is a strength or weakness.)

The autistic people with this skill enjoy systematizing a wide variety of information, objects, or activities. Some examples include food, textures, knitting, sports, music, art, collectibles, calendars, timetables, mathematics, visual patterns, routes, furniture arranging, social systems, faces, weather, gardening facts, how gadgets work, linguistic rules, movies – the list is endless!

There are different types of systematizing.

Visual: Some autistics **tend to think in pictures,** and many of them have photographic memories, though **others need to see the objects and manipulate them in order to understand how they work** and/or fit together. Temple Grandin describes her bottom-up approach to designing equipment as follows, "*When I design equipment for the cattle industry, I can test-run it in my imagination, similar to a virtual reality computer program.*"

Verbal: Despite the inaccurate belief that all autistic people have delayed or impaired language processing, there are autistic people who are exceptional at analyzing and remembering verbal information. As Temple Grandin and Richard Panek note, **these verbal/logical thinkers love studying words, literature, and speech, and are frequently gifted at learning languages.** Many are *hyperlexic* – they start reading at a very early age (as young as 18 months) and are very fast readers as well as exceptional spellers. They may love making lists. While these kinds of thinkers may not be skilled at drawing or thinking visually, they can remember facts that others can't about topics of interest, such as celebrities, sporting events, books, or historical events.

Yael C., a verbal thinker, says, *"I see patterns in behavior and language. My husband calls me 'Mrs. Wordsmith' and has declared my pedantry an 'unmarketable commodity.' I just love words and I love what they teach us about the people who use them. Sure, I am a highly trained psychologist, but I know that my abilities as a clinician are because of my autistic talents. I pick up on patterns of what was not said, or how things were said."*

Creative: Many autistic people are incredibly creative and innovative, due in part to their unique thought processes and ways of experiencing the world. Three examples are musician Ahmir Khalib Thompson (a.k.a. Questlove), David Byrne of the Talking Heads, and the creator of Pokémon, Satoshi Tajiri. These **creative thinkers often have extraordinary imaginations and express their novel ideas in surprising ways.** Audrian F. reports, *"Creating characters and massively detailed stories is one of my greatest skills and definitely a social interest."*

Indeed, a drive to **experience novel forms of complexity** seems to be a part of the autistic experience for some. *"My brain needs novelty so I am always eager and willing to learn new things. I can knit very complicated lace because easy lace charts are not engaging,"* says Allie S.

From the experts: Reflections on system(at)izing

I'm really good at figuring out what the problem is, and coming up with effective solutions. I think it's systemizing – and, in particular, I think it's systemizing around people. It's noticing the patterns in what people say and do, and figuring out how to predict outcomes based on those observations.
                                                            –Charlotte R.

I am very pattern oriented and will pick out errors in knitting chart patterns that have been missed by many others for years.
                                                            –Allie S.

Analytical thinking

Some autistic people excel at **reasoning through a problem in a logically consistent manner**. As mentioned above, they may be less likely to bring preconceived notions to bear during the decision-making process, leading them to consider all the facts at hand when determining what to do. These enhanced abilities are notable in the domains of reasoning, judgment, and decision making, in which autistic individuals often show *enhanced rationality* by exhibiting more rational and bias-free decision making than do non-autistic individuals.

For example, research has demonstrated that autistic people may rely less on intuition and more on deliberative reasoning; they tend to be more consistent in their choices, they are less likely to be influenced by costs that have been incurred and cannot be recovered (sunk costs), and they learn equally from desirable and undesirable information. Furthermore, as Rozenkrantz, D'Mello, and Gabrieli noted in their 2021 paper, autistic people are less likely to assume that individuals are like other members of a group to which they belong, and they evaluate information based on the facts, rather than on how those facts are presented or framed. This means that they may be less likely to make irrational decisions. As Sherlock Holmes famously said in *A Scandal in Bohemia*, "I have no data yet. It is a capital mistake to theorize before one has data. Insensibly one begins to twist facts to suit theories, instead of theories to suit facts" (Doyle, 2005).

In a crisis, some autistic people who exhibit enhanced rationality **prioritize logic over emotions**. This means that autistic people can be quite helpful in situations that could overwhelm a non-autistic person.

We recall a striking example of this ability to ignore emotions from John Elder Robison's book, *Switched On*. In the book, he relates a story of driving late at night and encountering a scene on a deserted road in which a man had been crushed to death while changing a car tire. The deceased man's companion was sitting six feet away, rocking back and forth, in shock and unable to speak. Robison calmly walked to a nearby house, knocked on the door, and said to the person who answered the door, "Call the cops .... There's a wreck out there, and someone's dead." When the person closed the door in his face, Robison returned to the accident and waited for the police to arrive.

From the experts: Reflections on analytical thinking

> I'm naturally very curious so I want to ask questions about everything, needing to know why it is important. Because of that, I can deep dive into the most random topics at a rapid pace. I also learned how to ask the right questions. Whenever a new project starts up at work, I can ask the right questions for scenarios we overlooked, which saves time down the line.
>
> –Noelle B.

> I am good at solving problems. My job is looking at worst-case scenarios. Who better than an anxious and autistic person to think of all the worst-case scenarios and come up with ways to avoid them?
>
> –Financial planner, Andrew K.

> I'm adopted, and after doing DNA tests and searching online databases, I found a second cousin twice removed. I was able to figure out who my birth mother was in about six hours. Obituary searches, internet digging, connecting dots, finding

faces, phone calls, and so on. And once a new third cousin once removed was added to one of the databases, I was able to find my birth father in about four hours.

−Carol B.

We were up at the University of Alberta, working with some scientists to measure the flow of oil through porous media like shale. Instead of looking at gross measurements, I looked at the detailed measurements and realized that it propagated through the core by sending out straight, flat fingers that moved in a steady and straightforward way through the shale. Eventually the fingers fill up a segment, and the oil will then proceed to move into the next segment in the same manner. If you map its flow, it looks like a step function. No one had ever understood that before I figured it out.

−Bob W.

Intense interests

Autistic people who have intense interests are able to bring many strengths to bear in the pursuit of exploring them. These include an **intense curiosity** that spurs a **deep desire to learn**, an **intensity of focus,** and the energy and memory to **develop an encyclopedic understanding** of the topic. This drive propels them to **become highly skilled through intense, self-directed study.** Interestingly, when talking to others about their area of interest, autistic people's social communication skills are often more reciprocal, flexible, and engaging. They report enjoying the thoughtful deep conversations that come with exploring their interests with others through immersive and focused conversation.

From the experts: Reflections on intense interests

I am extremely autodidactic for things I am interested in, especially in handcraft. I taught myself to knit, spin, crochet, hand and machine sew, all at a very high level through reading books and watching YouTube videos.

−Allie S.

I am like a dog with a bone for anything I can remotely get myself to care about. I double majored in college while working a full-time third shift job in the ER and while playing college rugby and launching an entire goat dairy from scratch because I was interested in all those things. Sleep? Relaxation? Relationships? Irrelevant. I know very little in the way of middle ground. Moderation is not my strong suit. I do or I do not. When work needs a hero, something puzzled out, something vast and challenging modeled and forecast in the nick of time, I will excitedly toss away the semi-false barriers between myself and my obsession and spend the next 30 hours saving the day.

–Jesse P.

I have a knack for picking up new skills in a technical topic of special interest extremely rapidly.

–Eric O.

Consistency

A more positive way to view *inflexibility* is through the lens of *consistency*. The **ability to follow a consistent schedule repeatedly without getting bored** can be a strength in an environment where a worker must do the same task day in and day out. This can be an important advantage in tasks where it is critical to precisely follow rules that are created by others, such as air traffic control or running a nuclear reactor. And while some people find it off-putting to be around a person who likes to support others in following and remembering the rules, these skills are crucial for sports referees who keep game play within agreed-upon bounds.

Refereeing gives me a sense of purpose. It allows my love for fairness and order to come into play. I was into sports as a kid, but had no future as a competitor; being a referee allows me to be part of sports. And now I'm good enough to be a referee for professional games.

–Ilya Z.

Different social communication style

The social aspects of autistic connection can be an enormous strength potentially due to two factors: (1) the work autistic people do to understand how to connect and communicate with non-autistics sometimes leads to exceptional abilities in this area; and (2) the very nature of their wiring can be an asset.

As noted in the chapter on reciprocity, *social camouflaging* involves using strategies in social situations with the general goal of appearing less autistic. Earlier, we described how camouflaging can create challenges; yet it can also bestow advantages. Because autistic people have had to critically analyze and explicitly delineate how non-autistic people behave, some of them can understand social dynamics better than non-autistic people, giving them an **uncanny ability to read and use social pragmatic cues.**

> *A lifetime of masking and having to work hard to read other people's body language means that I am unusually good at both. When I'm fully engaged, I can read intentions better than most people, and I can signal complex intentions such as "I'm lying and trying to hide it." It's exhausting to be fully engaged like that, but when I am, the fact that I'm doing it deliberately gives me a competitive edge. I only usually do it when it matters – providing support counseling when people are upset or angry, interviews, important social events, networking at conferences, and winning social deduction games.*
>
> –Drew R.

This skill likely explains why Gollwitzer, Martel, McPartland, and Bargh observed in 2019 that autistic people are on average **better at predicting social psychological phenomena**, especially in settings where an immediate response is not required. This is one reason that online communities can work so well for some autistics. When interacting with others in writing, you can take your time to process what another community member writes, understand what they are trying to communicate, and respond in a thoughtful, considered manner.

Ironically, one of my strengths is taking someone else's perspective. It doesn't really work in direct communication, reading hints and all that. But to compensate, I developed elaborate "little role plays" that allow me to retrospectively or hypothetically construct someone else's viewpoints, which can be really helpful in situations of prolonged or institutional conflict.

–Elena-María G.

We have observed that there are some autistics who are, by the very nature of their wiring, **keenly attuned to the emotions of others** (i.e., they possess tremendous affective empathy). Extreme compassion, when present, can be quite an advantage in the right context. Who doesn't want a highly empathic friend or therapist?

I find that my high empathy makes me a very good support system for loved ones.

–Audrian F.

Clubs, live music gigs, and any excited moments – such as someone winning a prize or a gold medal at the Olympics – or just seeing people happy really boosts me up. I have a very high level of "compersion" – being happy when my partner is happy – which makes our relationship amazing.

–Alis C.

There are autistic people whose affective empathy is particularly strong with animals. They connect deeply with their pets and are drawn to careers where they get to work with animals.

This keen empathy can also extend to issues of **fairness and a strong sense of justice**.

Greta Thunberg is a well-known young autistic woman who is passionate about addressing environmental issues, especially global warming. In 2020, Thunberg's mother, Malena Ernman wrote: "In the end, she simply couldn't reconcile the contradictions of modern life. Things simply didn't add up .... She saw what the rest of us did not want to see. It was as if she could see our carbon dioxide emissions with her naked eye …. She saw all of it – not literally, of course, but nonetheless she saw the greenhouse gases streaming out of our chimneys, wafting upwards with the winds and transforming the atmosphere into a gigantic, invisible garbage dump. She was the child, we were the emperor. And we were all naked."

Greta Thunberg is not alone. We have many clients who are deeply affected by injustice. We have both known many autistic children who get extremely angry at a teacher when other children are unfairly punished. Sarah has an autistic friend who nearly lost her job because her productivity suffered when she could not stop thinking about her Black friends and the injustices revealed by the Black Lives Matter movement. The intensity of the concern can be all-encompassing, and this concern can be channeled to **action that really can make a difference.**

This ability to speak out against injustice is made possible in part because some autistic people are willing to question social norms and challenge assumptions because they are **less hierarchical and less susceptible to peer pressure.**

This profound need for fairness and equity is inextricably tied to **a strong sense of integrity.** The SASSI (Survey of Autistic Strengths, Skills, and Interests) assesses this trait with the question: "Can you describe times where you have been willing to go against the majority because of something you believed in or because of something that was important to you?" When faced with a situation that goes against their ethical code, the autistic people with this trait are willing to challenge people's opinions and oppose the majority. Furthermore, they will avoid people whom they feel are untrustworthy.

Autistic people with a strong sense of integrity and desire to get things right can **do extremely well academically** when the work is in an area of strength. They take deadlines seriously, they want their work to be excellent, and they are not defensive when a *respected* teacher or supervisor corrects them.

The autistic people with this strong sense of integrity and fairness are frequently **accepting of difference and open to other marginalized and misunderstood groups**. Perhaps because of their own experiences, they are willing to befriend people who are different and to work to understand them. The SASSI asks, "How willing are you to be friends with people from different age groups? Cultures? Walks of life? Ability levels?" The SASSI also asks about friendships with other neurodivergent people.

> *I think, maybe, for me, a core part of being a person of integrity is treating others as you would wish to be treated .... It is necessary, as a matter of integrity, to accept others as they are, regardless of their differences – because that's what I want for myself, and for those I love.*
>
> –Charli R.

Because they want to treat others well, these autistics can be very open-minded, compassionate about the impact of difference, and less likely to judge. When combined with intense curiosity, these autistic people are able to understand others with radically different life experiences.

> *Accepting differences in thought and background has helped me a great deal in my career.*
>
> –Eric O.

> *My other strengths ... are deep compassion, fascination with psychological and sociological research, and a very accepting, non-judgmental mind. I don't buy into social constructs of status or gender and have an easy time connecting with my clients of all ages and genders.*
>
> –Yael C.

As you might imagine, these traits can make autistic people **incredibly thoughtful friends**. Indeed, when parents are asked about the positive traits they see in their autistic children, they frequently report that their children are loving, kind, and highly loyal. Also, perhaps because they must think so carefully about what makes a good friend, they will do things for their friends that non-autistic people might not.

> Susan never forgot a birthday and always sent thoughtful handwritten cards on anniversaries and other special occasions, whether happy or tragic. She loved thinking about what would be a perfect gift for her friends and family members. She would compose songs for them and buy presents that she knew they would find both delightful and useful. Because she was so attentive, she only had time for three close friends, though they loved and appreciated her generosity and thoughtfulness.

Many autistic people have a **direct, straightforward communication style,** and prefer to be honest about what they observe, especially if they think you have done something rude or inappropriate. This can lead to more **genuine and honest interactions** without the complexity of trying to figure out unspoken reactions or conflicting signals.

I am very genuine and straightforward, and clients relax with me right away. I love my work because I am blessed to have authentic, meaningful conversations all day and to connect at a profound level within the safe, predictable boundaries of the client–therapist relationship.

–Yael C.

I never understood the "drama" around relationships, listening to someone go back and forth with themselves about "should I break with him, or not?" My brain is very black and white. I would say to friends, "If you just spent 45 minutes telling me about all the things that bother you about this person, then this person is not right for you, nor you for them."

–Carol B.

A trait that proved highly beneficial during the COVID-19 quarantines of 2020 and 2021 was **the ability to enjoy solitude.**

During much of the quarantine in the USA, Sarah's oldest son was happier than he had been in years because there was no pressure to socialize outside of the family.

Some autistic people really like spending long periods of time alone doing things they enjoy. Indeed, many autistic people *need* long periods of time alone. Non-autistic people sometimes view this as worrisome, because there are studies showing that mental health outcomes are better for people who have a rich network of social connections. However, we are not aware of any studies that have looked at the impact of social connections on mental health outcomes for the subset of autistic people who prefer to be alone.

> *In my 52 years of life, my experience has been that healthcare professionals are very, very pro-relationship and, whether they mean to or not, their questioning and discussion of relationships assumes that a person is "less than" if they aren't in a relationship or aren't actively dating and seeking out someone to be with for the long haul.*
>
> –Carol B.

Humor

One absurd misconception about autistic people is that they lack a sense of humor. Both of us can think of autistic people we have loved, worked with, and lived with who are absolutely hilarious!

When we recently asked a group of 33 autistic people about their sense of humor, we noted some themes worth highlighting. One theme involved **deliberately using flat affect** to make it less clear that they were being deliberately provocative. Indeed, it seemed that some of the autistic people in the group enjoyed it when other people did not understand their jokes (*"That was definitely a good joke, but I'd say easily missed. Which only adds to the joy of it for me,"* says Eoin W.). Of course, some people simply have flat affect (*"This is just how I talk. It accidentally went well with the jokes"* reports comedian Steven Wright).

One-third of the group reported enjoying **humor that involves wordplay**. This included puns (*"Punny thing you ask!"*), deliberate mispronunciations (*"pronouncing* Sophocles *like* cuticles, *or vice-versa"* or *"fork, spoon, and ker-niffee"*), Spoonerisms (saying *"hackjammer"* instead of *"jackhammer"*), using homophones or ambiguous meanings to create confusion (*"If a phrase is ambiguous, or if a word has multiple meanings, I'll deliberately take the unintended meaning, and double down if the other person tries to clarify"*), reversing portmanteaus (*"Why spork and not foon?"*), saying words as they would be pronounced if spelled in reverse (*"I will ask if there is mail in the 'xobliam' instead of in the 'mailbox.:"*), or combining words in fun ways.

> A friend of the family is named William, though he goes by Bill. Grace could not decide whether to call him the more formal William or the more casual Bill, so she calls him "Billiam."

Thirty percent mentioned **dark humor**, especially when combined with **sarcasm or satire**.

> *My sense of humor is dark, sarcastic, satirical. This is more times than not met with looks like, "Did he really just say that?" Sometimes, I'm not even trying to be funny and I'll realize people are laughing nervously.*
>
> –Jon W.

Eighteen percent specifically mentioned **sarcasm** as their favorite form of humor, especially when combined with spotlighting logical fallacies.

> *My favorite humor involves saying what, to me, are obviously stupid or incorrect things as if I wholeheartedly believe them. For example, noting that dishwashers use an indefensible amount of water and that I therefore prefer to throw dirty dishes straight into the garbage even if it is a little expensive.*
>
> –Fabian B.

Several group members also mentioned enjoying **harmless irreverent humor that violated unwritten rules.**

One morning, Meaghan's parents woke up to find that all the family photos in their house had been replaced with pictures of the *Star Wars* character Chewbaca.

Last, but not least, a few people mentioned that they found out-of-place details hilarious.

It's interesting that many comedians identify as autistic, including Dan Aykroyd, Tig Notaro, and Hannah Gadsby. Apparently, we aren't the only people who find autistic humor hilarious.

Grit

Some of the most impressive qualities we see in the autistic people we know are the **astonishing resilience and perseverance** they have for living in a society that was not built for them. Indeed, a number of autistic people have a **strong work ethic.** Consider the kid who goes to school day after day, even when the stress of trying to fit in and do well is overwhelming. Or the adult who goes to work, even when they know their coworkers don't understand or appreciate them. It takes immense **tenacity and courage** to do this, and yet countless autistic people do – at a tremendous cost. We want to recognize this determination, while also advocating for a kinder world that acknowledges the challenges and gifts of autism, supporting and encouraging neurodivergent people so they can flourish and contribute to the world as only they can.

From the experts: Resilience and tenacity

A big strength of mine is my perseverance! When I really want something, I never give up. I have a huge ability to learn from mistakes. I'm a completely different person from when I was young because I've learned so much.

–Leen V.

Tenacity and resilience in the face of a grinding institutional bureaucracy for 17 years with one employer – also commitment there too!

–Eric O.

If there were a score for tenacity and resilience, I think I'd score high on that one too. I don't give up easily. I always figure if Plan A doesn't work, I'll find a Plan B or a Plan C.
                                                              –Charlotte R.

Frequently asked questions

- **What good is a trait that is both a strength and a challenge?** People can't choose their traits. What they can do is determine the environments in which a trait operates as a strength, and work to be in those environments as much as possible. Playing to our strengths while acknowledging our challenges is part of being a well-adjusted human.

- **Why do people focus on challenges instead of strengths when talking about autism?** There are many reasons for this. One reason is that healthcare professionals usually see people when they aren't doing well. This leads them to focus on what is going poorly, so they can figure out how to help. Another reason is that humans are wired to notice problems. If things are going well, there's no need to change. If things aren't going well, best to attend to the reasons, so you can make adjustments. There are other reasons, but instead of paying attention to negative, perhaps we should instead focus on how to get the word out about the positive side of being autistic.

References and related reading

Baron-Cohen, S., Ashwin, E., Ashwin, C., Tavassoli, T., & Chakrabarti, B. (2009). Talent in autism: Hyper-systemizing, hyper-attention to detail and sensory hypersensitivity. *Philosophical Transactions of the Royal Society B: Biological Sciences, 364*(1522), 1377–1383. https://doi.org/10.1098/rstb.2008.0337

Berkman, L. F., Kawachi, I., & Glymour, M. M. (2014). *Social epidemiology.* Oxford University Press.

Bertone, A., Mottron, L., Jelenic, P., & Faubert, J. (2005). Enhanced and diminished visuo-spatial information processing in autism depends on stimulus complexity. *Brain, 128*(10), 2430–2441. https://doi.org/10.1093/brain/awh561

Brosnan, M. J., Gwilliam, L. R., & Walker, I. (2012). Brief report: The relationship between visual acuity, the embedded figures test and systemizing in autism spectrum disorders. *Journal of Autism and Developmental Disorders*, 42(11), 2491–2497. https://doi.org/10.1007/s10803-012-1505-0

Cost, K. T., Zaidman-Zait, A., Mirenda, P., Duku, E., Zwaigenbaum, L., Smith, I. M., ... & Vaillancourt, T. (2021). "Best things": Parents describe their children with autism spectrum disorder over time. *Journal of Autism and Developmental Disorders*. https://doi.org/10.1007/s10803-021-04890-4

Davies, W. J. (2019, November 30). Autistic listening. Aural Diversity Conference 2019, Leicester, UK. http://auraldiversity.org/conferences.html

Doyle, Arthur Conan (2005). Leslie Klinger (Ed.), The new annotated Sherlock Holmes (Vol. 1). W.W. Norton.

Ernman, M. (2020, February 23). Malena Ernman on daughter Greta Thunberg: 'She was slowly disappearing into some kind of darkness.' *The Guardian*. www.theguardian.com/environment/2020/feb/23/great-thunberg-malena-ernman-our-house-is-on-fire-memoir-extract

Fletcher-Watson, S., & Bird, G. (2020). Autism and empathy: What are the real links? *Autism*, 24(1), 3–6. https://doi.org/10.1177/1362361319883506

Gollwitzer, A., Martel, C., McPartland, J. C., & Bargh, J. A. (2019). Autism spectrum traits predict higher social psychological skill. *Proceedings of the National Academy of Sciences*, 116(39), 19245–19247. https://doi.org/10.1073/pnas.1911460116

Grandin, T. & Panek, R. (2013). *The autistic brain: Thinking across the spectrum*. Houghton Mifflin Harcourt.

Grandin, T. (2009). How does visual thinking work in the mind of a person with autism? A personal account. *Philosophical Transactions of the Royal Society B: Biological Sciences*, 364(1522), 1437–1442. https://doi.org/10.1098/rstb.2008.0297

Grandin, T. (2013, May 23). How an entirely new, autistic way of thinking powers silicon valley. *Wired*. www.wired.com/2013/05/silicon-valley-coders-and-autism-and-asperbergers-maybe-its-a-new-kind-of-design-thinking/

Holt-Lunstad, J., Smith, T. B., & Layton, J. B. (2010). Social relationships and mortality risk: A meta-analytic review. *PLoS Medicine*, 7(7), e1000316. https://doi.org/10.1371/journal.pmed.1000316

Howlin, P., Goode, S., Hutton, J., & Rutter, M. (2009). Savant skills in autism: Psychometric approaches and parental reports. *Philosophical Transactions of the Royal Society B: Biological Sciences*, 364(1522), 1359–1367. https://doi.org/10.1098/rstb.2008.0328

Kaufman, S. B. (2014, February 25). Where do savant skills come from? Scientific American Blog Network. https://blogs.scientificamerican.com/beautiful-minds/where-do-savant-skills-come-from/

Li, J., Zhu, L., & Gummerum, M. (2014). The relationship between moral judgment and cooperation in children with high-functioning autism. *Scientific Reports*, 4, 4314. https://doi.org/10.1038/srep04314

Logan, B. (2017, June 26). Steven Wright, master of meh: "This is just how I talk. It accidentally went well with the jokes." *The Guardian*. www.theguardian.com/stage/2017/jun/26/steven-wright-comedy-interview-emoji-movie

Mottron, L., Dawson, M., Soulières, I., Hubert, B., & Burack, J. (2006). Enhanced perceptual functioning in autism: An update, and eight principles of autistic perception. *Journal of Autism and Developmental Disorders*, 36(1), 27–43. https://doi.org/10.1007/s10803-005-0040-7

Murray, D., Lesser, M., & Lawson, W. (2005). Attention, monotropism and the diagnostic criteria for autism. *Autism*, 9(2), 139–156. https://doi.org/10.1177/1362361305051398

O'Connor, K. (2012). Auditory processing in autism spectrum disorder: A review. *Neuroscience and Biobehavioral Reviews*, 36(2), 836–854. https://doi.org/10.1016/j.neubiorev.2011.11.008

Panek, T. G. R. (2013, October 7). Temple Grandin: What's right with the autistic mind. *Time*. http://content.time.com/time/subscriber/article/0,33009,2153096-3,00.html

Ponnet, K., Buysse, A., Roeyers, H., & De Corte, K. (2005). Empathic accuracy in adults with a pervasive developmental disorder during an unstructured conversation with a typically developing stranger. *Journal of Autism and Developmental Disorders*, 35(5), 585–600. https://doi.org/10.1007/s10803-005-0003-z

Rawlings, D., & Locarnini, A. (2008). Dimensional schizotypy, autism, and unusual word associations in artists and scientists. *Journal of Research in Personality*, 42(2), 465–471. https://doi.org/10.1016/j.jrp.2007.06.005

Remington, A., & Fairnie, J. (2017). A sound advantage: Increased auditory capacity in autism. *Cognition*, 166, 459–465. https://doi.org/10.1016/j.cognition.2017.04.002

Remington, A., Hanley, M., O'Brien, S., Riby, D. M., & Swettenham, J. (2019). Implications of capacity in the classroom: Simplifying tasks for autistic children may not be the answer. *Research in Developmental Disabilities, 85*, 197–204. https://doi.org/10.1016/j.ridd.2018.12.006

Rimland, B., & Fein, D. (1988). Special talents of autistic savants. *PsycNET*. https://psycnet.apa.org/record/1988-97460-025

Robertson, A. E., & Simmons, D. R. (2013). The relationship between sensory sensitivity and autistic traits in the general population. *Journal of Autism and Developmental Disorders, 43*(4), 775–784. https://doi.org/10.1007/s10803-012-1608-7

Robertson, C. E., Kravitz, D. J., Freyberg, J., Baron-Cohen, S., & Baker, C. I. (2013). Tunnel vision: Sharper gradient of spatial attention in autism. *Journal of Neuroscience, 33*(16), 6776–6781.

Robison, J. E. (2016). *Switched on: A memoir of brain change and emotional awakening*. Speigel & Grau.

Rozenkrantz, L., D'Mello, A. M., & Gabrieli, J. D. E. (2021). Enhanced rationality in autism spectrum disorder. *Trends in Cognitive Sciences, 25*(8), 685–696. https://doi.org/10.1016/j.tics.2021.05.004

Samson, F., Mottron, L., Soulières, I., & Zeffiro, T. A. (2012). Enhanced visual functioning in autism: An ALE meta-analysis. *Human Brain Mapping, 33*, 1553–1581. https://doi.org/10.1002/hbm.21307

Santini, Z. I., Koyanagi, A., Tyrovolas, S., Mason, C., & Haro, J. M. (2015). The association between social relationships and depression: A systematic review. *Journal of Affective Disorders, 175*, 53–65. https://doi.org/10.1016/j.jad.2014.12.049

Shah, P., Catmur, C., & Bird, G. (2016). Emotional decision-making in autism spectrum disorder: The roles of interoception and alexithymia. *Molecular Autism, 7*(1), 43. https://doi.org/10.1186/s13229-016-0104-x

Sparrow, M. (2020, March 19). Autistic in the pandemic: A call to action. *Thinking Person's Guide to Autism*. www.thinkingautismguide.com/2020/03/autistic-in-pandemic-call-to-action.html

St. John, T., Woods, S., Bode, T., Ritter, C., & Estes, A. (2021). A review of executive functioning challenges and strengths in autistic adults. *The Clinical Neuropsychologist, 36*(5), 1–32. https://doi.org/10.1080/13854046.2021.1971767.

Treffert, D. A. (2009). The savant syndrome: An extraordinary condition. A synopsis: past, present, future. *Philosophical Transactions of the Royal Society B: Biological Sciences, 364*(1522), 1351–1357. https://doi.org/10.1098/rstb.2008.0326

Woods, S. (2020, October). Seeing the big picture: Incorporating strengths into effective autism assessments across the lifespan. adult and child versions of the Survey of Autistic Strengths, Skills, and Interests (SASSI). Continuing education course presented through the Chicago School of Professional Psychology, University of Washington, Virtual.

The end

We will end where we began, namely by asking, "Why did we write this book?"

We wrote this book because we wholly believe that all people deserve to be seen. To be understood. To be accepted and validated. To be allowed to move through the world in the ways that work for them, and to be valued for their unique contributions. To understand themselves, to feel safe, and to pursue a well-rounded life with connection and purpose.

We all deserve these – regardless of gender, race, age, religion, sexual orientation, *or neuro-style*. We hope that the information in this book – and particularly the words of the autistic individuals who shared their lived experience – moves us slightly in the right direction.

DOI: 10.4324/9781003242130-14

Index

Made in the USA
Columbia, SC
04 April 2024

34018264R00161